PRINCE OF PERSIA

PRIMA OFFICIAL GAME GUIDE

WRITTEN BY:

CATHERINE BROWNE

Prima Games
An Imprint of Random House, Inc.
3000 Lava Ridge Court, Suite 100
Roseville, CA 95661
www.primagames.com

Product Manager: Todd Manning
Associate Product Manager: Sean Scheuble
Digital Product Manager: Lex Scheuble
Copyeditor: Sara Wilson
Design & Layout: Bryan Neff, Jody Seltzer
Manufacturing: Suzanne Goodwin

Ubisoft *Prince of Persia* Illustration Team:
Art Director: Mickaël Labat
Art Production Manager: Martin Schelling
Illustrators:
Bruno Gentile, Maxime Desmettre, Patrick Lambert, Thierry Doizon, Ulrich Brunin, Xavier Thomas

ISBN: 978-0-7615-6116-3
Library of Congress Catalog Card Number: 2008935304
Printed in the United States of America

08 09 10 11 GG 10 9 8 7 6 5 4 3 2 1

CONTENTS

RETURN OF THE PRINCE 2
MOVES IN MYSTERIOUS WAYS 8
DYNAMIC WORLD 19
DESERT 30
RUINED CITADEL 38
THE VALE 70
ROYAL PALACE 107
CITY OF LIGHT 144
TREE OF LIFE 180
SECRETS 189
THE MAKING OF A NEW PRINCE 192
ART GALLERY 209

ABOUT THE AUTHOR:

atherine grew up in a small town, loving the proverbial "great outdoors." While she still njoys hiking, camping, and just getting out under the big sky, Catherine also appreciates the ne art of blasting the Covenant in Halo as well as arranging a perfect little village in Animal rossing. (Seriously, you cannot just plant apple trees all willy-nilly. Neat rows, people!)

We want to hear from you! E-mail comments and feedback
to cbrowne@primagames.com

Stranger in a Strange Land

A storm whips across the land, catching in its fury a young man and his donkey. When the howling winds subside and the skies clear, the young man, a Prince in a faraway land, does not know where he is—and his donkey is nowhere to be seen. Eager to find the pack animal, her burden a king's ransom in gold, the Prince starts calling her name. His voice echoes through a narrow canyon. He thinks he is alone, but his shouts are not fading into the distance unheard. They are picked up by the ears of men on a hunt—men determined to capture their quarry.

These men are closing in on a young woman named Elika. She runs from these guards frantically, avoiding their eyes by darting between the shadows of sharp rocks in the canyon. Escape is almost within her grasp. But just when she is about to slip beyond the fingers of her hunters, she hears the call of a young man looking for his donkey. He's going to get himself killed. And worse, get her captured.

Elika runs into the Prince, clasping her hand over his mouth to keep him quiet. But she doesn't reach him soon enough and his voice reveals her position to the hunters. Now, the Prince and Elika must run together, keeping one step ahead of these dangerous men. While the Prince runs for his life, she runs for the life of all humankind. She runs to keep a dark power hidden, buried so deep in history that it's been turned into a story to scare children into behaving.

What the Prince doesn't know is that Elika is the daughter of a once-great king, now known sadly as the Mourning King. The Mourning King is about to make the third in a series of tragic mistakes that threatens to undo all of the universe, perverting the pure into the corrupt and casting the light into the shadows. He is going to resurrect Ahriman, the horrible God of Darkness. And only Elika can stop him. But she has to get to a sacred temple first.

The temple is the site of the fabled Tree of Life. In the children's story, the tree is the prison of Ahriman, bound there by his brother and God of Light, Ormazd.

In the beginning, there was only Ahriman and Ormazd. The light and the dark. And as dominion spread, Ahriman learned to covet the half of the universe controlled by his brother. Ahriman derived power from darkness, and so he sought to corrupt the hearts of humans. Lured with false promises of riches or fooled into distrusting their fellow men, these souls turned grotesque. As each heart fell into blackness, Ahriman grew in strength. Thanks to the ease with which the human heart can be made impure, it was not long before Ahriman controlled almost the entirety of the universe.

Before the last light of good was eclipsed, Ormazd launched his attack on his brother. Ahriman had corrupted so many souls that his power was no longer concentrated in his own being—it had been spread throughout his slavering followers. And so Ormazd charged into these twisted souls, striking them down before Ahriman could withdraw his power from their vessels. Unable to collect himself, Ahriman was cut to the quick. By the time Ormazd tired, only four of Ahriman's grim soldiers remained—the Hunter, the Concubine, the Alchemist, and the Warrior.

RETURN OF THE PRINCE
MOVES IN MYSTERIOUS WAYS
DYNAMIC WORLD
DESERT
RUINED CITADEL
THE VALE
ROYAL PALACE
CITY OF LIGHT
TREE OF LIFE
SECRETS

Ormazd used the last of his strength to trap these four blighted spirits inside the Tree of Life, one of the last pure objects in the universe. With his servants under chains, Ahriman himself was now tethered to the Tree of Life. With his last pulses of power, Ormazd drove Ahriman into the Tree of Life and sealed him inside. Before disappearing into the cosmos, Ormazd placed his chosen people, the Ahuras, in charge of maintaining the Tree of Life. As long as the tree lived, Ahriman and his wicked soldiers could not spread their shadows.

But time weakens all bonds, and Ahriman's whispers are escaping the Tree of Life. The Mourning King has fallen victim to Ahriman's lies. The duty of the Ahuras is about to falter. The Tree of Life must survive.

And so Elika runs.

And now the Prince runs beside her.

The Cast

The Prince

He is the hero without a name, but his deeds do not need a name to be legendary. However, the Prince was not always a hero. He wasn't even always a Prince. In the beginning, this young man only dreamt of riches as he wandered the world in search of adventure. The young man never considered the lessons of yesterday—only the promises of the road ahead of him. So concentrated on himself was he, that he had no true friends and no true home—just a life on the road, learning only what he needed to get by and see another day in the hopes that it would be the day that made him rich beyond his wildest dreams.

What makes a man a hero? Is it bravery? Is it courage? Is it a firm grasp on the difference between right and wrong?

Or is it sacrifice? Is it finally getting everything you wanted, only to give it up for something greater than yourself? The man who would one day become a Prince is about to learn this hard lesson and have his heart tested in ways that reveal the true material of a man. He will hurt. He will suffer. But he will stand taller for it and become the hero the world needs, lest it crumble.

Elika

As the Ahuras slide into the folds of history, this last descendant of the once-legendary people must do all she can to prevent the cosmic disaster of Ahriman's return. Whereas the Prince is still a stranger to the transformative power of sacrifice, Elika knows it all too well. Her life has been beset by tragedy too many times, but instead of retreating into bitterness, she has turned her pain into something great. She has turned it into duty.

As one of the last Ahuras, only Elika knows what is at stake if Ahriman finds a way to loosen the bonds of the Tree of Life. She is, at first, hesitant to open her trust to the Prince, but to save the world, she must learn to rely on this brash young man who is good with a sword. Between his sword and her magic, the pair might be able to force back the darkness. If there is a hero inside this young man, let her be the one to bring it out so that humankind can survive.

Mourning King

Elika's father is the last of the Ahura kings. With the dwindling of Ahuras, the royal lineage enters its sunset. The Mourning King earned his sad name from the tragic death of his wife, Elika's mother, a devastating loss from which he never quite recovered. As a result of the tragedy, the king's fate has taken a dark turn. His own daughter flees from him, determined to reach the Tree of Life before the Mourning King. The king is supposed to be the true vanguard of the Tree of Life, so why is Elika's father so intent on stopping his beloved daughter from even stepping foot in the temple that houses the mystical tree?

The Corrupted

Ahriman's power is spread across his minions. To turn back Ahriman, the Prince and Elika must strike down the God of Darkness' four soldiers, known as the Corrupted. These grotesques were once humans. But their hearts were weak at just the wrong moment, allowing Ahriman to slither inside and ruin them. Can they be redeemed? Or must each be dealt one final blow to bring Ahriman to his knees?

The Hunter

Pride has its price. The Hunter was once a prince consumed with the sport of the hunt. But after bringing down one of each beast in all of creation, the prince believed himself to be a hunter unrivaled. This was the opening that Ahriman needed. The God of Darkness offered the prince a quarry unparalleled in this world. The prince greedily traded his soul for such game, but instead of finding himself chasing down a fantastical animal, the prince was transformed into a monster. Now he himself is the hunted, a lure for the world's greatest sportsmen. With his grim traps and three-bladed sword, the prince will forever fight men on behalf of his new dark master.

The Hunter stalks his prey, patiently waiting for the right moment to lunge.

THE CONCUBINE

There is no cruelty greater than love that is not returned. There was once a woman who so loved a man, but he did not share such affection. Though she desperately sought to be what he wanted, the man's heart never softened. And so the woman allowed herself to be fooled by Ahriman's promise to turn her into what the man would love. She was given the gift of shape-shifting and was able to discover the form that best pleased her beloved. But she soon discovered this talent had its limits.

Each night, she was forced to retreat from the man and become an entirely new woman. And so each night she had to try to woo the man all over again. Each new form pushed her further from her true self until all that was left was the Concubine, a writhing mass of jealousy and rejection.

From behind her wicked veil, the Concubine still has the power the exert a siren song.

THE ALCHEMIST

There is great honor in the pursuit of knowledge, but to do so at the cost of compassion or ethics is an equally great sin. Long ago, there was a scientist so consumed by his quest that he was ultimately rejected from society. As he grew old, the scientist realized that his vast knowledge would cease with his death. And so the scientist set about discovering a way to trump the finality of death. But no man can stop death, and so when Ahriman offered the scientist the formula for eternal youth in exchange for his soul, the man accepted.

But Ahriman is the ultimate trickster. The formula was so complicated that the scientist expired while trying to make sense of it. But he was not angered by this trick, because through eternal service to Ahriman now, he would truly live forever, able to continue his experiments.

As wicked as he is intelligent, the Alchemist has outsmarted centuries of opponents.

The Warrior

The desire for peace can lead men to unspeakable acts of war. And so the king of a pacifist tribe turned to violence when his peaceful people were attacked without mercy. But his enemies were better at the art of death than the king and his small cadre of soldiers. When all hope was lost and his beloved people were about to be destroyed, the king accepted an offer from Ahriman. In exchange for his soul, the king would inherit the power to visit death upon his enemies. After ripping apart his enemies, the king became a symbol of violence and was cast out by his peace-loving people.

Now the king is Ahriman's instrument of war. Capable of incredible acts of violence thanks to his twisted form and superhuman strength, the Warrior is the most feared of the God of Darkness' horrors.

The Warrior's massive frame makes him a force to be reckoned with. But beneath that corrupted armor lies a heart in eternal turmoil.

Moves in Mysterious Ways

During his travels, the Prince has achieved great mastery over his body. He is capable of some astounding acrobatics—at times, it looks like he is able to shake free of gravity. During his adventures with Elika, the Prince is able to call upon not only some impressive solo moves, but also some incredible duo maneuvers. And just when the Prince is ready to be impressed with his own skills, Elika has a few moves of her own that put the Prince in his place.

Princely Moves

From the desert outside the temple of the Tree of Life, you can see incredible skylines of the regions corrupted by Ahriman. Huge windmills scrape the skies. Crumbling towers make defiant last stands against the horizon. Hot air balloons gloomily sway in a sinister wind. Those are just the tip of the landscapes the Prince must successfully negotiate in order to strike at the heart of Ahriman's power: the Corrupted.

There are very few direct lines from one location in this world to the next. Since the regions controlled by the Ahuras have fallen into disrepair and the presence of the corruption has only served to accelerate that decay, the Prince and Elika must be clever in sniffing out new routes through the wreckage and ruins. With floors fallen away, columns that still hold up a dangerously unstable rooftop must substitute as a means of crossing corridors. Poles that once held proud royal banners are now there to be swung around. Scaffolding exposed by severe weathering is now the only way to ascend a tower with collapsed stairs.

But even though the mission is dire, the Prince cannot entirely write this off as a sour experience. He knows how well he moves. And these exposed fixtures and vine growths are a means for showing off a little. Sure, there is a centuries-old monster waiting for him at the end of the line, but why not at least have some fun leaping from pole to post like a child turned loose on a brand-new playground?

The Basics

You have primary control over the Prince. Use the left control stick to move the Prince. Lightly pressing the stick makes the Prince gingerly move, but pressing it farther in any direction breaks the Prince into a brisk run. The face buttons of the controller are assigned to the Prince's elemental moves, which can be turned into some pretty spectacular moves when linked together properly.

**Please refer to the PC manual for PC controls.*

Move	Xbox 360	PLAYSTATION3
Sword	X	■
Jump/Dodge	A	×
Elika/Magic	Y	▲
Gauntlet	B	●
Guard	RT/RB	R1/R2
Talk to Elika	LT/LB	L1/L2

Action/Jump: While exploring, this button makes the Prince jump. In battle, this button pulls off one of the Prince's acrobatic moves, such as sliding between the enemy's legs.

Attack: This button is only used in combat. It slashes an enemy with the Prince's sword.

Magic: This is Elika's cue. Depending on how you use this, Elika will perform a number of different moves, such as assisting in battle or utilizing one of the mysterious power plates you'll encounter while exploring the regions.

Gauntlet: The gauntlet is used in both exploration and combat. While exploring, the gauntlet is used to "link" moves, such as transitioning from a wall run to grabbing a brass ring and then back to a wall run. In combat, this button grabs an enemy and throws it into the air.

Descend/Guard: To slide down a vertical surface while exploring, hold the right trigger. In combat, though, this button doubles as your guard command.

Acrobatics

Watching the Prince in motion is like having a front-row seat to the circus, except the clowns have been replaced by thousand-year-old monsters. The Prince has a series of basic acrobatic moves for negotiating tricky landscapes. You must master these moves if you want to close in on Ahriman's vicious henchmen and restore order to a universe that is about to fall into ruin.

Jump

The Prince is outrageously nimble, able to make fantastic jumps through open space like a cat. To make one of these astounding leaps, just run toward anything the Prince can grab on to—a column, vines, scaffolding—and press the jump button right when his feet reach the edge. The Prince throws himself through the air and instinctively grabs on to the target surface.

CAUTION

If the target is too far away, the Prince falters without Elika's help. Check out Elika's special moves to see how she can assist him.

Climb

The Prince is an accomplished climber, able to find a foothold in even the shallowest crack on a sheer surface. When approaching a wall, inspect it for any imperfection—that's a potential grip. Jump onto the wall and then scrabble up it by moving the Prince over any hold.

Horizontal cracks can be gripped with relative ease, and exposed woodwork is as good as a ladder. In fact, it's so easy for the Prince to climb up surfaces like these, he can often afford a free hand to help Elika get up a wall, too.

RETURN OF THE PRINCE
MOVES IN MYSTERIOUS WAYS
DYNAMIC WORLD
DESERT
RUINED CITADEL
THE VALE
ROYAL PALACE
CITY OF LIGHT
TREE OF LIFE
SECRETS

The Prince can even run directly up a flat wall. Eventually, gravity does kick in while running up a wall, so look for features you can grab on to. Brass rings or scaffolding are perfect grips. Just climb up the wall, grab the ring or scaffolding, and then either kick away to scamper up another wall opposite from your current surface, or grab onto another textured surface with the gauntlet and continue your ascent.

Beams are perfect springboards for launching the Prince across open spaces.

With his special glove and incredible upper body strength, the Prince can climb up columns and posts. To rotate around the post, press left or right on the left control stick. Ascend or slide down the post by pressing either up or down on the left control stick.

Grab vines for support when climbing walls. Elika hops on the Prince's back and hitches a ride.

The Prince can even use vertical cracks to climb up walls. Just make sure you have your grip before trying to ascend.

Use the jump button to kick away from columns and walls and land on the opposite landing, provided you checked first and there is one.

Wall Bounce

The Prince can bound between two vertical walls to reach high ledges, as long as the walls are close enough together. To pull off this move, run up one of the walls. At the height of the Prince's climb, kick off with the jump button. When the Prince finds temporary purchase on the opposite wall, kick off again. Repeat your jumps until the Prince is at the top of the shaft and able to pull himself up to the ledge.

If the walls are too far apart for the Prince to jump alone, use Elika's assistance to cover the extra distance.

Wall Run

The Prince not only can run up a wall, but he can even run along a wall for a short distance. Thanks to his ability to shift his weight combined with a gauntlet that can "bite" into walls, you can cross chasms with little worry. To wall run, just run toward a wall and jump into it. Keep pressing forward with the left control stick. Watch for the Prince's loosening grip, though.

When you see the Prince's feet and gauntlet start to slide, he's about to peel away from the wall. If you're still over a hole, press the jump button to kick away from the wall. The Prince uses the last of his momentum to push off and either hop down to a platform or grip the opposite wall. Just keep pressing forward to continue wall running.

Look for horizontal scratches on a wall—they're a hint that the Prince can perform a safe wall run.

Roofing

In some circumstances, the Prince can almost wholly defy gravity. With brief bursts of speed, the Prince can clamber across a ceiling. However, there must be something for the Prince to quickly grab on to, such as a brass ring, or he will completely lose his grip. To grab the ring and keep roofing, press the gauntlet button just as the Prince grabs the ring.

Roofing is one of the Prince's "linking" moves. You can cross a room without touching the floor with this maneuver. For example, try scrambling up a column. At the top, kick free of the column and scramble across the ceiling using rings before jumping down to another column. This is perfect for situations where the floor is either dangerous—or simply not there.

Grip Fall

Sometimes the Prince needs to drop down to a lower level but there is nothing to grab onto and safely descend. In situations like this, the Prince can use his special glove to find purchase and slow a fall. Just lower the Prince over the edge of a wall and then squeeze the right trigger to hook the wall with the glove. Sparks fly as the Prince battles gravity. There is no limit to how long the Prince can use a grip fall, but you had better make sure there's something at the bottom to land on.

TIP

The Prince can kick away from a grip fall to reach a ledge on the opposite side of a room or canyon. Just press jump near the bottom to put your feet on the wall and push away.

Return of the Prince
Moves in Mysterious Ways
Dynamic World
Desert
Ruined Citadel
The Vale
Royal Palace
City of Light
Tree of Life
Secrets

Slide

The soles of the Prince's sandals let him slide effortlessly down sloped surfaces, such as carved stone and rooftops. The only catch is that once the Prince starts to slide, it's impossible to stop. The only way out of a slide is to jump away from the surface, so before committing yourself to a slide, make sure there's something on the other side that you can catch—or that will catch you.

TIP

While sliding, you can move from side to side with the left control stick, directing the Prince so he can safely jump to the next surface at the end of the slope.

Linking Moves

Because each area is constructed of so many poles, pillars, slides, walls, and rails, you will need to often "link" together moves to keep from falling. This requires using the gauntlet at the right time to link together different activities. In an extended run through a number of environmental features, like wall runs

Linking Moves

(continued)

and rings, using the gauntlet almost feels a bit like a rhythm challenge. Hitting the button at just the right moment transitions the Prince out of wall run and across a ring. In time with the Prince, you press the gauntlet button again to release the ring and grab on to a ledge. There is no jamming buttons here—success comes only to the smooth.

Here's an example of linking some moves:

The Prince and Elika use a power plate to fly to a new area, but their arc drops them off just below the next power plate.

Pressing and holding the gauntlet button makes the Prince scramble up to the power plate.

Now you can use the magic button to activate the power plate and blast off for the next plate.

There is one time where it's especially tricky to know when to use the gauntlet button to transition between moves. A few rings are on runners. When the Prince grabs this type of ring, it slides along the wall. You must tap the gauntlet button right as the ring reaches the end of the runner to wall run away from it successfully. If you hesitate, the Prince loses his grip on the ring runner.

Elika's Moves

Elika is hardly helpless—she too has a range of acrobatic gifts. Many of her moves are similar to the Prince's, so don't worry about her falling behind when you scramble across a tricky landscape or dart around a puzzling room. But Elika also has her own skill set, plus a few moves she can use in conjunction with the Prince when he dares gravity a little too much.

Save

The greatest magic at Elika's disposal is her ability to pull you back from the brink whenever it looks like you are about to fall to your doom. As you lose your grip and start to tumble into the void, Elika's hand reaches out to grab yours. She yanks you back up to stable ground, giving you a second (or third, or fourth) chance to get it right. Elika also rescues you if you stumble into a pit of corruption. This gift is automatic. You do not need to activate it with the magic button and there is no limit on the number of times Elika can save you.

Compass

When you're unable to see the best way out of a trouble spot—maybe the solution to a particular room is eluding you—Elika's magic gives you a hint at how to escape. Elika raises her hand, releasing a blue trail that highlights potential routes. She shows you things like places you can wall run, cracks to climb, and where you can safely grip fall. To use the compass, just come to a standstill and press the magic button.

NOTE

To use compass effectively, you must first set a destination on your map screen. Please see the next chapter for a complete expianation of using the in-game map and setting destinations.

Cooperative Jump

Sometimes the distance is just too great to cross alone, so Elika and the Prince team up to perform this high-wire move. Jumping through the air, the Prince and Elika join hands to gain momentum and propel each other across a wide divide. To use this move, jump across a particularly wide chasm. As the Prince starts to descend from the apex of the jump, press the magic button to call on Elika. She propels you to your next landing point.

Want a good indication of when you need Elika's help? The screen will start to turn gray, indicating that the Prince is about to take a nasty fall. Quickly press the magic button to salvage the jump.

TIP

Elika's magic is strong. Even if the next landing surface is too high above you and you don't press the magic button soon enough, Elika will still safely hurl you up to the landing zone. Use this whenever you're not sure about a gap that may be too wide. Give it a try and see if Elika can help you cover the distance. If not, well, then Elika can use her magic to save you instead of helping you complete a jump.

Power Plates

Return of the Prince
Moves in Mysterious Ways
Dynamic World
Desert
Ruined Citadel
The Vale
Royal Palace
City of Light
Tree of Life
Secrets

The magic of Ormazd, the benevolent god that lost out against the wickedness of Ahriman, is still alive in the world of the Ahuras. This magic can be unlocked by collecting Light Seeds after purifying different areas of the world. (For a complete description of Light Seeds and the different magics, please see the next chapter.) Once Elika unlocks one of Ormazd's four magics, the corresponding power plates in the world light up. Each magic is associated with a specific color, and there are four different colored power plates: red, yellow, green, and blue. For example, if you unlock the Breath of Ormazd first, that will activate the green power plates. You cannot use the other three until you gather up enough Light Seeds to unlock the corresponding magics.

To use a power plate, grab it by either wall running across it or climbing up to it. When you pass over the plate, you automatically hesitate as Elika reaches to the sky, ready to unleash the power plate's magical move, should you press the magic button in time. If you press the magic button while the Prince and Elika are on top of a power plate, the pair pirouettes into the sky. There are often networks of power plates you must use to reach the end of each area and challenge the Corrupted.

CAUTION

If you fail fall while jumping around a series of power plates, Elika carries to back to the last solid platform you were standing on before you used Ormazd's magic.

Since you unlock the different magics throughout the adventure, you must sometimes return to previously visited areas and try out power plates that were dormant on your first pass.

Combat

During his travels, the Prince has become quite handy with a sword. His skill with a blade will be put to the test as Ahriman's forces rally against him and Elika. The combat system, however, is more involved than that just slashing with a sword. In addition to his regular slice and parry attacks, the Prince can now link together a series of attacks and acrobatic moves. A simple sword attack can dovetail into an aerial maneuver, with the Prince flinging an enemy into the air before calling upon Elika to use her magic to strike a monster down to the ground with a thunderous thud.

Mastering this new combo system—the art of chaining moves—is both the key to success in the fight against the forces of darkness as well as a feast for the eyes. Especially when the acrobatics result in a phenomenal death blow that sends one more of Ahriman's minions back to the underworld.

Individual Moves

Before getting into combos, you must understand the essentials of the Prince's individual attacks and moves. Once you have these down, then you can start experimenting with combos to pull off insane attack chains.

Attack

The Prince's default attack is a sword slash. Approach an enemy and press the attack button to strike. Steel flashes across the screen, connecting with the target and dishing out a little damage. Pressing the attack button four times is a basic sword combo that is effective at pushing back against an enemy and cleaving away a solid amount of the enemy's stamina.

CAUTION

Make sure you are within range of the enemy before attacking. If you attack out of range (about three steps back), you leave yourself open to a harsh counterattack.

If, while attacking, you push a smaller enemy up against a wall, you can throw them over your shoulder by pressing the attack button. The Prince automatically grabs the enemy with his gauntlet and tosses them back into the arena. This move not only causes damage to the enemy, but also leaves the enemy open for a second. Use the dodge button to close the gap and launch an new string of attacks.

NOTE

If you back a Corrupted up to a wall (or it backs you into one), you begin a small struggle minigame.

Block

Holding the guard button raises the Prince's arm so he can block an incoming attack. Using the sword as a shield, the Prince can block most attacks, but cannot launch an attack from this position. If the Prince is wounded, he auto-generates health over time, but holding this defensive position slows his recovery.

If you are severely hurt, the corners of the screen turn red. Seek cover to revive the Prince's flagging spirits. While hurt, you are vulnerable to lethal strikes from enemies. If you do not block an incoming blow, the enemy may force you to the ground and try to deliver a lethal strike. You can recover from this by pressing the button flashed on-screen. If you hit the button in time, the Prince jumps to his feet and is back in the fight.

However, if you miss the button timing, the enemy will indeed slice and stab you. Elika must use her magic to rescue you from certain death. While Elika is using her magic to assist you, the enemy retreats and recovers a significant amount of lost health.

Deflect

A properly timed block can effectively counter an enemy attack, opening a window to launch a counterattack that can evolve into a mighty combo. When you spot your enemy launching an attack, such as raising a sword or rearing back a massive fist, get ready to block. If you block just as the enemy's blow is coming down, you brush it aside. Now, you are not guaranteed a free hit on your enemy just because you successfully deflected an attack. Your enemy can do the same to you. It is not uncommon, when fighting the Corrupted, to see a series of blows and deflections before one of you misses the timing and breaks the cycle.

Dodge

If you need to put some distance between you and an enemy (perhaps you've been injured), use the dodge button to quickly hop in the direction you are pressing the left control stick. Repeatedly tapping the dodge button while pulling away from your enemy will draw some distance, but that won't necessarily stop your foe from trying to close the gap you're busily creating. You can also slide to the left or right, which is particularly useful when you are fighting an enemy that can be pushed over a ledge. Keep sliding until you have the enemy with its back against the ledge and then launch your series of attacks.

RETURN OF THE PRINCE
MOVES IN MYSTERIOUS WAYS
DYNAMIC WORLD
DESERT
RUINED CITADEL
THE VALE
ROYAL PALACE
CITY OF LIGHT
TREE OF LIFE
SECRETS

If you press the control stick toward the enemy and tap the dodge button, you slide between your enemy's legs and pop up on the other side. This little bit of acrobatics is a good launching pad for an attack combo, but it can also be used to quickly get an enemy to make it back toward a ledge or breakable object.

Gauntlet/Lift

The same gauntlet that lets you slide down sheer walls also digs into the corrupted hides of enemies. When close to an enemy, tap the gauntlet button. The Prince lunges at the enemy and slams that glove into its torso. Now, the Prince launches the enemy into the air. From here, you can either jump back and dodge (useful for healing) or start an attack combo.

Magic

Elika can attack, too, but she does so with her magic instead of a physical weapon. Elika cannot zoom across the arena and attack from any distance. She uses your shoulders as a springboard for her magic attack, so you must be close enough for Elika to vault over you and deliver her magic blow. Now, the magic move by itself has very limited use (more on that in the Ahriman's Influence section), but it is a very important part of successful attack combos.

Special Attacks

Sometimes, Ahriman's minions will get the drop on you. Or they will fly into a rage and attack with a ferocity than can only be answered with lightning reflexes. These special attacks from your enemies are handled not with traditional moves, but by pressing buttons as they appear on-screen. You have a short window of opportunity to press the on-screen button before you are injured by the special attack.

Just like trying to avoid a lethal attack when you've been knocked on your back, you must respond to these rage-fueled attacks right away or suffer the consequences. For example, the Hunter will sometimes go berserk and start wildly flashing his blades. You must tap the sword button to parry each incoming blow.

The Warrior will also try to swipe you off him after you launch an acrobatic attack, so as you climb around his massive frame, tap the on-screen button as it's shown to keep moving around the body and attack where the Warrior cannot reach. These sequences typically last just four or five moves, but if you mess up the timing, the monster will punish you. Expect some real hurt—the kind that can get you in trouble with an incoming lethal attack if you do not back off and recover right away.

Struggles

Now, when you or an enemy get backed into a wall or a corner, you enter into a struggle. Depending on the enemy, you may have to try to pull away from the confrontation or at least keep a clash of weapons out of your face. In the case of the Concubine, as an example, the harpy uses her corruption powers to grab your sword and try to pull you close to her so she can attack you directly. When these struggle erupt, you must repeatedly tap the attack button as fast as you can to break free of the struggle. If you lose the struggle, you suffer injury. If you win, though, you put your enemy on its heels and can launch into a new attack on your terms.

Perimeters

The perimeter of each arena is a significant factor in the pacing of a battle. There are three kinds of perimeters: open edge, wall, and corruption. If you push a soldier or Corrupted into a wall (or they push you into one), you and your opponent immediately go into a struggle.

However, if you back a soldier up to an open edge and land a strike, you enjoy a quick kill. The Prince runs the soldier through with his blade, no matter the strength of the soldier.

Tip

You can even use this move on some of the Corrupted, such as the Hunter and the Alchemist—but expect them to work overtime to keep away from the edges of an arena.

Some arenas are lined with corruption, and that benefits your enemy. If you are shoved back into the corruption, Elika must save you. While Elika pulls you out of the poison, your enemy can regain any lost health. Pushing an enemy into corruption is actually something of a favor for the evil one. For example, if you back the Alchemist into a field of corruption in an arena, he just melts into the muck and then appears directly behind you. Now your back is to the corruption, leaving you extremely vulnerable.

Ahriman's Influence

Occasionally, your enemies will be overcome by an extra boost of power directly from Ahriman. This power manifests itself in three different ways. Each condition, called Ahriman's Influence, is linked to a specific Corrupted. When you first encounter that Corrupted, who then uses the influence, it is thereafter unlocked for all other Corrupted and soldiers to use. Influences must be battled with a specific attack. Using the wrong attack results is a terrific backfire.

Ahriman's Influence

(continued)

Ahriman's Fury: The enemy suddenly erupts in black corruption, covered with writhing tendrils or sharp spikes. Only Elika's magic dispels this state. Trying to attack with the sword or gauntlet injures the Prince.

Ahriman's Patience: The enemy goes into a defensive position that can only be disrupted with a gauntlet attack. Watch for yellow sparks to indicate the enemy in this state. Let the enemy attack, deflect the blow, and then tap the gauntlet button to dispel the influence.

Ahriman's Anger: A bright flash of blue envelops the enemy. Only a sword attack removes this powerful influence.

If you try to use Elika's magic on either Ahriman's Anger or Ahriman's Patience, she will be hurt. Elika is cast aside and must regain her strength before she can rejoin the fight. While Elika is out of commission, you cannot use any of her magic attacks in your combos. Because this severely limits your options, be sure that the influence is only Ahriman's Fury before tapping the magic button.

RETURN OF THE PRINCE
MOVES IN MYSTERIOUS WAYS
DYNAMIC WORLD
DESERT
RUINED CITADEL
THE VALE
ROYAL PALACE
CITY OF LIGHT
TREE OF LIFE
SECRETS

Combos

Now that the basic are out of the way, it's time to start linking attacks into devastating combo chains that leave your enemies reeling. Just like linking acrobatic moves while exploring seems to have a rhythm to it, so does chaining attacks. Depending on which move you start your combo with—sword, lift, dodge/acrobatic, or magic—you can try dozens of different chains.

The basic combo is to tap the sword button four times, unleashing a torrent of blows that knocks your enemy back. However, instead of tapping the sword button that fourth time (which ends the combo), tapping the magic button instead links your sword attacks with a magic attack from Elika.

Now, you have an entirely new set of options. If you were to tap the magic button two more times, Elika would strike the enemy with a total of three magic attacks. That would end the combo.

However, tapping the gauntlet button after invoking Elika's magic the first time sends the Prince in to grab the enemy and send it flying into air. Now that the enemy is in the air, you have another series of options. Hitting the sword button would slash the enemy as it falls and end the combo.

But if you instead tapped the dodge button, you could now chain this already fierce combo that started with some sword slashes, then added a magic attack before going for a lift move, with any number of combo endings. For example, hitting the magic button twice after the acrobatic move would close out this extended chain with two hard hits from Elika. A lesser soldier wouldn't survive and one of the Corrupted would certainly be rattled to the core.

Combo Tree

It may be easier to think of these combos not as just a bunch of attacks, but as branches of a tree. (In fact, if you look at the Options tab from the Pause screen, you can access a list of the combo moves in-game that's called the Combo Tree.) Every chain starts out with the normal combo. This set includes all of the starting moves for a chain, from a sword attack to a lift attack with the gauntlet.

From the normal combo, you have three choices: lift combo, Elika combo, and acrobatic combo. These moves are determined by how you link away from the normal combo. If you link away from your normal combo with the magic button, you then move into the Elika combo branch of the tree. You could end your chain with the Elika combo, or branch out into the two combos accessible from the Elika combo: lift combo and aerial combo.

Chaining into the aerial combo or throw combo branches of the Combo Tree are dead ends. All chains stop at the conclusion of one of the moves from this combo group. They are indeed powerful finishers, but they do end a chain.

Here is the entire Combo Tree, complete with the button presses that make up each move inside the individual branches of the tree. Branches that feed into each other are linked by arrows. Because the aerial combo and throw combo branches are chain-enders, they do not link to any other branch except by the arrow that feeds into them from other branches.

NOTE

If an arrow does not branch away from a group of button commands, then that move ends the chain.

TIP

It takes real practice to master the Combo Tree, but when you do link together a series of seven attacks for the first time, mixing up swords, magic, and throws, it feels like quite an accomplishment.

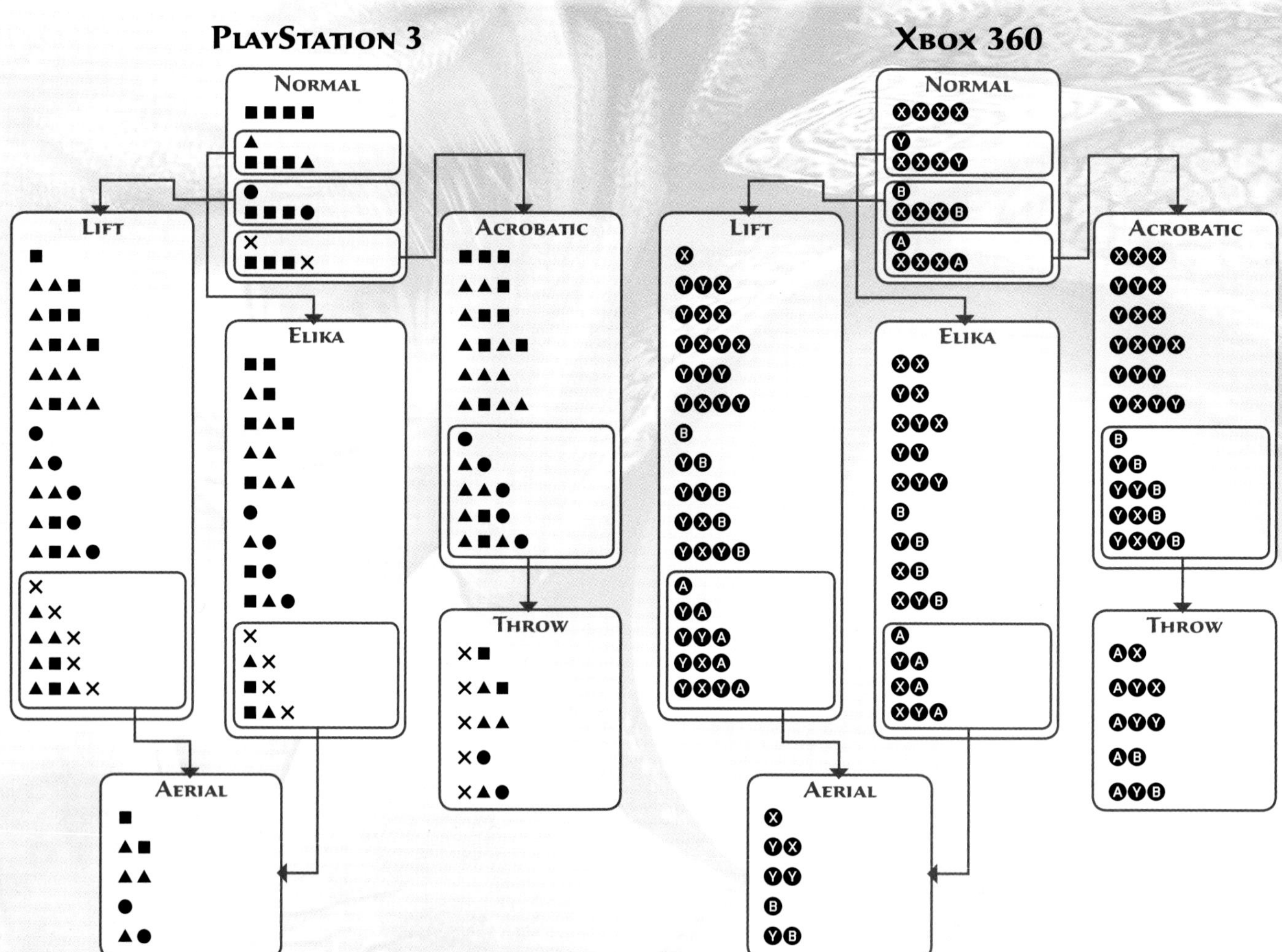

DYNAMIC WORLD

RETURN OF THE PRINCE
MOVES IN MYSTERIOUS WAYS
DYNAMIC WORLD
DESERT
RUINED CITADEL
THE VALE
ROYAL PALACE
CITY OF LIGHT
TREE OF LIFE
SECRETS

After Ahriman explodes from his bindings, the Prince and Elika must discover a way to put the dark god back in his eternal shackles. Since Ahriman thrives on corruption, the only weapon to use against the god is the power of purification. Throughout the land are patches of sacred ground, buried under the rot and stench of Ahriman's darkness. Elika possesses the power to turn the land before Ahriman's influence sinks in too deep. Should Ahriman be allowed to salt the earth with his wicked corruption for too long, it may be impossible to repel the god. And so the Prince and his companion must waste no time driving straight for the fertile grounds spread around the world. If the Prince and Elika can push back the Corrupted that guard each piece of fertile ground, Ahriman will have no choice but to retreat to his prison beneath the temple of the Tree of Life.

But how the Prince and Elika tackle their task is entirely up to you. After leaving the temple of the Tree of Life at the beginning of the game, you choose where the pair goes first. And second. And so on. Will you start your adventure by pushing through the Vale, home of the Alchemist? Or visit the Royal Palace and challenge the Concubine? Or will you actually explore different corners of the map instead of focusing on one particular region at a time? It's entirely up to you. But the decisions you make are not without consequence. The order in which you visit areas and defeat Corrupted has a ripple effect across the rest of the world. Stepping foot in certain areas releases traps that infect other parts of the world. Meeting one of the Corrupted affects the way the others fight. You could feasibly see this world through sixteen different lenses, depending on your decisions.

This chapter will explain exactly how to travel around the world of the Ahura and what changes occur when you reach specific destinations or battle each Corrupted. Use this as a travel guide and plot out your path. You can try to avoid trouble by triggering traps as late in the adventure as possible, or really increase your challenge by getting the Corrupted to share their powers early in the game.

TRAVEL

In the world of the Ahuras, you step to your own fate. Defeating Ahriman requires saving all 24 patches of fertile ground, but you choose the order in which you purify the corrupted soil. Routes through the world are unlocked by collecting the powerful Light Seeds, a magical source that allows Elika to unlock the four powers of Ormazd. Each of Ormazd's powers allows passage to four different fertile grounds throughout the world—two in each of the four regions of the world: Royal Palace, City of Light, the Vale, and the Ruined Citadel. Each of Ormazd's powers unlocks like-colored power plates, though, so you must return to purified areas after earning a new Ormazd power so you can grab all the Light Seeds and invest in another new power, until you have all four at your disposal.

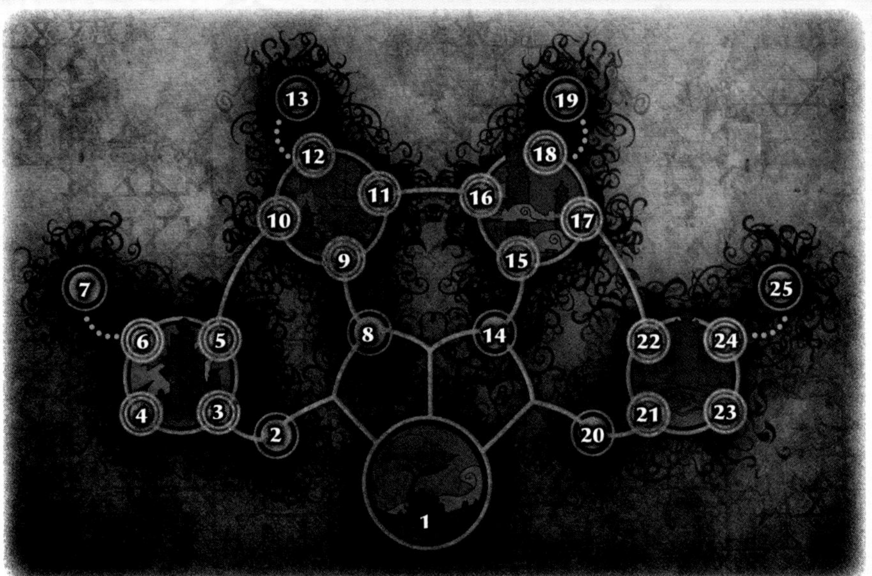

LEGEND

1 Temple
2 King's Gate
3 Sun Temple
4 Marhsalling Ground
5 Martyr's Tower
6 The Windmills
7 Hunter's Lair
8 The Cauldron
9 Construction Yard
10 Machinery Ground
11 Reservoir
12 Heaven's Stair
13 The Observatory
14 The Cavern
15 Royal Gardens
16 Royal Spire
17 Spire of Dreams
18 Coronation Hall
19 Concubine's Chambers
20 City Gate
21 Tower of Ahriman
22 Tower of Ormazd
23 Queen's Tower
24 City of Light
25 Warrior's Fortress

World Tour

The world is divided into four main regions, each branching off from the central temple of the Tree of Life. The first time you visit each region, it is under the dark influence of Ahriman's corruption. Purifying each region, though, reveals the bittersweet beauty of the declining Ahura civilization.

Ruined Citadel

Crumbling in the west side of the world is the Ruined Citadel. Once an incredible site of industrious innovation, the citadel is now silent. A brutal sandstorm rips through the air, stripping the citadel of its last remnants of glory. Here, the Hunter stalks his prey. The Prince and Elika must navigate the decrepit windmills and staging grounds, pushing back against the Hunter's lunges and feints. If the Hunter can be turned into prey, Elika can purify this region. It may not ever return to its zenith, but the citadel can at least stand as a reminder of days when the Ahuras were unrivaled in diligence and hard work.

The gateway leading into the Ruined Citadel is the King's Gate. The four areas of the Ruined Citadel are:

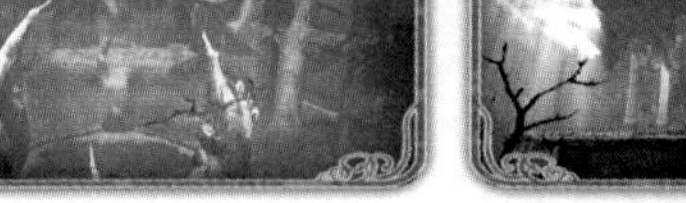

The Sun Temple

Marshalling Ground

Martyr's Tower

The Windmills

Vale

The once-peaceful Vale was the site of all the Ahuras' scientific discovery. Under beautiful blue skies, the best and brightest—which at one time included the Alchemist—set about unlocking the creative genius of the Ahuras. Incredible discoveries were made in the fields of flight and irrigation. But that was before the Ahuras fell into ruin. And now that Ahriman's corruption has rotted the region, the incredible observatory has fallen into absolute disrepair. The Prince and Elika must purge this region of the Alchemist to give the surviving Ahuras any hope of one day seeing their innovation rekindled.

The gateway leading into the Vale is the Cauldron. The four areas of the Vale are:

Construction Yard

Machinery Ground

Reservoir

Heaven's Stair

RETURN OF THE PRINCE
MOVES IN MYSTERIOUS WAYS
DYNAMIC WORLD
DESERT
RUINED CITADEL
THE VALE
ROYAL PALACE
CITY OF LIGHT
TREE OF LIFE
SECRETS

Royal Palace

Once the celebrated home of the Ahura royal line, the palace has fallen under the shadow of a dwindling lineage. The once-vibrant royal gardens were left to grow untended. The coronation hall has not heard the joy of the peaceful transfer of power from one generation to the next in many, many years. The palace is now in the grip of the Concubine, who is consumed with jealousy and self-loathing. Can the Prince and Elika cure the Concubine's twisted heart and let her pass to the other side in peace in time to save the kingdom?

The gateway leading into the Royal Palace is the Cavern. The four areas of the Royal Palace are:

Royal Gardens

Spire of Dreams

Royal Spire

Coronation Hall

City of Light

The City of Light was once a place to celebrate and honor the twin gods that birthed light and darkness. Even Ahriman earned a tower bearing his name, as there cannot be good in this world without the existence of evil. The City of Light is slowly being consumed by the fires of the earth, though. Lava swallows the once-grand city one inch at a time and nobody is left to keep the site from sliding into the molten earth. The City of Light is dominated by the Warrior. The tragic figure must be mercifully eliminated if the City of Light is to ever regain its illustriousness.

The gateway leading into the City of Light is the City Gate. The four areas of the City of Light are:

Tower of Ahriman

Queen's Tower

Tower of Ormazd

City of Light

World Map

Once you have escaped the temple of the Tree of Life, you can access the world map and see the different regions of the world. Each region is depicted as a ring with four nodes. Each node represents an area. Each region has four main areas as well as a gateway that's linked to the desert outside the temple and the final lair of the Corrupted that haunts each specific region.

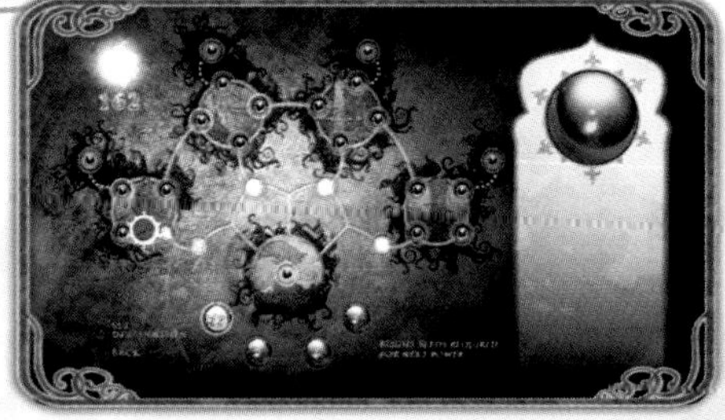

With the left control stick, you move a cursor around the map screen. Moving the cursor over a node shows you the name of the area and all relevant statistics about it. When the area is still corrupt, the map screen shows whether you have visited the location and which power is associated with the area. Once it has been healed, though, you can see how many Light Seeds are there and how many you have collected thus far.

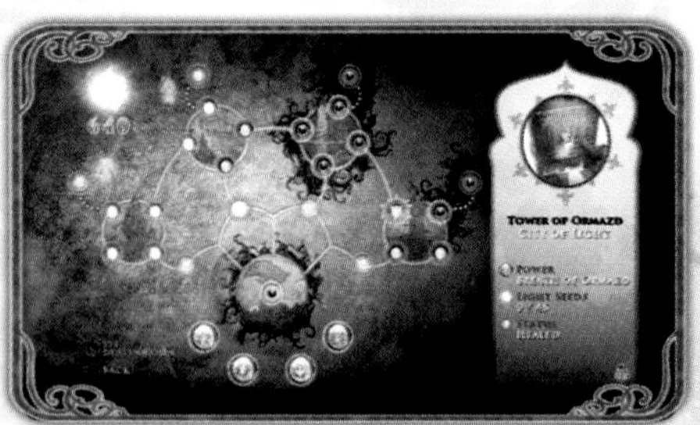

You can also set a destination on each area by pressing the jump button after placing the cursor on top of where you want to go. Setting a destination is extremely useful. Once this is set, Elika can use her compass skill to show you the way to your desired location. Press the magic button to see Elika release a burst of light that slithers along the route to your chosen destination.

TIP

After you have purified an area, you can instantly teleport to it from the map screen. Select a healed area with the cursor and press the magic button. The Prince and Elika are instantly warped to the fertile ground of the selected area. This is a great way to cover great distance when hunting down errant Light Seeds after earning a new power.

NOTE

The four crests at the bottom of the map are the different Ormazd powers. To learn more about those powers and how to unlock them, please see the Ormazd Power section of this chapter.

Breaking Through

At the start of the adventure, you chase Elika through a canyon and into the temple of the Tree of Life. After disastrous events play out, you have limited access to the world. There are three paths from the desert outside the temple that spider across the world. The paths are accessed via openings in the imposing cliff sides.

After one Elika-assisted jump across a wide chasm, the duo is on their way. The route soon forks. Each direction leads to the gateway area of each region. However, the regions cannot be accessed right away. You must first unlock the first of Ormazd's powers to move into the different regions. But earning Ormazd's powers is not going to be easy.

Ahriman has placed one of his Corrupted at each of these first nodes to block you from reaching the fertile ground. You must defeat the Corrupted in combat. Once the Corrupted has been dispelled from the area, Elika can purify the fertile ground and redeem the soil. After an area has been purified, not only does the color and splendor return, but the skies twinkle with the appearance of Light Seeds.

This process is repeated in each area of the four different regions. After negotiating the treacherous paths toward each area—all areas inside a specific region are interconnected—you must jump, climb, and balance your way to the next Corrupted battle. The Corrupted influences each area of a region, so you must face down the Corrupted four times before you can finally take him or her on in a battle for the fate of the entire region.

Approaches

As you can see from the map, all of the areas in a specific region are linked. The circle in the center is the location of the fertile ground that must be purified. That central location is without fail the scene of some incredible acrobatics and puzzle-solving, as you find a way to scale great heights or work ancient machinery that unlocks the path to the patch of fertile soil in need of purification. There, the Corrupted that poisons the areas waits.

But you can approach each area from at least two different directions. Each path leads directly to the starting point of the quest for the fertile ground, but offers different puzzles and obstacles. For example, here are two ways into the Spire of Dreams within the Royal Palace.

The path from the west requires balancing along a narrow beam over a bottomless chasm.

The path from the east is a long corridor, ravaged by both time and corruption. You must jump from one orphaned column to the next to negotiate the corridor.

NOTE

IT DOES NOT MATTER WHICH WAY YOU APPROACH AN AREA—THE GOAL IS ITS FERTILE GROUND AND THE ULTIMATE GOAL IS NOT AFFECTED.

LIGHT AND DARK

Because of the unleashing of Ahriman, the entire world has been splashed with corruption. To seal Ahriman, you must deprive him of his power by purifying the fertile grounds he has buried beneath layers of corruption and locked away behind the protection of his wicked Corrupted. But just fighting to the fertile ground and purifying an area does not end the challenge.

CORRUPTED LAND

Your first visit to any area is dreary. Paradise has been lost beneath the deadly film of Ahriman's corruption. Plants have withered. Sunlight has been snuffed out. While navigating to the fertile ground, you must avoid pulsing patches of corruption on walls and floors. Just touching the stuff threatens your life. Only the miracle of Elika's magic saves you before you are completely consumed by its evil force.

RETURN OF THE PRINCE
MOVES IN MYSTERIOUS WAYS
DYNAMIC WORLD
DESERT
RUINED CITADEL
THE VALE
ROYAL PALACE
CITY OF LIGHT
TREE OF LIFE
SECRETS

When you first enter an area that is corrupt, you face off against a living embodiment of that corruption, called a soldier. As you approach the crossroads that link two areas, you see the soldier not in corporeal form, but as a cloud of black. As you sidle up to the cloud, the soldier forms. These soldiers are found at the nexus between areas, where the routes leading toward and away from an area meet. To start pushing toward the fertile ground, you must first defeat the soldier. These battles are much shorter than your epic fights with the Corrupted, but that does not mean you can let your guard down. Deflect incoming blows with well-timed guard moves. Use Elika to blast away corrupt armor. And press these beasts up to the edge of platforms so you can drive your sword right through their dark hearts and dispel them forever. Not until the areas on each side of the crossroads have been purified do these soldiers stop spawning.

When you first spot the growing cloud of corruption, rush in and slice it with your sword. This instantly dispels the evil before the monster can form. If you hesitate for even half of a step, the monster will coalesce from the murk and muck.

PURIFICATION

After you defeat the Corrupted that guards the fertile ground at the heart of these initial gateways, Elika can purify the area. Move into the blue beacon that marks the fertile ground and activate Elika's magic to start the purification process. Elika steps into the light and rises into the air, becoming one with the beacon. To complete the purification, you must repeatedly tap the magic button until Elika forces back all of the corruption from the area.

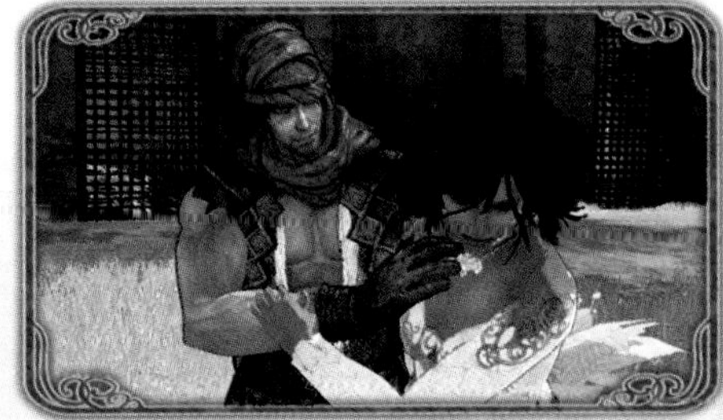

As Elika drops to the ground, exhausted from her work, you watch the purification unfold before your eyes. From the heart of the beacon, a wave of healing ripples outward. Shadow is washed away from the earth. Flowers return to bloom. Color soaks the landscape. The choked sky is cleared of darkness. It's quite a transformation.

But even though Elika is fatigued, there is no time for rest. Now the second half of the mission begins. It's time to collect Light Seeds.

NOTE

To open the path to the final battle with the Corrupted in a specific region, you must purify all four areas in that region first.

Light Seeds

Purifying a patch of fertile ground releases the Light Seeds, a concentrated magic that Elika uses to unlock new Ormazd powers. The Light Seeds are scattered around each area. Some of them are easy to pick up, but others are deftly hidden in corners or beneath platforms. You must search high and low to find all the Light Seeds in each area; there are 45 Light Seeds to find in each area. The final Corrupted battles give you 25 Light Seeds without your having to hunt them down individually.

The Light Seeds require you re-explore the area. Since the corruption is gone, new paths through the area are now open. Walls that were previously impossible to touch due to pulsing masses of corruption are now safe for wall running. The Light Seeds are not only spread across the area, but also stretch along the two paths that join the area to its neighboring areas in the region. You must explore that path until you reach the corruption of the neighboring area. If you are in an area that is connected to the next region as well, such as the Royal Spire in the Royal Palace region, you must also check the corridor that links the two regions for additional hidden Light Seeds.

With few exceptions, you cannot gather all 45 Light Seeds during your first visit to an area after Elika purifies it. A handful of Light Seeds are out of normal reach unless you have unlocked the Ormazd power back at the temple that activates the different power plates in each area. For example:

There are Light Seeds up on the ledge high above the cliff. However, because you have not unlocked the Breath of Ormazd power, the power plate is dormant. Come back after earning enough Light Seeds to unlock the power.

After unlocking the Breath of Ormazd power, the power plate is now active. Rush toward it and use Elika's magic to utilize the power plate and ascend the cliff side to grab the Light Seeds and complete the collection for this area.

NOTE

When you find all of the Light Seeds in an area the blue orb that denotes the purified area turns white.

Ormazd Powers

You cannot unlock Ormazd's powers without Light Seeds. You begin your adventure with none. To start banking Light Seeds, you must purify the gateways between the desert and the regions, such as the King's Gate. There are 45 Light Seeds in these areas. These go a long way to boosting your nascent Light Seed collection so you can start unlocking those much-needed powers.

The four powers are:

 ***Step of Ormazd***

 ***Hand of Ormazd***

Wings of Ormazd

 ***Breath of Ormazd***

You can unlock these powers in any order you desire. The cost of unlocking the next power goes up each time you unlock a new power—it does not matter which one you pick and when. The needed number of Light Seeds for each power is 70, 140, 340, and 540. There are 1,000 Light Seeds in the entire world, so you have ample opportunities for hunting down these precious orbs. When you reach a Light Seed threshold, definitely return to the temple so you can open new areas and seek out addition fertile ground for purification.

Once a power has been unlocked, you can start using the power plates associated with the particular power. Each power plate is colored so it matches up with the associated power anyway, but once you have unlocked the associated power, the physical plates light up out in the regions.

To unlock a power, step on the matching seal outside the temple and press the magic button, just as if you were trying to purify fertile ground. Elika will take care of the rest.

As soon as you unlock a new power, you are directed to a short tutorial of how to use the power.

Step of Ormazd

The Step of Ormazd activates the red power plates. These plates launch the Prince and Elika through the air, rocketing them toward previously unreachable platforms and landings. In some places, a system of three or four red power plates must be negotiated to reach the fertile ground.

This power unlocks:

 ***The Sun Temple***

The Windmills 

Machinery Ground

Reservoir 

Hand of Ormazd

The Hand of Ormazd activates the blue power plates. These plates send the Prince and Elika swirling into the sky along arcs. These plates often bounce the pair up to hard-to-reach Light Seeds or across treacherous bends.

This power unlocks:

 ***Tower of Ahriman***

 ***City of Light***

 ***Royal Spire***

 ***Spire of Dreams***

Wings of Ormazd

This Ormazd power blasts the Prince and Elika into the heavens from the yellow power plates. While zooming along a predetermined path, you must steer the pair around obstacles such as pillars with the left control stick.

This power unlocks:

 ***Marshalling Ground***

 ***Martyr's Tower***

 ***Royal Gardens***

 ***Coronation Hall***

Breath of Ormazd

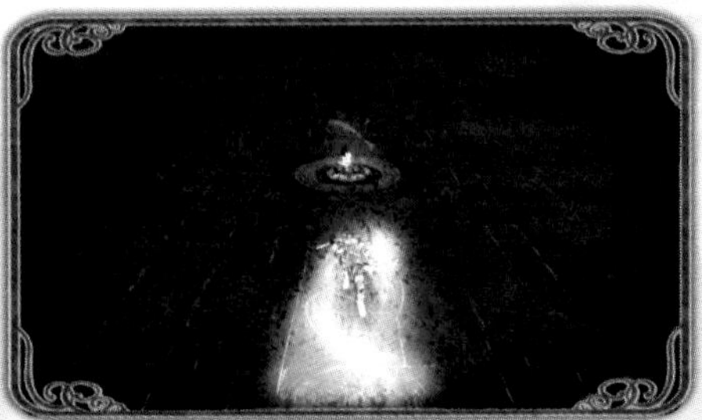

The Breath of Ormazd allows the Prince and Elika to use the green power plates. This power lets the Prince climb along vertical and horizontal surfaces free of gravity's grip. Often, several green power plates are linked to create a course or track through an area so the Prince can negotiate a tall building or a twisted piece of machinery.

This power unlocks:

Queen's Tower

Tower of Ormazd

Construction Yard

Heaven's Stair

The Changing World

As mentioned earlier in the chapter, the Ahura world changes depending on the order in which you explore the different areas and battle the Corrupted. The Corrupted are also affected by the order in which you visit areas and fight the other Corrupted, so be sure to know beforehand what you are about to unlock by entering a specific area or by challenging one of the Corrupted.

Traps

There are four traps that are unlocked as you explore the world—one per region. When a trap is unlocked by your visiting a specific area, the affects of the trap spread across the world. Different areas are infested by the trap, which can alter your approach to the area. Once a trap has been unlocked, you cannot contain it. It's out there permanently. You can manage the trap's rollout by avoiding the areas that unlock them. By visiting them as late as possible, you can keep routes through the world fairly clear. Here are the four different traps plus the areas they affect, so you can plan your approach on the different Corrupted. To avoid the traps for as long as possible, collect all of the Light Seeds you can from a healed area before moving on to the next. If you minimize the number of areas you visit to collect the required Light Seeds for unlocking the four magics of Ormazd, you can delay releasing the traps.

NOTE

The screens in this guide were taken from different plays through the game, which affects the traps you see in them. Depending on how you play, you will undoubtedly see different traps in different places. This does not change how you get through an area. The necessary acrobatics or puzzle solutions do not change. You just have to adjust your timing to deal with the traps as they come.

Tremor

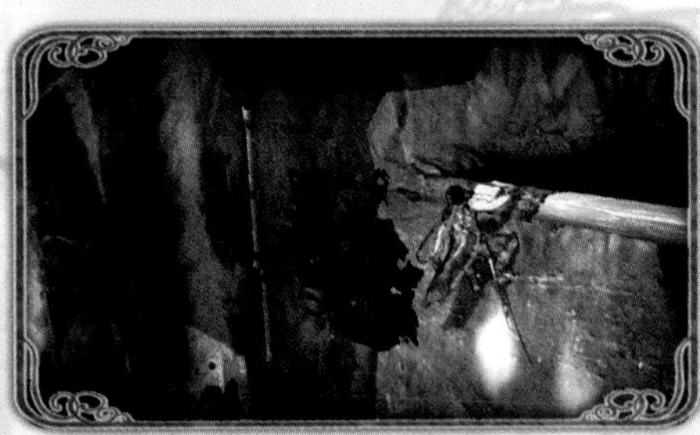

The tremors are unlocked by visiting the Sun Temple in the Ruined Citadel. Tremors are concentrated balls of corruption that roll up and down surfaces such as walls. If the Prince collides with one while wall running or climbing, he's sucked into the darkness. Elika must then save him, forcing him back to the start of the interrupted acrobatic sequence. Tremors essentially affect your timing. You must watch the rolling balls and then start your move when the route is clear. Unlocking the tremors affects the following areas: the Windmills, Martyr's Tower, Sun Temple, King's Gate, Machinery Ground, the Cauldron, Spire of Dreams, Royal Gardens, Coronation Hall, Royal Spire, the Cavern, City of Light—plus the routes between King's Gate, the Cauldron, and the Temple, the routes between the Cauldron, the Cavern, and the Temple, the routes between the Cavern, City Gate, and the Temple, and the routes between Martyr's Tower and Machinery Ground.

Gas

When you chase the Alchemist up Heaven's Stair in the Vale, you unlock the gas trap. The gas is an aerated form of corruption. It gets on the skin and seeps into the lungs when breathed. If the Prince remains for too long in an area poisoned by the gas, he fails. Elika must then save him. So, when the air looks thick with corruption particles, pick up the pace and keep an eye out for pockets of fresh air. As long as you keep moving through the gas, you should be fine. But if you stand still to gawk at your surroundings, you're going to be in serious trouble. Unlocking the gas in Heaven's Stair affects these areas: the Windmills, Martyr's Tower, King's Gate, Machinery Ground, Heaven's Stair, the Cauldron, Spire of Dreams, Royal Gardens, Queen's Tower—plus the routes between King's Gate, the Cauldron, and the Temple, the routes between the Cauldron, the Cavern, and the Temple, and the routes between the Cavern, City Gate, and the Temple.

Swarm

The Concubine releases the swarm trap in the Coronation Hall of the Royal Palace. The swarm is a swirling mass of corruption particles that chases the Prince like mad hornets. The swarm is persistent and will not let up until the Prince leaves the affected area. If the swarm closes in and manages to engulf the Prince, he falls and Elika must save him. So, if the swarm is on your tail, you can never stop. You must keep moving until the swarm dissipates. Once the swarm has been released in the Coronation Hall, the following areas are affected: Martyr's Tower, Marshalling Ground, Sun Temple, King's Gate, Machinery Ground, Heaven's Stair, Observatory, Construction Yard, Reservoir, Spire of Dreams, Coronation Hall, Royal Spire, the Cavern, Tower of Ormazd, Tower of Ahriman, City Gate—plus the routes between the Cauldron, the Cavern, and the Temple, and the routes between the Cavern, City Gate, and the Temple.

Tendrils

The tendrils trap is releases by the Warrior in the City of Light. This trap is similar to the tremor. Tendrils lurk on walls. Every few seconds, the tendrils explode from the wall and flail about. If the Prince is captured by the tendrils, he's violently yanked into the wall and then flung away. Like the tremors, this trap affects your timing. When wall running, for example, you must watch the tendrils ahead then start your acrobatic sequence so that you pass over tendrils as they pull back into the wall. When the Warrior releases the tendril trap, the following areas are affected: the Windmills, Martyr's Tower, Marshalling Ground, Sun Temple, King's Gate, Machinery Ground, Heaven's Stair, Construction Yard, Reservoir, Cauldron, Royal Gardens, Royal Spire,

Tower of Ormazd, Tower of Ahriman, Queen's Tower, City of Light, City Gate—plus the routes between King's Gate, the Cauldron, and the Temple, the routes between the Cauldron, the Cavern, and the Temple, the routes between the Cavern, City Gate, and the Temple, and the routes between Royal Spire and the Tower of Ormazd.

Return of the Prince
Moves in Mysterious Ways
Dynamic World
Desert
Ruined Citadel
The Vale
Royal Palace
City of Light
Tree of Life
Secrets

Tip

To delay the traps effectively, visit the four gateway areas—King's Gate, the Cauldron, City Gate, and the Cavern—and clear them of Light Seeds. Then, avoid the Sun Temple since it's the closest area to the desert that unlocks a trap. Keep away from the other three trap-unlocking areas as you purify the other three regions of the Vale, Royal Palace, and City of Light. If you keep on top of Light Seed collecting, you can reach about 350 Light Seeds before having to unlock more than one trap.

The Corrupted

The Corrupted are also affected by the order in which you fight them. Each Corrupted possesses one of Ahriman's Influences, which were detailed in chapter 2. As soon as one of the Corrupted uses its influence for the first time, all other Corrupted can then call upon that influence. The only exception to this rule in the Warrior, who can call upon Ahriman's Rage. No other Corrupted can use Ahriman's Rage and the Warrior cannot use Ahriman's Patience. (He's simply too big for your gauntlet.) As you fight the Corrupted, consider each of these influences and which ones you want to deal with.

Tip

Ahriman's Rage, for example, is unleashed by the Hunter and is dispelled with the sword. This is the easiest to deal with, so perhaps you want to tackle the Hunter first.

The Corrupted are always aware of each other. This manifests itself through the changing difficulty of each Corrupted battle. Every time you defeat a Corrupted in their lair and completely purify a region of the world, a signal goes out to the surviving Corrupted. Those Corrupted become more aggressive, and more likely to use their special attacks sooner. Each Corrupted you drive out of the world keeps raising the aggression levels of the other Corrupted until the fourth and final Corrupted is a real force to be reckoned with.

The order in which you fight the Corrupted also affects the different attacks they employ. Each Corrupted has complex attacks that require lightning reflexes to either repel or counter them. There are four types of complex attacks: weapon, corruption, grab, and jumping However, the same kind of attack manifests differently for each of the Corrupted.

For example, the weapon attack of the Hunter is the repeated slashing of his triple blade, while the Concubine twirls her staff into you. To fight back against these attacks, you have to hit the on-screen buttons as they flash. The required buttons are random.

Depending on which areas you visit and which Corrupted you fight, you can unlock these complex attacks in different orders. If you play the game a second time and visit the areas in a different order, you can avoid seeing the complex attacks sooner than if you took an alternate route. Here are the areas that unlock the complex attacks:

Area	Attack(s) Released
Martyr's Tower	Weapon attack
Tower of Ahriman	Jump attack
Queen's Tower	Jump attack
Machinery Ground	Corruption attack
Spire of Dreams	Grab attack
Hunter's Lair	All complex attacks
Observatory	All complex attacks
Concubine's Chambers	All complex attacks
Warrior's Fortress	All complex attacks

CAUTION

Defeating any of the Corrupted in the final area of a region, such as the Alchemist at the Observatory, releases all of the complex attacks for all of the remaining Corrupted. To avoid unlocking the complex attacks so soon, avoid finishing off a Corrupted for as long as you can.

TIP

The Breath of Ormazd unlocks access to the Tower of Ormazd and the Queen's Tower. Both of those areas release the jumping complex attack, so consider waiting as long as possible before converting your Light Seeds for that magic.

Mourning King

Unlocking Ormazd's Powers draws the attention of Elika's father. The Mourning King is descending into madness, which forces him to lash out against the Prince and Elika when they revisit the temple at the 140 and 540 Light Seed thresholds. After unlocking the next power and completing the short tutorial, the Mourning King launches his attack. You must repel the Mourning King each time to leave the temple and venture back to the corrupted regions.

The Mourning King not only unleashes the different Ahriman's Influences you unlock by meeting other Corrupted, but he can also call upon the special techniques of each encountered boss. For example, after the Concubine unleashes her seduction attack that reverses your controls, the Mourning King can use it, too, even though the other Corrupted cannot. The Mourning King is unique in this ability to harvest other Corrupted's special attacks.

First Mourning King Battle

After returning the temple to unlock your second power, the Mourning King appears. He cruelly casts aside his daughter and zeroes in on you. He recognizes you as a threat to Ahriman's power and decides to take care of you himself, despite Elika's pleading. You must fight back against the mad king to escape the temple with Elika and return to the corrupted regions.

CAUTION

Elika cannot help you in this battle, so don't try to string together combos with her magic attacks. Stick to acrobatics, swordplay, and the gauntlet.

The Mourning King uses a twirling strike to deal extensive damage against you. Fortunately, this attack has a warning sign. When the king's sword hand glows yellow, he is about to unleash a series of blows that concludes with him jumping into the air and swinging his sword at your torso. If you do not successfully deflect the first attack in this chain, hold the guard button to enter a defensive crouch and weather his blows.

RETURN OF THE PRINCE
MOVES IN MYSTERIOUS WAYS
DYNAMIC WORLD
DESERT
RUINED CITADEL
THE VALE
ROYAL PALACE
CITY OF LIGHT
TREE OF LIFE
SECRETS

Regular sword strikes are good for hammering away at the king's health, but look for openings to launch truncated combos. After deflecting the twirling attack, grab the king with your gauntlet and fling him into the air. Then slash with your sword as he comes down. Do not stop until he starts to recover.

If the king gets the drop on you, be ready to hit the on-screen command to negate his severe blow. If you miss, the king recovers health while you stagger.

TIP

Throw the king into walls and corner him. Attack with four sword blows so you can close in and physically grab the king. The combo ends with your throwing the king to the ground, which does solid damage.

Elika stops the battle before you can kill her father. She hits the Mourning King with a magic attack that knocks the fury out of him. For a moment, she sees the man that took care of her as a little girl and promised to split the heavens for her.

Second Mourning King Battle

The Mourning King is much more aggressive in this encounter. He attacks right away, coming at you with a brutal sword attack. You must quickly deflect the blow to avoid injury. This can actually lead to deflection exchanges where you parry each other's attacks several times before you can effectively land a slashing blow against Elika's father.

Back the Mourning King up to the wall with gauntlet attacks. Throwing the Mourning King to the wall puts you in an advantageous position, as long as you do not attack from too far away. That will sacrifice the upper hand, giving the Mourning King space to counterattack and throw you off your rhythm.

Once you have the Mourning King cornered, slash away. Eventually, you will grab him and hurl him over your shoulder, chiseling away a chunk of his health.

The Mourning King will explode in a fit of corruption. Spikes of blackness erupt from his body. In this temporary form, the Mourning King is invincible against sword or gauntlet attacks. You must get close enough for Elika to attack with her magic and dispel the darkness. As soon as the Mourning King is revealed, rush in and resume your attacks.

At the end of the battle, the corruption completely consumes the Mourning King, pulling him into the ground.

The Beginning

Desert

A sandstorm consumes the desert, enveloping a lone traveler. It is the Prince, in search of his beloved donkey, Farrah. The storm has divided the two companions, and the Prince is eager to find Farrah before she wanders too far. But, unable to see his way across the dunes, the Prince also finds himself just as lost. The Prince soon stumbles into a canyon.

Obscured from the rest of the world by the gritty maelstrom, the canyon acts as the gateway to the world of the Ahuras. The Prince knows nothing of the Ahuras on this day, but before his adventure is complete, the traveler will play a central part in the very fate of not only the Ahura people, but also the survival of their world and all those beyond it.

The Canyon

The walls of the canyon keep the sandstorm at bay, allowing the Prince to regain his bearings. This is a strange place—as unrecognizable to him as the glyphs carved into the canyon walls. Hoping his donkey was smart enough to seek refuge in this canyon, the Prince begins calling out for his faithful animal. But there is no answer. The canyon is quiet. All is still. But not for long.

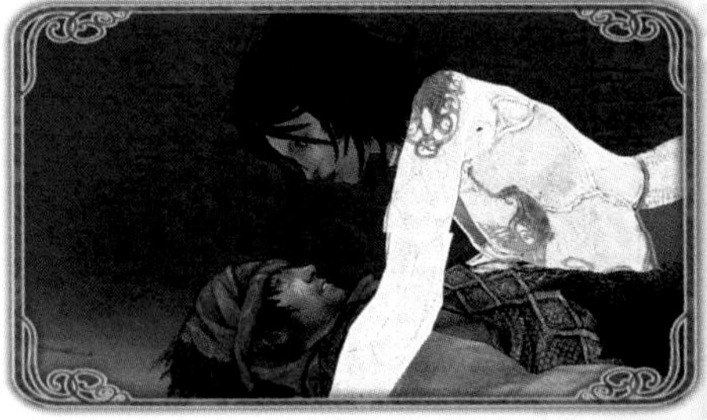

Suddenly cast in shadow, the Prince looks up to see what has passed in front of the sun. It's the unmistakable shape of a woman. She crashes down on top of the Prince, knocking him to the ground. The Prince instinctively starts unloading his small talk, but this woman has no time nor interest in a silver tongue. She clasps her hand over the Prince's mouth and slams him against the wall of the cliff she has just hurled herself over.

The woman is fleeing a trio of guards armed with deadly pikes.

After the guards retreat from the wall to look elsewhere for the escaping woman, she pulls away from the Prince and flees deeper into the canyon. The Prince has no choice but to follow this enchanting person before she gets too far ahead. Who is she? Why is she on the run? And, by any chance, has she seen a lonely donkey anywhere?

NOTE

Chasing Elika through the canyon acts as a tutorial of sorts, giving you a chance to test out the basics of running, jumping, wall running, and even a little taste of combat.

Follow Elika through the first part of the canyon, hopping over the small gaps in the ground. Don't worry if you accidentally take a tumble. These gaps are shallow and you can easily scramble back to higher ground by pressing against the wall and hitting the jump button. When the Prince grabs the ledge above, just press up on the left control stick to continue your pursuit.

Wall run along the sides of the canyon, mimicking Elika's movements. Use her steps as a guide while chasing her.

The guards have spotted Elika. And now they've spotted you, too.

As you keep after Elika, you must combine wall running with jumping. Wall run along the scratches in the walls of the canyon. At the end of the wall run (typically near the end of the scratch marks), press the jump button to kick away from the wall and drop down on a ledge on the opposite side of the canyon. Follow Elika around the next bend in the canyon.

The guards have Elika surrounded. You don't like those odds.

When you drop down to assist, one of the guards engages you. This is your first fight, so use it to get the feel for the combat system. The guard is a little timid, so you definitely can be aggressive without too much worry. Get close to the guard and tap the sword button to see a basic attack. Your sword cuts across the guard. Sparks fly. The guard loses some health, as noted by the health bar at the bottom of the screen.

Try out some easy combos here, too. After slashing the guard, use the dodge button perform an acrobatic move and actually run up the front of the guard. After starting this move, segue back into attacks by tapping the sword button again.

RETURN OF THE PRINCE
MOVES IN MYSTERIOUS WAYS
DYNAMIC WORLD
DESERT
RUINED CITADEL
THE VALE
ROYAL PALACE
CITY OF LIGHT
TREE OF LIFE
SECRETS

TIP

Don't be too eager to beat the guard. Use this encounter to test out moves and get down the timing of attacks.

Wait for the guard to attack. When you see the pike moving, press the guard button to deflect the attack. Notice how the screen flashes gray. That means you successfully deflected and can now counter. Press the sword button to assail the guard.

Back the guard up into one of the walls and hammer him with a sword combo. If you get him completely against the wall before the fourth tap of the sword button, you throw the guard over your shoulder and back into the center of the little clearing.

While you watch the guard flee, Elika handles his companion in her own special way. The guard tries to slam Elika with his pike, but a blue field repels the attack. She cannot be killed? Scared by this display of sorcery, the guard runs. You mistake his flight as fear of your blade, unaware of Elika's powers just yet. Elika doesn't let on. Instead, she orders you to leave the canyon before you get too deep-as if you would actually do that...

Instead, follow Elika up the vertical shaft in the rear of the clearing. Jump from wall to wall. Holding the jump button when you land on the opposite wall makes you run up it a few steps. Before losing traction, tap the jump button again to kick away to the opposite wall. Repeat this until you reach the top of the shaft.

Follow Elika through the canyon, slowing only when you catch your first glimpse of a magnificent ancient tree rising out of the otherwise arid desert. It's breathtaking in its size and majesty. But you should also take a peek at the nearby rock outcropping. More men are on the ledge. They are pursuing Elika, so you had better quit sight-seeing and continue following her, just in case those guys reach her first.

As the Prince crosses the bridge to pursue Elika, one of the guards rolls a giant stone down on top of him. The Prince dodges the stone, but it shatters the bridge he is on. The bridge collapses, taking the Prince down with it. Elika has no choice but to reveal her secret to the Prince now. Summoning an ancient Ahura magic, Elika jumps into the abyss after the Prince. She reaches out and takes his hand before he falls too far. Her magic pulls both of them back from the abyss, depositing the pair on the opposite side of the bridge. There is no going back now. The Prince is now stuck on this side of the canyon.

Using this magic in such a selfless way—throwing herself toward certain death and counting on a mystical power to prevent such a grisly fate—saps Elika of her strength. She wilts in the Prince's arms. The Prince carries her through the canyon, promising to stay with her in gratitude for saving his life. And besides, it really doesn't look like he can go back the way he came.
At the end of the trail, another guard challenges the Prince.

Try out the gauntlet in this battle. Get in close and tap the gauntlet button. You grab the guard and fling him high into the air. This is the start of a potential combo, so give some extra moves a try while the guard is airborne.

Tapping the gauntlet button again grabs the guard again and throws him to the ground.

Corner the guard and lay into him with a sword combo that ends with you throwing him over your shoulder and back into the center of the arena.

After you defeat the guard, Elika agrees to follow you to the canyon's end. Jump from ledge to ledge through the remainder of the canyon. Use the scratches on the wall as indicators of where to wall run and kick away to bound to the opposite side of the canyon.

RETURN OF THE PRINCE
MOVES IN MYSTERIOUS WAYS
DYNAMIC WORLD
DESERT
RUINED CITADEL
THE VALE
ROYAL PALACE
CITY OF LIGHT
TREE OF LIFE
SECRETS

At the very end of the canyon, you must perform two wall runs in succession. This can be tricky at first. Jump to the right wall and wall run until the scratches end. Then kick off to the other wall. Keep holding the jump button so you run as soon as you touch the wall. At the end of the wall run on the left side, tap the jump button to leap away from that wall.

Two guards attack at the far end of the canyon, although, they do so one at a time. Use the dodge button to start acrobatic attacks. Jumping over the guards leaves a nice opening for launching furious sword attacks.

CAUTION

If you're struck by a guard, fall back. If you hold down the guard button, you recover from your injuries slower than you will if you just keep your distance and move normally.

Lay into these guards with sword combos to keep them on their heels.

After you defeat the two guards, a third figure appears on the ridge above you. This is the Mourning King.

He calls to Elika by name. The king warns Elika about going to the giant temple at the base of the desert tree, but he is too far behind to stop her. What's more, she seems determined. Why she needs to go there is unknown to you, but since you still owe her your life, you should do everything you can to make sure she reaches the temple safely.

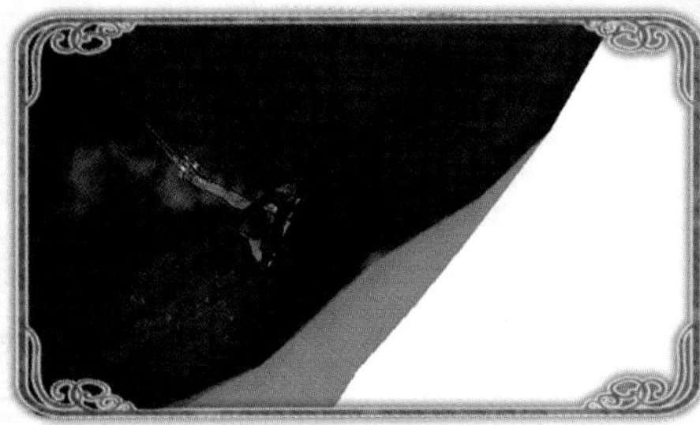

Use the grip fall to slide down the cliff and reach the desert floor.

Elika takes off in a sprint as soon as you touch down on the desert floor. Follow her across the dunes to the base of the temple. Run up the winding stairs on the left side of the temple to keep following Elika to the door of the temple. The door is firmly locked. You must find a mechanism to open it.

Climb the wall next to the door by using the exposed scaffolding. Scramble from one horizontal beam to the next by pressing up on the left control stick and tapping the jump button.

There is a crank at the top of the wall. Press the gauntlet button to grab the crank. Turn the crank with Elika's help to open the door. Now, descend the wall with a grip fall to enter the temple.

The Temple

The temple is silent. It looks as if it has been untouched for years. The great corridor leading into the heart of the temple is completely empty of life, save for its newest visitors. The Prince and Elika must run down the corridor and force open the next door in order to reach the heart of the temple before the Mourning King can catch up.

As the pair runs down the corridor, Elika tells the Prince about the temple's purpose. It's to contain the wicked power of Ahriman. The Prince had always dismissed tales of Ahriman as a sort of fable used to scare misbehaving children. But Elika dispels the myth. Ahriman is real. And if they do not reach the temple's center before the Mourning King, the Prince will find out just how real Ahriman is.

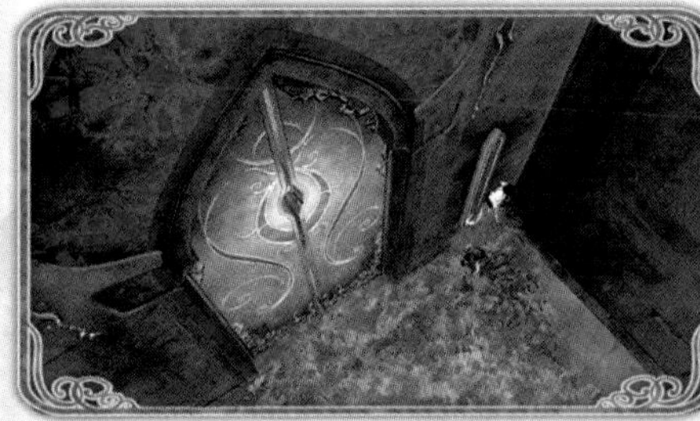

Jump on the ring next to the door. Your weight pulls it down, forcing open the door.

Rush down the steps in the next room to reach the center of the temple.

The Prince and Elika slowly approach the Tree of Life. The tree grows out of a patch of sacred ground—fertile soil that holds back the stink and rot of Ahriman's corrosive power. As long as the Tree of Life thrives, Ahriman cannot escape his prison. But the tree is weakening due to the Ahuras' decline. Elika must revive the tree to make sure Ahriman's influence does not do any more damage than it already has.

RETURN OF THE PRINCE
MOVES IN MYSTERIOUS WAYS
DYNAMIC WORLD
DESERT
RUINED CITADEL
THE VALE
ROYAL PALACE
CITY OF LIGHT
TREE OF LIFE
SECRETS

Before Elika can tell the Prince how she will nurture the Tree of Life, the doors to the central chamber are thrown open by the Mourning King. Flanked by two guards, the Mourning King endeavors to stop Elika from curing the tree. To do that, though, he must fight his way through the Prince, who already has his sword at the ready to defend Elika from the king's threats.

The Mourning King drops to the bottom floor of the temple. You must fight him. The Mourning King is a tougher opponent than the guards, but he is not without weaknesses that can be exploited. The king must cover a bit of distance to engage the Prince. While the king approaches, move so that the king is caught between the Prince and the Tree of Life.

Deflect the Mourning King's first attack and then hit him with an immediate counter. This slams the king up against the Tree of Life.

Hit the sword again to grab the king and draw him close. You instinctively butt heads with the king, doing a solid amount of damage. The king is then tossed aside.

The Mourning King has a special move—a twirling attack that knocks you to the ground if it connects. Fortunately, there is a "tell" for this attack: When you spy a yellow light around the king's sword hand, he is getting ready for the four-part attack. If you deflect the first attack, you stop the king's combo.

If the first attack connects, hold the guard button and just weather the remainder of the king's volley. You do not regain full strength very quickly while in this defensive crouch, but if the king connects the rest of the attack, he will go for a lethal attack.

CAUTION

If the king goes for a lethal attack, a random button flashes on screen that you'll need to press. If you miss, the king goes for the kill. Elika's magic repels him from you, but during the breather, the king recovers a lot of stamina.

Toss the king into the air with your gauntlet and start an acrobatic combo.

Slice up the king with sword attacks until his health meter is empty.

The Prince has defeated the king in combat, but the man still draws breath. And before he does expire from his wounds, he makes one final stand. But instead of raising his sword to the Prince, the Mourning King hacks at the Tree of Life. His great blade cleaves the fragile trunk of the Tree of Life in two. Elika screams for her father to stop, but it's too late. The Tree of Life has been cut down. The shackles of Ahriman have been loosened.

Why on earth would the Mourning King do such a thing? Why would he doom the world to the horror of Ahriman?

The death of the Tree of Life releases Ahriman's wretched corruption from the heart of the temple where it was kept prisoner for so long. The wave of escaping evil rushes from the temple, spreading across the world within seconds, plunging it into shadow, and choking life from the final remnants of the Ahura civilization. The Prince sees the effects of Ahriman's corruption right away. A monster made of pure corruption rises from the ground.

NOTE

Elika unleashes her magic attack against the first monster, knocking it back. You can now call upon Elika's magic in battle. Use her magic to chain together combos even stronger than those you used against the guards and the Mourning King.

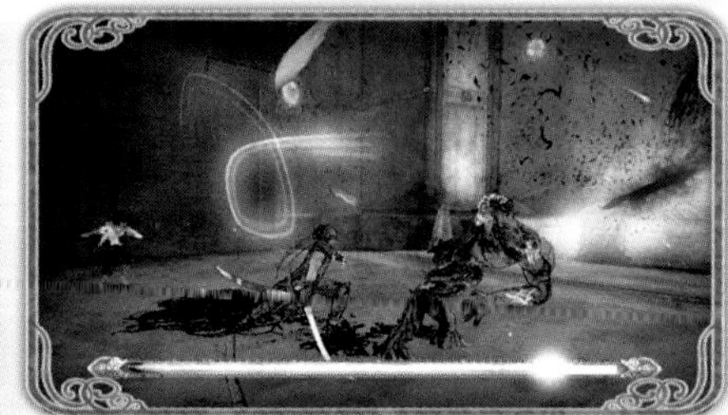

Waste no time engaging the monster. When within range, start a combo with a sword attack. From there, call in Elika to pounce on it with a magic attack.

CAUTION

The monster is skilled at counterattacks. It can deflect your blows, so be ready to exchange deflections in this battle. There is a rhythm to deflecting and counterattacking. You'll soon start to feel this deflecting groove when you see the incoming attack, and then counter when you enemy recoils.

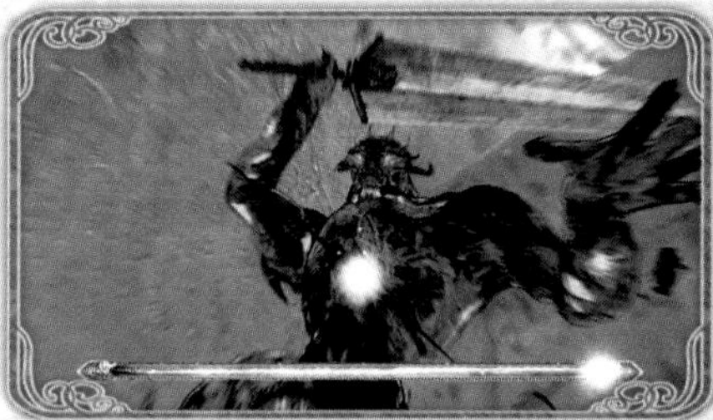

If the monster injures you and then gets the drop again, you must hit the on-screen command right away so Elika can repel the monster. If you miss, the monster regains strength and the fight is prolonged.

Back the monster up to one of the ledges and unleash a flurry of attacks. If you overwhelm the monster when its back is against the ledge, the Prince finishes the combo by driving his sword into its heart. The monster instantly dies.

Escape

Now that the monster is dead, you must flee the temple. Jump across the stones rising from the pool of corruption. (If you fall into the inky mass, Elika will rescue you.) Wall run at the end of the stones to reach a fissure in the platform beneath the temple door.

RETURN OF THE PRINCE
MOVES IN MYSTERIOUS WAYS
DYNAMIC WORLD
DESERT
RUINED CITADEL
THE VALE
ROYAL PALACE
CITY OF LIGHT
TREE OF LIFE
SECRETS

While you climb along the fissure, the two guards that joined the Mourning King inside the temple lose their lives to another monster. Wall run to the left at the end of the fissure to drop down to the base of the stairs that lead up to the monster—and the exit.

Fight the brute to the edge of the platform and then hammer it so you finish it off with the same death blow as the previous monster's.

You must now escape the temple, as it is being consumed by Ahriman's corruption. The floor of the corridor that leads out to the desert cracks and buckles as the pulsing corruption rises from an evil core beneath the temple. Wall run along the wall to cross the pits and kick away to jump to the opposite side of the corridor.

The end of the corridor shatters as the poison pushes its way to the surface. The gap is just too far for the Prince to jump. However, Elika's magic again proves more than just useful—it's essential. Jump straight across the chasm. At the end of the jump, as the Prince starts to come down and the screen turns gray, tap the magic button to call upon Elika. Elika grabs the Prince in midair and tosses him to the safe landing on the other side of the gap.

The temple doors slam shut behind the Prince and Elika. This is Ahriman's territory now. And the wrathful god is entirely too strong for even Elika's powerful magic to stop. As the Prince recovers from the jump, he cannot believe his eyes. The world outside the temple is barely recognizable. The once-blue sky is now an expanse of shadow. The great regions of the Ahura civilization are now blanketed in corruption.

Elika tells the Prince that they must now endeavor to stop Ahriman. The world that Ahriman has corrupted must now be purified. The four regions must be cleansed of the poison by visiting the fertile ground in each.

Traveling to the outer regions will not be easy. Elika uses a map at the base of the temple to show the Prince how they must fan out to the different regions via a system of corridors and bridges. Unfortunately, most of those paths have fallen into ruin, and on top of that, they've been affected by Ahriman's corruption. In order to reach the four regions and purify them, they must first cross the desert and slip between the giant columns that mark the start of three different paths.

From these paths, they can branch out to the four regions. But nothing is that simple. Even these gateway regions must first be purified before the pair can move through them. And once they have accomplished this, they must find a way to unlock the dormant magic of Ormazd to access the four different areas of each region. Perhaps if Elika can harness the power of the fertile ground, she can find a way to appeal to Ormazd and learn his ancient magics....

Ruined Citadel

Across the swirling sands of desert and beyond a canyon crawling with corruption is the Ruined Citadel. In better days, the military might of the Ahuras marshalled here. The Ahura warriors were known as the fiercest in the world, but they only used their force for good—never to advance selfish interests. But now the citadel has fallen. And filling the void is the Hunter. He lurks in the crumbling ruins, setting traps and waiting patiently for his prey. For thanks to Ahriman, the Hunter has all of eternity to play this most dangerous game.

What's Unleashed

Upon visiting the Ruined Citadel, the Prince and Elika release a multitude of complications into the wild. Not only is there a trap to be triggered—the tremors—but confronting the Hunter unlocks one of Ahriman's Influences for the benefit for soldiers and any remaining Corrupted.

The Hunter

Your eyes are not playing tricks on you—the shadows of the Ruined Citadel move. In the corners. Along the ceiling. They are creeping ever closer. And when you convince yourself that there's nothing there, that's the moment the Hunter strikes. The spoiled prince, who was addicted to the thrill of the hunt, is now forever sentenced to playing this game. As a powerful Corrupted, he is able to bring down prey of any size. But now humans hunt him, too, stalking him to the ends of the earth in the hopes of claiming the glory that will go to the one that snares the Hunter. Can you be that hero?

The Hunter uses traps to get the drop on his quarry. His favorite trick is to spit black ink in the eyes of his prey, disorienting them just before he strikes. While dueling the Hunter, watch for this attack. Suddenly, your vision is blotted out. You can see only the corners of the arena. You can maybe see the legs of the Hunter as he is closing in on you. You have two choices at this point. You can guard until the ink wears off in several seconds. But, if you land an attack against the Hunter, the ink immediately vanishes.

NOTE

As soon as the Hunter uses the spit attack for the first time, the Mourning King inherits the move.

The Hunter also unlocks one of Ahriman's Influences: Anger. When Ahriman's Anger is in effect, the Hunter in engulfed in blue fire. Only a sword attack dispels the state change. If you try to use the gauntlet, you fail and are injured. Calling upon Elika is a serious mistake, too. When she lunges into Ahriman's Anger, the effects of the state change overwhelm her and she is tossed aside for a few moments. So, when you spy that blue fire, put up your guard and wait for your opening. Hit the Hunter with a sword attack to remove the influence and then launch into a combo to drain his health.

NOTE

From the first time the Hunter calls upon Ahriman's Anger, the influence is unlocked for all other Corrupted and soldiers to use.

The Traps

When you arrive in the southern area of the Ruined Citadel, the Sun Temple, the Hunter unlocks one of the dynamic traps that infects the rest of the world: tremors. Tremors are rolling balls of corruption that slide up and down or left and right across your paths, making the timing of moves a touch trickier. For example, you may need to pause on some vines for a second to let the tremors in front of a power plate roll out of the way. Should you accidentally touch a tremor, you're pulled into it and Elika is forced to save you. When you recover, you return to the last instance of solid ground. When you unlock the tremors, the traps appear in the following areas:

The Windmills, Martyr's Tower, Sun Temple, King's Gate, Machinery Ground, the Cauldron, Spire of Dreams, Royal Gardens, Coronation Hall, Royal Spire, the Cavern, City of Light -- plus the routes between King's Gate, the Cauldron, & Temple, the routes between the Cauldron, the Cavern, & Temple, the routes between the Cavern, City Gate, & Temple, and the routes between Martyr's Tower & Machinery Ground.

King's Gate

RETURN OF THE PRINCE
MOVES IN MYSTERIOUS WAYS
DYNAMIC WORLD
DESERT
RUINED CITADEL
THE VALE
ROYAL PALACE
CITY OF LIGHT
TREE OF LIFE
SECRETS

Before the Prince and Elika can enter the Ruined Citadel, they must pass through the King's Gate. This outpost to the south of the Ruined Citadel was once a stronghold and excellent scouting spot for the Ahuras, but now it is sliding into the sand. Deliver the King's Gate from Ahriman so the Prince and Elika can stalk the Hunter in the Ruined Citadel.

Corrupt

Approach

When you reach the fork in the road leading away from the desert, take the left route to start moving on the King's Gate. Jump across the gap in the path and swing around the lone flagpole to reach a ledge below a series of brass rings. Use the rings to ascend the wall and scramble up to the higher path through the canyon.

The walls of the canyon pulse with corruption, so mind your step. Jump across the next two flagpoles and then settle on the ledge overlooking a post. Step out to the end of the post and jump to the next ledge.

Rush to the next post and use it as a springboard to reach the wall with a vertical fissure.

After climbing the fissure, hop across the series of posts to access some scaffolding.

Use the scaffolding to shimmy across the void and close in on the gate.

After pulling yourself up to the wooden ledge, jump along the system of posts and poles sticking out of the stone wall. The King's Gate is to your right.

King's Gate

To enter the King's Gate, step out on the post directly in front of the stronghold. Jump out to the column in front of you and swing around so your back is toward the structure. Jump away from the column to drop down on a safe ledge.

Use the vines on the wall to crawl to your left. Grip fall off the vines when you reach the corner.

Use the next two columns to continue circling the King's Gate.

Around the next corner, wall run to the vines. Crawl across the vines to the left and then wall run to the next ledge.

Jump out to the next column. Climb the column up to the next story of the gate. Swivel so your back is to the left and then kick away to land on a walkway that continues circling the gate. Corruption gnaws at the edges of the ledge, so stick close to the wall.

Jump to the next column and then roof along the ring to keep climbing the stronghold exterior.

Leap across the posts and then use the column to round the next corner of the gate.

You're almost to the top of the King's Gate. Jump across the columns and then wall run to the vines growing across the curved wall. Use the vines to crawl around the wall. The vines end in a patch of corruption, so wall run up.

The Hunter waits for you just inside the iron gate.

The Hunter

As soon as you approach the Hunter, the iron gate slams shut, locking you inside the arena. The top of the King's Gate is a large arena, giving you plenty of room to maneuver. There is no corruption on the ground, so you do not need to worry about backing the Corrupted opponent into a potentially advantageous position. However, even though you do have room to exchange blows, definitely work to keep the Hunter near the middle of the arena.

RETURN OF THE PRINCE
MOVES IN MYSTERIOUS WAYS
DYNAMIC WORLD
DESERT
RUINED CITADEL
THE VALE
ROYAL PALACE
CITY OF LIGHT
TREE OF LIFE
SECRETS

The Hunter wastes little time in attacking. Immediately put up your guard and let the Hunter's first volley play out. After the hunter's fourth attack with his giant blade, you have an opening to launch a combo of your own.

If the Hunter backs you into a wall, he opens his triple blade and tries to run you through. This is the struggle. Repeatedly tap the sword button to keep from getting skewered.

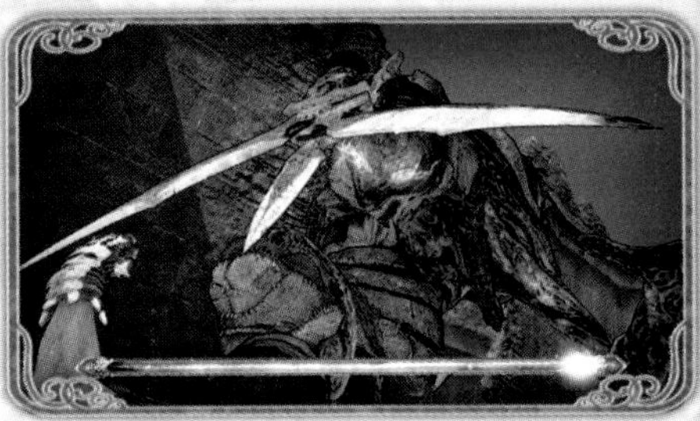

If the Hunter gets the drop on you while injured, be ready to hit the on-screen button to repel his attack.

CAUTION

If you miss repelling the Hunter's lethal attack, the Corrupted can heal his wounds while Elika' saves your hide.

Your sword is powerful, but linking a sword attack with Elika's magic—and then furthering it with the gauntlet—is the best way to handle the Hunter. Keep him on his heels with big combos. Since this is an early encounter, he does not strike back as hard as he will later on. Enjoy this while you can.

If the battle nears the wall, toss the Hunter into the air with your gauntlet and then reverse the course of the battle with an acrobatic move. Push the Hunter back to the arena's center with sword attacks.

When you empty the Hunter's health meter, he retreats to plot his next move. You let him go. The priority is to purify the fertile ground and liberate King's Gate. Now, collect some Light Seeds so you can earn Ormazd's magic.

Healed

Two paths lead away from the King's Gate: north and south. After healing the fertile ground and dispelling the corruption, search these routes in addition to the King's Gate to locate Light Seeds.

King's Gate

Healing the sacred ground returns color to the King's Gate. Sparking Light Seeds scatter across the stronghold. Follow the trail of Light Seeds across the King's Gate rooftop arena and pull down the ring next to the gate to unlock the exit.

When you step outside the arena and onto the post, you can see a collection of Light Seeds. Jump out to the column in front of you and then jump to the vines in the alcove directly ahead. Grip fall from the bottom of the vines to the floor to pick up the Light Seeds below.

Retrace your steps around the exterior of King's Gate to collect the Light Seeds hanging in the air and along the outer walls.

Red Power Plate

After you unlock the Step of Ormazd, you can access the red power plates at King's Gate and collect the remaining Light Seeds. Wall run out to this power plate and use Elika's magic to bound away from the wall.

You are launched to the next red power plate, just above the large door. There is a Light Seed right on top of the plate that you automatically pick up as you zoom past it.

Red Power Plate (continued)

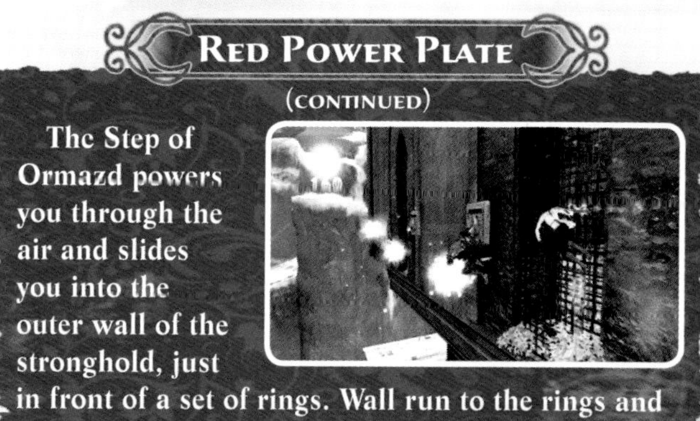

The Step of Ormazd powers you through the air and slides you into the outer wall of the stronghold, just in front of a set of rings. Wall run to the rings and link with each of them to pick up another three Light Seeds.

North Path

From the entrance of King's Gate, look to the left. That's the north path that leads to the Sun Temple. Jump away from the entrance and scramble up the wall. Now, jump out to the flagpoles and swing around them as you travel north. There is a Light Seed on the post between the flagpoles.

Use Elika's help to jump from the last flagpole to the vines on the cliff. Grab the Light Seed as you climb the vines. At the top of the wall, look north to see the loop you must make to grab the rest of the Light Seeds along this path.

Wall run up the rocks next to the ledge to pick up a Light Seed.

After jumping across the flagpole, slide down the tilted platform. Jump out at the end to wall run through the next Light Seed.

Jump between the cliffs as you run north to reach the crossroads between King's Gate and the Sun Temple. There is a soldier here that can be pushed to the edge of the arena and eliminated with a quick kill. On the way back to the King's Gate, wall run up the cliff to grab the hanging Light Seed.

Look to the right as you return to the entrance. Two Light Seeds are in an alcove. Jump out to them with Elika's help.

Follow the slides back to King's Gate. Swing across the flagpoles from the turret to collect more Light Seeds.

South Path

RETURN OF THE PRINCE
MOVES IN MYSTERIOUS WAYS
DYNAMIC WORLD
DESERT
RUINED CITADEL
THE VALE
ROYAL PALACE
CITY OF LIGHT
TREE OF LIFE
SECRETS

More Light Seeds await collection on the path back to the desert. Jump back across the posts and poles to gather up the prizes. When you reach the entrance of the canyon, wall run out to the ring and then to the ledge. Follow the vertical fissure down to locate another Light Seed.

Continue along the canyon back to the fork in the road to collect three Light Seeds.

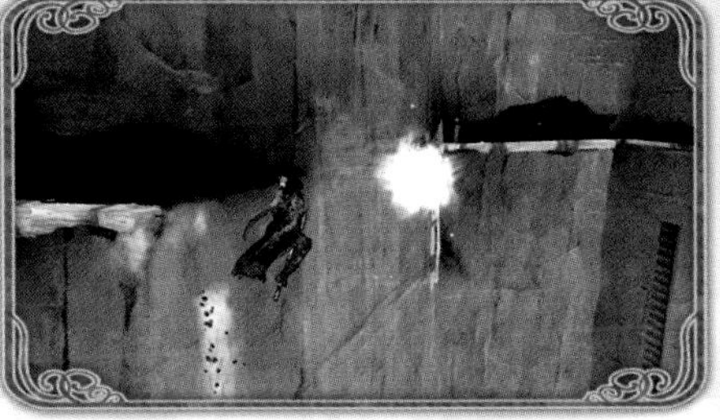

Return to the King's Gate via the fissures as before. When you reach the ledge at the entrance to the area, jump on the vines on the stone wall. Climb up them and wall run out to the column. Jump to the column to pick up one Light Seed. Now, leap the vines to pick up two more.

Sun Temple

The Sun Temple dominates the south of the Ruined Citadel region. This proud temple is now in utter decay and crawling with the Ahriman's poison. The Hunter could be anywhere in this maze of walls, posts, and poles, so the Prince and Elika must be ready at any moment for a surprise attack from the Corrupted.

Corrupt Approach

If you are approaching the Sun Temple from the King's Gate, use the network of tilted platforms to slide to the entrance of the area. If coming from the east or west, negotiate the system of columns and flagpoles to eventually reach the launching pad of the Sun Temple—a red power plate activated by the Step of Ormazd.

Rush along the post and cooperatively jump through the air to reach the red power plate on the rock outcropping.

The red power plate blasts you through the air toward another red power plate. Hit the magic button when you reach that power plate to continue deeper into the Sun Temple.

As you fly through the sky above the Sun temple, the Hunter strikes. He intercepts your trajectory and slams you to the arena below.

The Hunter

As soon as you land, the Hunter begins his assault. Hold guard to put up your blade and parry any incoming attacks. Let the Hunter's salvo play itself out. When the Hunter finishes his first set of attacks, launch into your counteroffensive.

Watch for the Hunter to put distance between you. When the Hunter backs away, he may be getting ready to spit his ink attack. If you see his head rear back and then quickly jut forward, he's about to spit.

The screen is blanketed with an ink splotch, limiting your visibility. Hold guard—especially if this is the first time you encounter this special attack.

TIP

Watch the Hunter's feet and blade. When you see the blade flash just outside the splotches, he's about to attack. Hit guard as the blade disappears under the ink to deflect the blow and dispel the ink.

Keep the Hunter juggled with aerial combos. Use the gauntlet to launch the Hunter and then keep him aloft. When you drain half of the Hunter's health, he retreats again. The Hunter holds court at the fertile ground high above the arena. You must use the power plates to reach him and finish your fight.

Power Plates

A red power plate faces the arena. Run over to it and use Elika's magic to activate the plate. You are bounced to another plate. Hit the magic button to use that plate and drop back down to solid ground, near the entrance of the Sun Temple.

The Hunter releases the tremor trap now. Balls of corruption roll along the walls, complicating your approach to the fertile ground. Not only is the Sun Temple now affected by the tremor trap, but the Hunter's gift spreads around the world.

CAUTION

There is no way to close Pandora's Box on a released trap. Be sure you want to release this trap before challenging the Hunter.

Wait for the tremors to roll out of the way as you use the scaffolding to close in on the Hunter.

Return of the Prince
Moves in Mysterious Ways
Dynamic World
Desert
Ruined Citadel
The Vale
Royal Palace
City of Light
Tree of Life
Secrets

At the end of the fissure network, wall run out to the red power plate.

The power plate bounces you up to a ledge in the middle of some corruption. Wall run up to the scaffolding and then climb to the top of the vertical fissure. Kick away from the wall to land on a column. Shimmy up the column and then jump back to the wall. Scramble up to the next fissure. Jump from the fissure back to the column. At the very top of the column, turn back to the wall and leap. Scramble up to the horizontal fissures along the top of the cliffs.

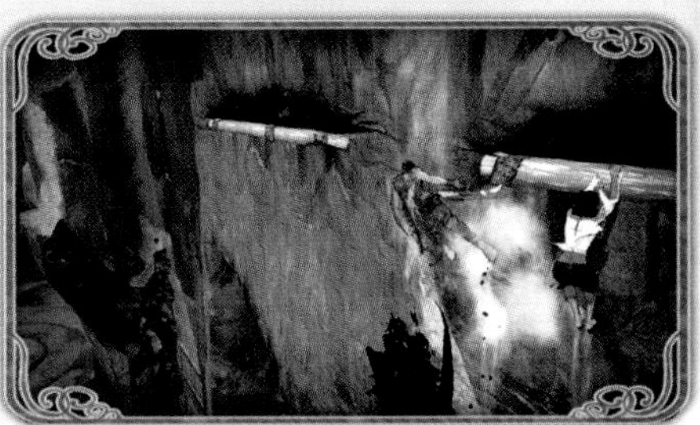

Watch for the tremors to pass as you wall run to the left.

Grip fall down to the ledge below, avoiding the tremors as you descend.

Next, wall run out to the red power plate and activate it with Elika's magic. The power plate launches you across the Sun Temple to another red power plate. Use it to bounce closer to the fertile ground.

When you land against the cliffs, wall run to the right and jump out to grab a column. Swivel around the column and then jump across the two flagpoles to reach the fertile ground … and the waiting Hunter.

Your battle with the Hunter resumes. The Hunter is at half health, still smarting from your earlier encounter. Hold guard as the Hunter closes in. This time, try to deflect the Hunter's first attack and then counter with a combo. After swatting the Hunter's blade away, send in Elika to pummel him with magic attacks.

CAUTION

Did the Hunter use the ink spit attack in your first encounter? Expect to see it again and in every fight with the Hunter from here on out.

The Hunter will try to slam you into the walls and initiate a struggle. Be ready to tap the sword button and repel this attack.

Basic sword attacks are certainly better than nothing, but always go for a combo when you have an opening against the Hunter. After eliminating the Hunter with your combo attacks, heal the fertile ground to banish the corruption and release the Light Seeds.

Healed

(see map on next page)

There are three paths leading away from the Sun Temple: east, west, and south. There are Light Seeds along each routes, as well as all over the Sun Temple.

Sun Temple

Three Light Seeds on top of the fertile ground. After collecting the trio, use the red power plate on the wall to the left. The power plate bounces you over to another plate, which gently drops you back down to the entrance of the area.

Use the red power plate in front of the first arena to leap through the air and reach the high ground above the entrance of the Sun Temple. You are bounced across three plates before you land on a ledge.

Cooperatively jump with Elika back and forth between the walls in this alcove to grab three Light Seeds.

Follow fissures to the right of the ledge to pass through two more Light Seeds.

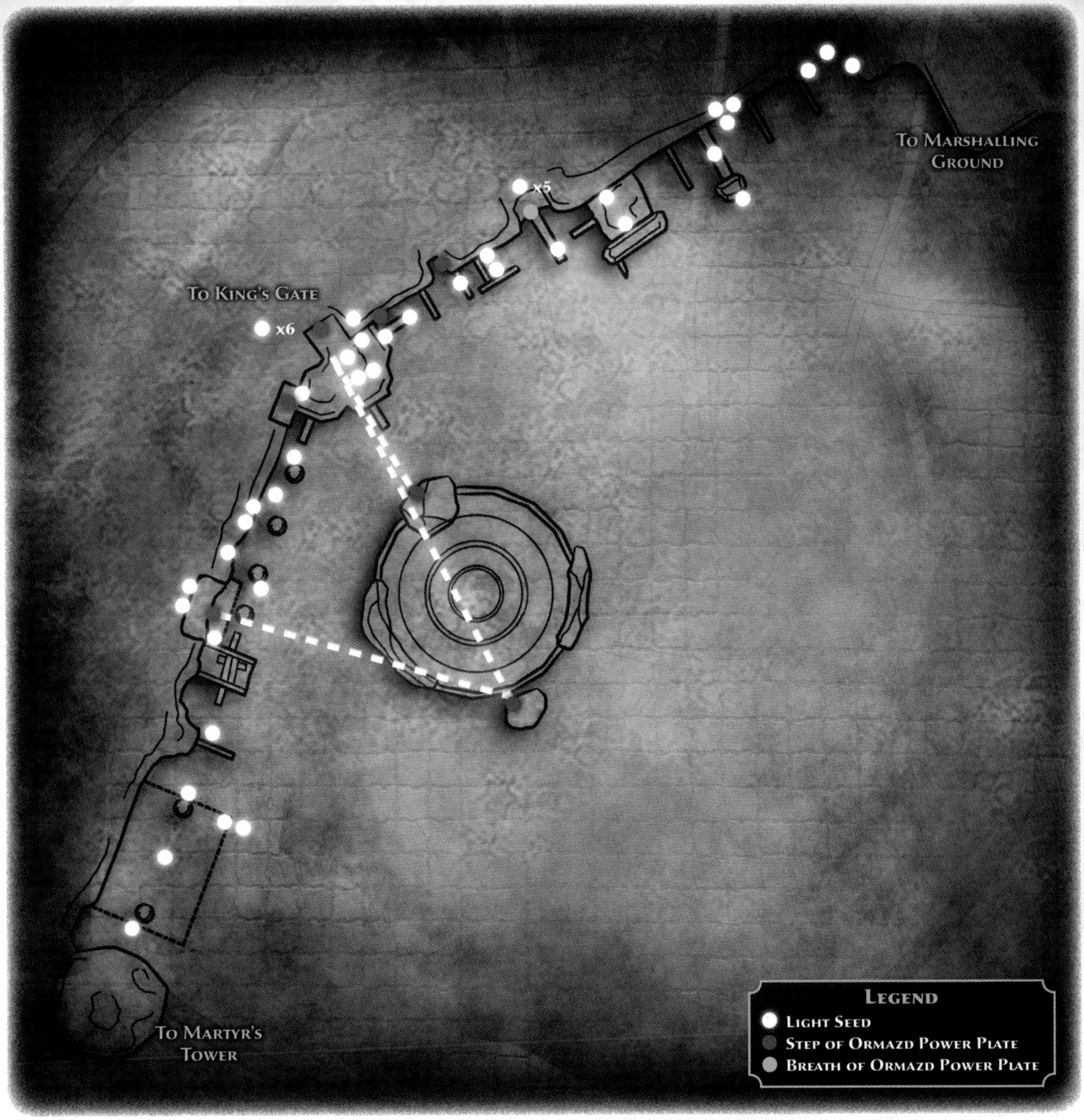

To Marshalling Ground

x5

To King's Gate

x6

To Martyr's Tower

Legend

- Light Seed
- Step of Ormazd Power Plate
- Breath of Ormazd Power Plate

The red power plate at the end of the fissures sends you flying across the Sun Temple. You land on the ledge with the tall column. Wall run up the wall from the fissures above the ledge and then bounce back and forth between the column and the cliffs to reach the scaffolding at the very top of the rocks. A single Light Seed is at the top of the column.

Grip fall down the wall to collect two Light Seeds. Hang off the ledge at the bottom to grab a dangling Light Seed.

Wall run out to this red power plate. Activate it to lurch across the Sun Temple. When you drop to the cliffs above, wall run to the right and jump out to the column to pick up a Light Seed.

East Path

From the starting point of the Sun Temple, look to the east. There are several Light Seeds in plain sight, stretching off into the horizon. Jump along the network of columns to pick up the first three Light Seeds along the route.

To pick up the Light Seed against the wall, jump to the cliff and then immediately hop back to the column.

Walk to the end of the post and then leap to the flagpole. You pick up a Light Seed on the pole, as well as another on the column just beyond. However, instead of roofing along to rings ahead, rotate around the column so that your back is facing away from the cliff. Jump out to the post and then wall run up to a pair of Light Seeds. Now, jump back to the column and then roof over to the crossroads.

South Path

The route to the King's Gate is lined with Light Seeds. Cooperatively jump out to the slide on the left, picking up the Light Seed along the wall. At the bottom of the slide, jump out and scramble up to the ledge. Two Light Seeds are on a post to the right, so hang down over the post and grip fall down to pick them up.

A lone Light Seed is on the rocks here. Jump out to the rock and wall run up it to claim the treasure, then jump back to the ledge.

Continue wall running back to the crossroads between King's Gate and the Sun Temple to grab another Light Seed.

On your way back to the entrance of the Sun Temple, slide down the left side of this tilted platform to gather a Light Seed.

West Path

Snare the Light Seed at the end of the post that points to the west. Jump out across the two flagpole to reach a series of posts. There is a Light Seed on the posts. There is a green power plate on the wall next to the last post. If you have unlocked the Breath of Ormazd, you can collect the Light Seeds above you.

Bounce between the wall and the rocks to pick up the pair of Light Seeds up here.

RETURN OF THE PRINCE
MOVES IN MYSTERIOUS WAYS
DYNAMIC WORLD
DESERT
RUINED CITADEL
THE VALE
ROYAL PALACE
CITY OF LIGHT
TREE OF LIFE
SECRETS

Green Power Plate

Wall run up to the green power plate fixed on the cliff. This sends you stomping up the side of the sheer rocks. Steer around the wooden planks to reach a secret stash of five Light Seeds at the very top of you run. Grip fall down the cliffs to safely reach the platforms below.

Two Light Seeds wait for you inside this arch. Wall jump back and forth to reach the top of the arch and collect them.

Jump across the flagpoles to grab another Light Seed. At the end of the network of poles, you reach a wall with three Light Seeds and some scaffolding. Cooperatively jump to the scaffolding and then shimmy beneath the high Light Seeds. Wall run up to each and the safely grip fall back to the scaffolding.

Marshalling Ground

Imagine the pride of the Ahura guards staging at the Marshalling Ground, ready to defend the honor of the Ahura nation from encroachers. Now, the only warrior defending the Marshalling Ground is the Hunter. Perhaps generations from now, after the Prince and Elika liberate the world from Ahriman's corruption, the banners of proud warriors will flap in the breezes above this region once again.

Corrupt

Approach

When approaching from the Sun Temple, follow the fissures along the cliffs, avoiding any unleashed traps. Grip fall to gently reach the scaffolding below you as you inch along the cliffs to the right. When you reach the platform at the right of the cliffs, wall run across the rocks to reach some vines. Use these vines to close in on the entrance to the Marshalling Ground.

If you come at the Marshaling Ground from the north, use the rings along the ceiling of the ruins to roof through the dark passages. Wall run through the narrow passages as they zigzag toward the entrance of the Marshalling Ground.

Wings of Ormazd

To reach the fertile soil at the heart of the Marshaling Ground, start your journey from the yellow power plate at the broken wall overlooking the area. Use Elika's magic on the power plate to begin soaring over the Marshalling Ground. This is not going to be an easy pass, though. You must dodge rocks, walls, and columns as you fly through the air.

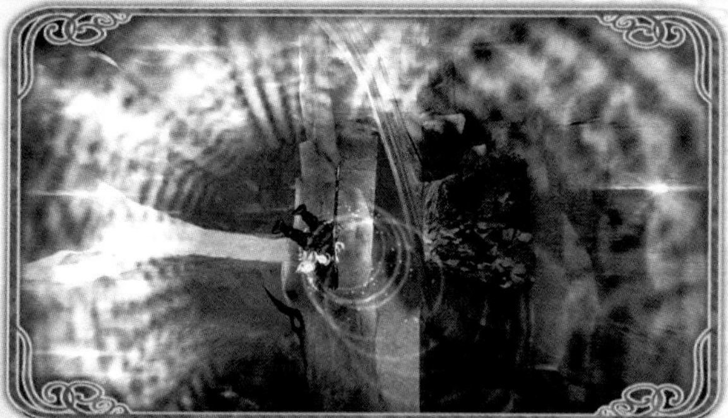

Veer around the stone arches and walls as you glide through the skies around the Marshalling Ground.

You land directly in front of another yellow power plate. Wall run up to the plate and use Elika's magic to resume your skyward travels.

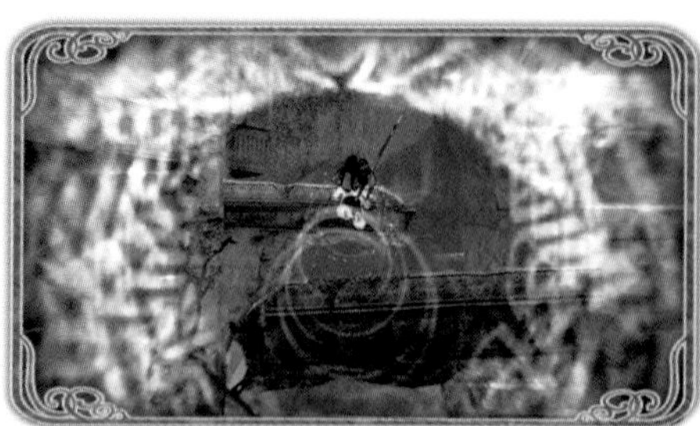

Duck under and steer over the broken walls as you circle the Marshalling Ground.

The next yellow power plate sends you rocketing toward the fertile ground. However, there are many obstacles during this flight, so be ready to duck and dodge. Veer around the stones and columns. The passages tighten, so make sure you don't oversteer and just slam into another wall while avoiding a hazard.

The Hunter

As soon as you touch down from your flight, the Hunter attacks. Throw up your guard as the Hunter closes in for his first strike. Deflect his incoming blade and start a counter-attack. This is a small arena with open edges, so try to keep the Hunter close to the middle. If the Hunter backs you up to an edge, you enter a struggle.

CAUTION

Be mindful of the columns on this arena. If you push the Hunter into a column while in the middle of a combo, the combo ends.

There is an excellent chance the Hunter will reveal Ahriman's Anger in this encounter. When you see the Hunter throw his head back in rage as his body becomes wrapped in blue fire, keep Elika back. Only a sword attack can disrupt this state change.

After dispelling Ahriman's Anger with a sword attack, immediate segue into a combo with Elika.

Return of the Prince
Moves in Mysterious Ways
Dynamic World
Desert
Ruined Citadel
The Vale
Royal Palace
City of Light
Tree of Life
Secrets

Keep the Hunter in the arena's center so that you can effectively juggle him in the air with your gauntlet.

TIP

If you back the Hunter up to the edge of the arena, you enter into a struggle. This is a perfect way to end this battle early. Beat the Hunter in the struggle by rapidly tapping the attack button. If you win this hard struggle, you knock the Hunter clean off the arena.

After defeating the Hunter, climb the wall of the arena using the ring. The fertile ground is at the top of the wall on a very small stone block. Heal the fertile ground to push the corruption out of the Marshalling Ground and spread some much-needed color around the region.

HEALED

There are just two routes leading away from the Marshalling Ground: north and south. Follow each of those routes to collect Light Seeds and add to your steadily increasing supply.

MARSHALLING GROUND

Once you heal the land, the Light Seeds come out. There are no Light Seeds on the arena, but three are right on top of the fertile ground. Two of them are on the block. The third is in front of a newly revealed yellow power plate. (It was smothered in sludge before you healed the fertile ground.)

The yellow power plate delivers you back to the entrance of the Marshalling Ground.

The flight paths between the yellow power plates you used to reach the fertile ground are full of Light Seeds. Follow the loop of power plates again, but steer into the Light Seeds as you race through the skies over the Marshalling Ground and beneath its cliffs.

At the second yellow power plate, jump out to the wall to the left to pick up three Light Seeds.

Hang off the ledge in front of the power plate to gather three slightly hidden Light Seeds.

SOUTH PATH

From the entrance to the Marshalling Ground, turn south and strike out for the Sun Temple. Wall run out to the huge patch of vines along the cliff. There are Light Seeds on the vines, so crawl over them to pocket them. Wall run to the left of the vines and jump across the waterfall to pick up a Light Seed and continue scrambling for another patch of vines.

From the ledge at the end of the vines, turn back and jump out to the short wall to claim a Light Seed.

Next, wall run out to the scaffolding along the cliffs. Follow the fissures back to the crossroads between the Marshalling Ground and Sun Temple.

Climb the cliffs carefully to reach the crossroads and collect even more Light Seeds.

When you return to the entrance of the Marshalling Ground, climb all the way to the top of the large vine patch. Jump away from the vines to reach an orphaned platform. There are three Light Seeds on this platform.

North Path

Wall run to the north of the Marshalling Ground, along the cliff beneath the blue power plate. A Light Seed is next to the ring in the rocks. Jump out to the next wall after swinging through the ring. There is another ring at the corner (and a Light Seed). Swing around it to wall run out to a flagpole.

Jump to the flagpole and swing out to the next wall. Wall run through the narrow passage, bouncing between the walls to keep aloft.

RETURN OF THE PRINCE
MOVES IN MYSTERIOUS WAYS
DYNAMIC WORLD
DESERT
RUINED CITADEL
THE VALE
ROYAL PALACE
CITY OF LIGHT
TREE OF LIFE
SECRETS

Wall run along the diagonal walls to collect another three Light Seeds. Use the column to stabilize yourself between the wall runs.

Tip

When you reach the column, stop. Look to the left. There are two Light Seeds in the alcove. Cooperatively jump to the Light Seeds and then immediately cooperatively jump back to the column.

Blue Power Plate

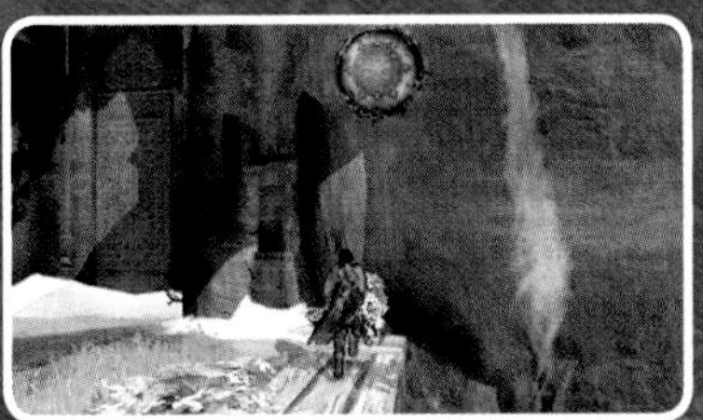

If you have the Hand of Ormazd, you can pick up the five Light Seeds that taunt you from the wall right above the first yellow power plate in the Marshalling Ground. The blue power plate bounces you up to the top of the wall. Walk along the wall to pick up five Light Seeds.

Martyr's Tower

By definition, a martyr is somebody who willingly sacrifices themselves for the betterment of others. And the Ahuras have a long tradition of respecting that the needs of the many far outweigh the needs of the few. Indeed, Elika herself knows about this first-hand. To further liberate the Ruined Citadel, the Prince and Elika must again strike at the Hunter and drive him back, ridding the Martyr's Tower of his infernal presence.

Corrupt

Approach

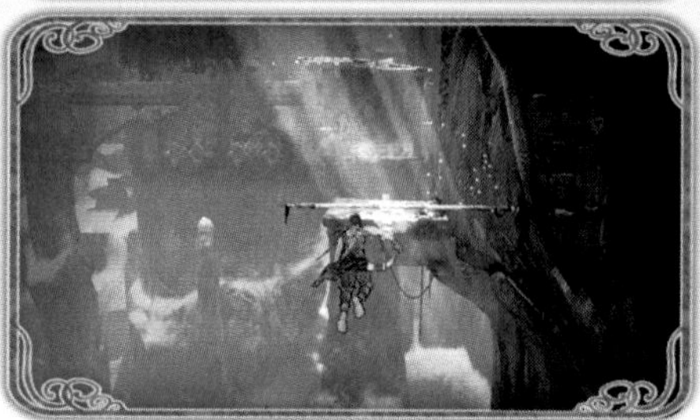

The entrance to Martyr's Tower is a single yellow disc at the nexus of the north and south approaches to the area. If you're coming from the south via the Sun Temple, use the rings to roof through the first half of the path. When you reach the flagpoles, you're getting close. Swing to the posts and ledges and follow the path all the way to the yellow power plate. There are plenty of fissures to negotiate as you near the power plate.

If you approach the Martyr's Tower from the north, wall run along the stone walls and swing between the flagpoles to close in on the yellow power plate.

When you're ready, use the yellow power plate to fly above Martyr's Tower.

You land just shy of the next power plate, so hold down the magic button and press up to scramble over the plate.

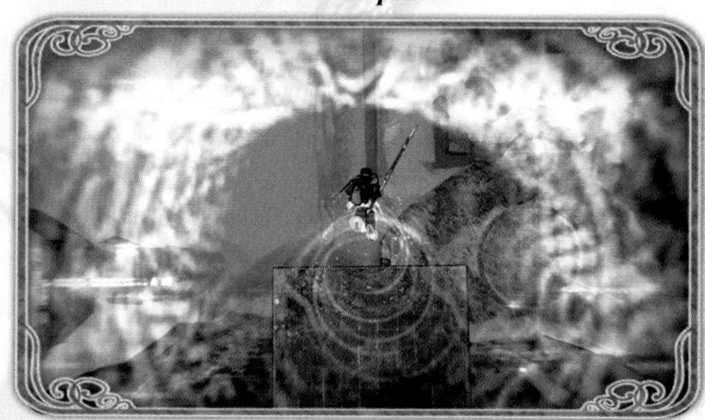

As you fly though the air, dodge stones and walls to avoid being sent back to the beginning of your flight path.

You drop just shy of another yellow power plate. Rush up to it to continue your approach on the tower.

Duck under the arches as you fly to the top of Martyr's Tower.

The Hunter is waiting for you on top of Martyr's Tower. He throws out his arms and roars, taunting you to attack him. Unfortunately, the Prince falls for the trick. As he rushes the Hunter, the floor falls out from under his feet and the pair crashes to the bottom of Martyr's Tower.

Into the Darkness

Your visibility is limited inside Martyr's Tower since there are so few light sources. The corruption that seethes on the walls seems to absorb whatever light does manage to sneak through the cracks in the walls. Grip fall from the ledge to the bottom floor of the tower.

The basement of the tower is flooded with corruption. You must stay out of the muck by keeping to the poles that jut out of the walls. Wall run over the corruption and then jump out to the flagpoles.

Use the fissures to get your grip and shimmy along the basement walls.

Circle the basement until you reach the wooden crates.

RETURN OF THE PRINCE
MOVES IN MYSTERIOUS WAYS
DYNAMIC WORLD
DESERT
RUINED CITADEL
THE VALE
ROYAL PALACE
CITY OF LIGHT
TREE OF LIFE
SECRETS

Jump up to the post above the crates. Turn to the center of the room. Jump across to the network of posts in the center of the room, and follow the posts as they close in one the center of the basement.

Cooperative jump to the wall and scramble up to this fissure to climb out of the basement.

Wall run to the right of the fissure at the top and then swing around the flagpole to reach some scaffolding.

The scaffolding leads to a series of poles. Swing from pole to pole until you cross the basement ceiling. Use the fissure to hold onto the wall. Follow the scratches up to the next floor.

The Hunter

The Hunter appears out of the darkness He has a bit of distance to close, so put up your guard as the he slinks toward you. The Hunter circles you as he approaches, stalking you as he looks for an opening. Keep your guard up as the Corrupted finishes his first set of attacks. Try to deflect an incoming blow to turn the tables and launch into your own combo.

The Hunter relies on Ahriman's Anger to keep you from using acrobatic or magic moves at the start of a combo. When the Hunter bursts into blue flames, keep Elika out of the fray and rush in to dispel that state change with a sword attack. If you try any other maneuver, either you or Elika will be injured.

As if the room wasn't dark enough already, the Hunter spits black ink at you to further obscure your vision. Guard until the ink vanishes.

When the Hunter rears back and spreads his three blades, put up your guard. This comes as a lightning fast attack that is tough to deflect.

The Hunter is determined to eliminate you in this fight, so look for an aggressive attack. You view this attack from above. The Hunter repeatedly slashes with his blade and you must counter every incoming blow by tapping the on-screen button. If you survive the attack, the Hunter reels for a second. This is a prime opportunity to launch a counter-offensive.

When the Hunter really loses his cool, he jumps into the air. Guard the second you see the Hunter leave the ground because he's about to turn into a makeshift saw blade. The Hunter tucks into a ball and rolls through the air with his sword outstretched. This is a tough attack to counter, so rely on your guard.

When you have the Hunter on the ropes, he starts to rely on his spitting attack. Guard until the ink disappears. Or try to hit the advancing Hunter with your sword, if you think you know his footwork well enough by this point.

Always attack with combos. Use Elika to pummel the Hunter from above. Then, toss the Hunter into the air and keep him up there with more magic attacks. Use acrobatic moves to keep him away from the wall (an instant combo killer) and finish him off in the center of the arena.

Escape

After defeating the Hunter, you must still make your way back to the top of the tower to heal the fertile ground. Use the fissures in the wall to ascend to the next story of the tower. Wall run across the flagpoles as you circle the room.

Make your way to the vertical fissure to climb to the next floor.

The ground is soaked with corruption. Carefully step around the poison.

Jump across the two posts that the span the hole in the floor. Use the scaffolding on the other side of the room to launch a wall run to the left. Slide along the slotted ring to swing over the corruption on the floor. Wall run from the ring to the fissure in the corner.

RETURN OF THE PRINCE
MOVES IN MYSTERIOUS WAYS
DYNAMIC WORLD
DESERT
RUINED CITADEL
THE VALE
ROYAL PALACE
CITY OF LIGHT
TREE OF LIFE
SECRETS

Slide along the fissure to the adjacent wall. Wall run to the flagpole and then leap to the post. Turn back to the center of the room. You are now perfectly lined up to hop across a set of posts and reach a yellow power plate on the opposite wall.

The Wings of Ormazd only take you far enough to reach a series of flagpoles along the ceiling.

Jump to the fissure in the corner of the room. Then wall run straight up to escape the interior of Martyr's Tower. You can now heal the fertile ground on the roof.

Healed

As soon as you purify the fertile ground in Martyr's Tower, you can collect Light Seeds not only in the immediate area, but also along three paths: north, south, and east.

Martyr's Tower

Four Light Seeds are on the roof of Martyr's Tower. Three of them are right around the fertile ground. The fourth is on a yellow power plate that, when activated, sends you flying through the skies and back to the area's entrance. From the entrance, you can easily break out to any of the three paths leading away from the tower.

When you land on the platform in front of the very first yellow power plate, you can see a number of Light Seeds that are easy grabs to north.

Turn to the south to see another collection of Light Seeds within easy range.

Ascend the outside of the tower via the fissures to grab a pair of Light Seeds on a narrow ledge.

Green Power Plate

Once you have the Breath of Ormazd, ascend the tower's exterior via the fissures. Wall run up to the green power plate above the top fissure.

This power plate lets you run along the side of the tower. Follow the scratches in the wall so you don't stumble. There is another green power plate on the cliff. Activate it to climb vertically to another power plate. There is a Light Seed on that plate.

Activate the green power plate to climb back across the tower. This leads you to one more power plate. Use Elika's magic on the plate to reach a hidden balcony on Martyr's Tower, which is festooned with three Light Seeds.

After collecting the Light Seeds on the tower exterior, follow the yellow power plate network to return to the top of Martyr's Tower. Dive back into the tower via the tall vertical shaft. It's dark inside, making it easy to see the Light Seeds below. Grip fall through them as you drop.

The basement of the tower is clear of corruption, so now you can walk on the ground. Cooperatively jump between the central pillars to pick up the Light Seeds in the middle of the room. Follow the posts and fissures up to the next floor.

Follow the flagpoles around the walls to grab a dangling Light Seed.

Use the fissures on the next floor to reach a balcony outside the tower.

Follow the length of the balcony to pick up three Light Seeds.

Another Light Seed in front of the yellow power plate on the top floor of the tower interior. Jump across the posts in front of the power plate to grab it.

East Path

Return of the Prince
Moves in Mysterious Ways
Dynamic World
Desert
Ruined Citadel
The Vale
Royal Palace
City of Light
Tree of Life
Secrets

Duck into the side passage near the yellow power plate to start trekking east to the Vale. There is a Light Seed in the narrow passage (it's in the dip in the floor). The path then opens up into a canyon. One more prize is on a rock platform off to the left. Jump over to the ledge to pick up the Light Seed. Then, cooperatively jump off to the right to push deep to the east.

Follow the rock ledges to the east to pick up Light Seeds. There are two on the left side of the canyon that are accessible by cooperatively jumping out to the rocks and then wall running to keep from falling.

North Path

Wall run along the rocks to the south to pick up a Light Seed. The cavern ahead is loaded with sparkling treasures, too. Wall run along the right wall and then jump out to the flagpole. Once you reach the flagpole, jump to the next wall and then link across the rings to pick up three Light Seeds in rapid succession.

If you have not liberated the Windmills, there's a solider waiting for you at the crossroads.

Wall run up the stone pillar at the crossroads to collect two Light Seeds. Since you come up a bit short, jump away from the pillar. Cooperatively jump to the opposite wall and then bounce back (also with Elika's help) to get the needed height to pick up the Light Seeds.

South Path

Grip fall down the cliff to the south of the tower to start along the path to the Sun Temple. Wall run up the cliff at the ledge below to pick up a Light Seed and then swing around the flagpoles to the south.

Roof over to the columns. Visit all three of these columns to pick up Light Seeds.

Jump out to the column farther from the cliffs. Swing around so your back is away from the cliffs. Jump with Elika out to a fissure in the rocks opposite of the column. Now, shimmy around to the back side of those rocks to discover two more Light Seeds.

Windmills

The Windmills push up over the rocks to collect the wind that rips through the Ruined Citadel. But the blades of the Windmills are now tattered and torn, and the structure is soaked in corruption. The Prince and Elika must rush to the top of the Windmills and challenge the Hunter to liberate the area and close in on the door to the Hunter's Lair.

Corrupt

Approach

You can close in on the Windmills from either the east or the west. The paths are similar, with column-lined corridors opening out into flagpoles. Swing around the poles to approach the entrance of the Windmills. Use the rings or wall jumps to bounce up to the platform directly in front of the Windmills.

To enter the Windmill, rush down the wooden ramp and leap to the red power plate. Scramble up to it and then use Elika's magic to bounce across a series of power plates.

When you land on the side of the Windmill, wall run to the left and use the rings to swing around the corner of the building.

Use the power plate on the side of the Windmill to fly across the void and slam into the wall south of another red power plate. Scurry up to the power plate via the ring.

The power plate launches you back across the abyss, depositing you on a ledge just outside the Windmill. From here, you can peek inside a see a pair of red power plates. You must unlock the secret of these power plates to further ascend the Windmill. Jump across the gap in the floor to solve the puzzle of the plates.

Climb the Windmill

One of the power plates is exposed, the other is tucked behind a gate. You must open both power plates to reach the second floor of the Windmill. The crank on the left side of the floor does not adjust the grates—it flips the two signs on the wall between the power plates. The arrows on these signs show how the grates will spin when rotated. To then actually rotate the grates in front of the power plates as directed on the signs, turn the crank on the right side of the floor.

An arcing arrow just rotates the grates a quarter-turn. A U-shaped arrow rotates the grates 180 degrees. A blank sign does not affect the grate. The sign on the left side affects the right grate. The right sign affects the grate on the left.

Rotate the grates into this position.

Turn the signs so the power plate on the left remains exposed while the grate on the right is rotated 180 degrees.

Turn the crank to unlock both plates, solving the puzzle.

The two power plates bounce you off the walls and launch you up to the next floor of the Windmill. Wall run to the right, grabbing the ring to swing to the next power plate. This launches you to the adjacent wall. When you land, wall run to the right and drop down on a stone platform.

Swing across the two flagpoles and then wall bounce up the vertical shaft.

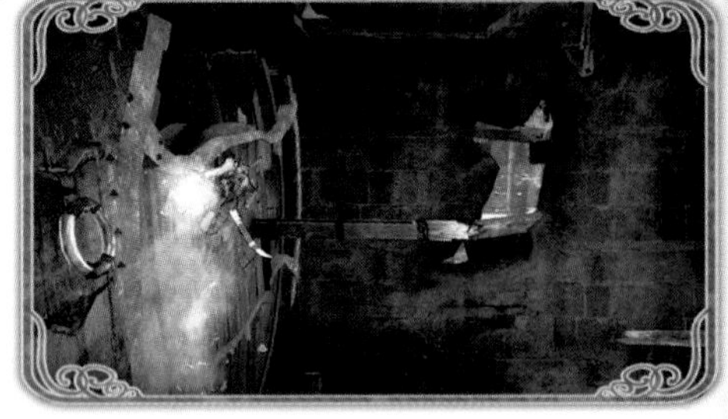

You must time this next wall run. There is a wooden plank on the rotating disc in the corner. You must swing from the ring at the end of your wall run onto the disc just as the plank turns horizontal. If you swing to the disc when the plank is vertical, you fall and Elika must save you.

Once you reach the post sticking out of the disc, turn around and face the wall. When the plank rotates so that it's vertical, wall run up to the top of the disc and then kick away to grab a post.

From the post, jump out to the next power plate puzzle.

Three power plates are in this puzzle. The crank on the left switches the signs in the center of the plates, which shows how the three grates rotate when you twist the crank over on the right.

Rotate the plates into this position. You want the middle plate exposed.

Change the signs so the middle plate remains still, but you lock the left and right power plates into position.

RETURN OF THE PRINCE
MOVES IN MYSTERIOUS WAYS
DYNAMIC WORLD
DESERT
RUINED CITADEL
THE VALE
ROYAL PALACE
CITY OF LIGHT
TREE OF LIFE
SECRETS

Rotate the grates to unlock all three power plates.

Rush up to the power plate on the right. Activate the plate with Elika's magic to bounce across the three power plates in the room. The third plate bounces you up to the next story of the Windmill.

Wall run across the exterior of the Windmill. Use the ring to link over to the ledge that is covered in corruption. Stick close to the wall to avoid the poison.

Jump out to the walkway to the right. Follow it up to the rings. Scramble up the rings and pull yourself up the wall. At the very top of the wall, hoist yourself up to the post that overlooks the central axle of the Windmill. Jump down to the axle to meet the Hunter face-to-face.

The Hunter

The Hunter wastes no time in attacking you as soon as you touch down next to the axle. The arena is moderately sized, giving you plenty of room to launch extended combos. Just make sure you keep the Hunter juggled in one area because if you accidentally slam the Hunter into the axle in the middle of the arena, your combo ends. Guard against the Hunter right away and then wait for your opening.

The Hunter launches into his furious attack if he gets the drop on you. Counter each blow by tapping the on-screen button as it appears.

When you see the Hunter's blade split open, get ready to deflect the incoming attack.

When the Hunter spits ink on the screen, throw up your guard and keep it up until the ink dissipates.

Keep on the lookout for the Hunter to call upon Ahriman's Anger. When the blue flame erupts around the Hunter, back off. Keep Elika safe and only use the sword attack. Once Ahriman's Anger goes away, then call on Elika to keep the combo going. Just make sure you keep the Hunter off the wall by using acrobatics to switch places.

After you defeat the Hunter, he leaps over the wall and escapes, determined to fight another day. Now that the fertile ground has been abandoned by the Corrupted, have Elika heal the area.

Healed

There are two routes that lead away from the Windmills: east and west. Search each path for Light Seeds, as well as the entire Windmills area.

Windmills

Once Elika recovers from healing the fertile ground, the Light Seeds appear around the Windmill. A stretch of Light Seeds leads away from the fertile ground and back to the area's entrance. Before jumping out to the poles directly across from the fertile ground, though, travel back down around the Windmill to collect Light Seeds.

Jump across the flagpoles to pick up some Light Seeds on your way back to the broken wall.

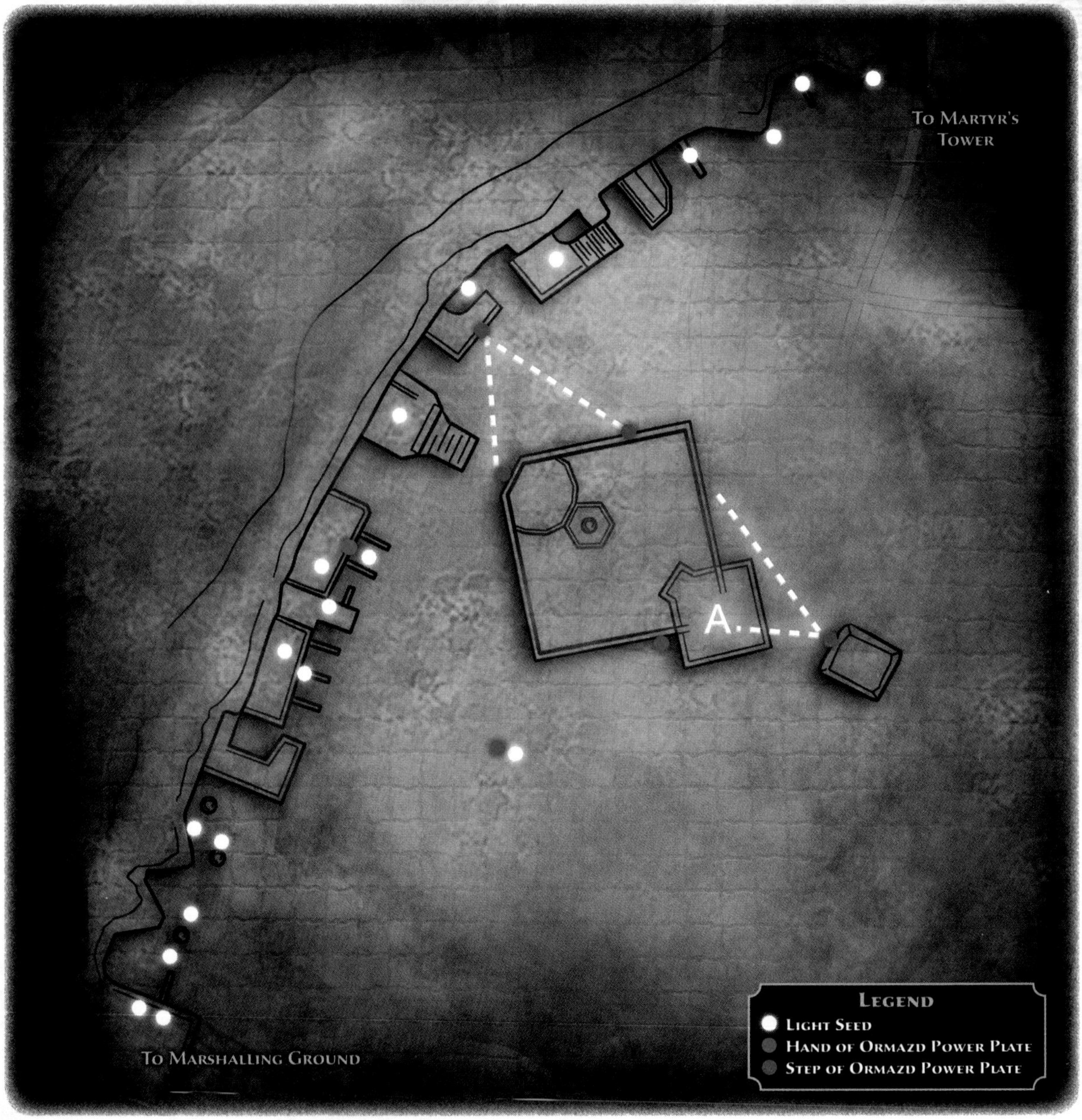

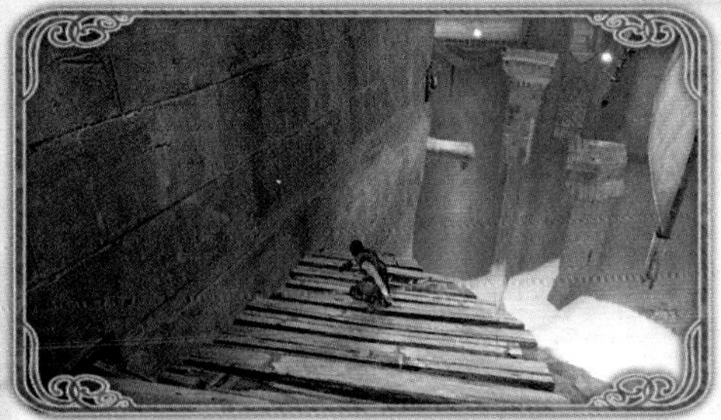

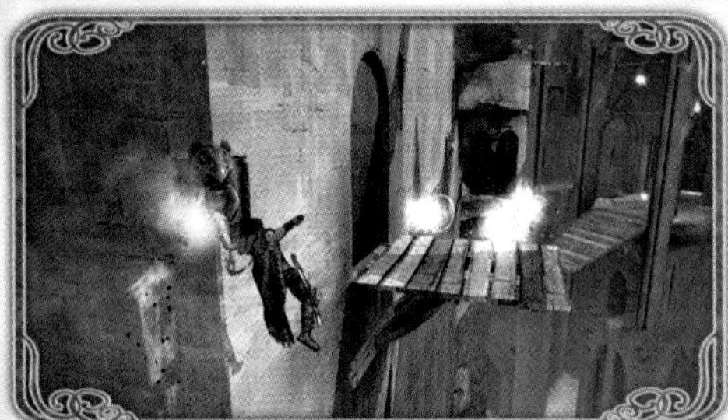

Follow the poles around the building and then slip down the tilted wooden platform. Wall run out to the ring at the corner of the building and then rush to the wooden ledge with three Light Seeds.

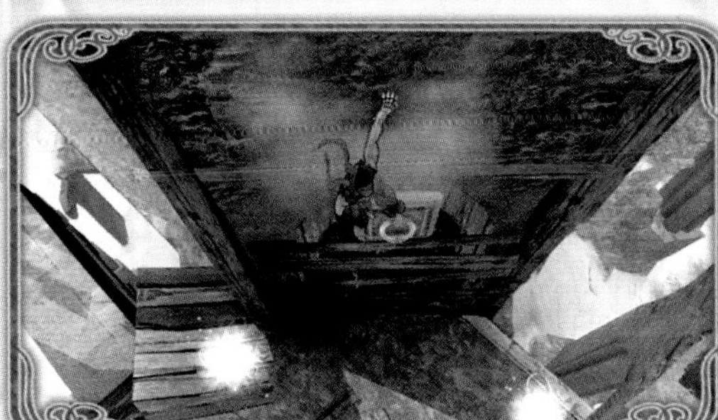

Slide down the building with a grip fall. Two Light Seeds are just below it.

RETURN OF THE PRINCE
MOVES IN MYSTERIOUS WAYS
DYNAMIC WORLD
DESERT
RUINED CITADEL
THE VALE
ROYAL PALACE
CITY OF LIGHT
TREE OF LIFE
SECRETS

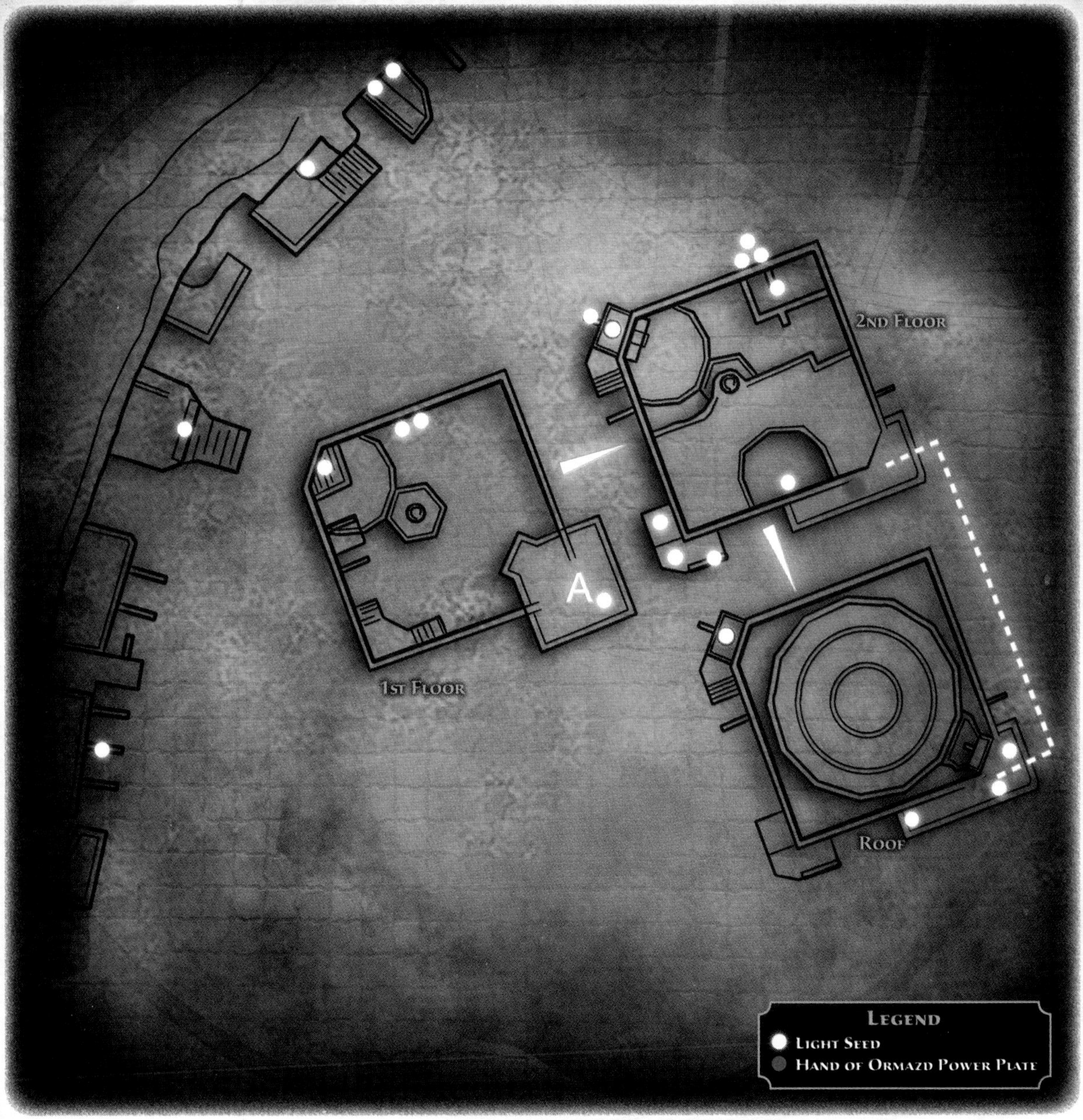

Slip down the wooden planks to grab a Light Seed tucked behind a wall at the end of a balcony. Now, return to the entrance of the Windmill.

At the crossroads, turn back to the Windmill. Use the fissures on the wall to climb up to the Light Seeds hanging from the scaffolding.

Enter the Windmill and use the red power plates to spiral back around the inside of the building. Follow the course of wall runs and poles to cross back across the power plate puzzles. Once you reach the top of the Windmill, jump out to the poles and grip fall down to the base of the huge black gate.

West Path

From the entrance, turn west and jump out to the slides. Follow the slides, sticking close to the wall to pick up a Light Seed. At the bottom of the slide, head out along the corridor leading away from the slides. Jump out to the column and then use the rings along the ceiling to roof out to the crossroads.

East Path

From the entrance of the Windmill, turn to the east and jump down to the slides. Follow the slides through the Light Seeds and then leap out to the flagpole. Swing around the flagpole and then run through the ring to swing around toward the crossroads.

On your way back to the crossroads, scramble up the wall with the ring. At the top of the wall, jump out to the post behind you to grab two Light Seeds. Then, wall run back to the entrance, using the flagpole to swing down to the black gate.

RETURN OF THE PRINCE
MOVES IN MYSTERIOUS WAYS
DYNAMIC WORLD
DESERT
RUINED CITADEL
THE VALE
ROYAL PALACE
CITY OF LIGHT
TREE OF LIFE
SECRETS

Blue Power Plate

Run out to the blue power plate along the outer wall of the Windmill. The power plate arcs you through the air, dropping you against a wall. Wall run between a series of surfaces. At the end of the walls, swing around the ring on the corner of the building. There is a blue power plate just around the corner.

This launches you through the air again to pick up a Light Seed and then drops you through another sequence of blue power plates. Follow these power plates to collect the remaining Light Seeds in this area.

Hunter's Lair

After cleansing the Ruined Citadel, the Prince and Elika have finally cornered the Hunter in his lair. The Hunter will not evacuate the Ruined Citadel without a fight, though, so the heroes must steel themselves for any of the Hunter's devious tricks and traps.

The Approach

To reach the Hunter's Lair, you must negotiate a series of power plates, starting with the red power plate next to the seething corruption just beyond the black gate. Activate the red plate to bounce over to a yellow power plate just above the gate.

Swing wide of the tower as you zoom through the air en route to another red power plate.

The red power plate bounces you across the void to a platform with a yellow power plate. When you reach the platform, wall run up to the power plate and blast off in a direct flight to the Hunter. The path is not free and clear of obstructions, though, so steer around the walls, cages, and towers that slide into view.

Final Showdown

The Hunter's arena is large—perfect for juggling without any interruptions. Plus, there is no corruption around the wall, so you only need to avoid pushing the Hunter into regular walls and launching into a struggle. When the fight begins, the Hunter is on the far side of the arena. Hold back and let the Hunter close the distance. While you watch him move, hold guard.

Tip

Feeling good about your deflecting skills? Meet the Hunter halfway and swat away his three-bladed sword to create an opening.

The Hunter never hesitates to slip into state changes, especially Ahriman's Anger. When the Hunter goes full blue, keep Elika back and plan a sword attack to dispel the influence. Hold guard while waiting for your opening.

One of the Hunter's favorite moves to counter a successful deflection is to spit ink in your eyes.

The four-hit sword combo is certainly nothing to be sniffed at, but you should always aim for performing big combos—especially when the Hunter is getting close to the walls. Lunge over the Hunter with an acrobatic move so your next attack (Elika's magic?) pushes him back to the arena' center.

When the Hunter's is close to losing half of his health, he leaps into the air and crashes down to the ground. The shattered arena buckles under the impact and you fall into a much smaller arena. It is much easier to get backed into the wall down there, so concentrate on keeping the Hunter somewhere near the center of the scene.

Continue hammering the Hunter with repeated attacks whenever you see an opening. The more you attack, the less chance the Hunter has to respond with his blades.

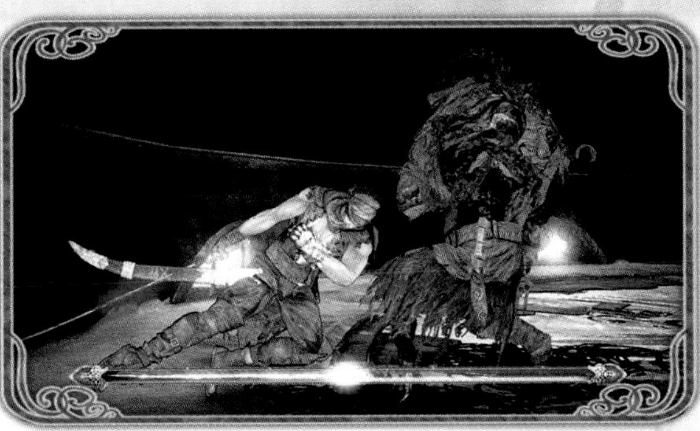
The Hunter is determined to back you into the walls so you must enter a struggle. If you win the struggle, you elbow the Hunter into the center of the arena.

The Hunter is small enough to launch into the air with your gauntlet—a great way to lead into an aerial combo.

When the Hunter's health drops to only a quarter, he flees again. He breaks through the arena as he scurries away to his final stronghold. To catch up with the Hunter, you must jump over a river of corruption and follow a series of slides. At the bottom of the slides, cooperatively jump out to a pair of walls. Wall run along the first and then bounce to the opposite wall. At the end of the second wall, jump to another slide and drop down into the final arena.

NOTE

Use a cooperative jump to leap over the corruption that lines the arena.

RETURN OF THE PRINCE
MOVES IN MYSTERIOUS WAYS
DYNAMIC WORLD
DESERT
RUINED CITADEL
THE VALE
ROYAL PALACE
CITY OF LIGHT
TREE OF LIFE
SECRETS

Because the arena is so small and it is surrounded by corruption, your priority is to keep the Hunter as close to the center as possible. Bounce back and forth over his shoulders with acrobatic moves, or launch him into the air with a gauntlet attack and juggle him with Elika's magic.

Expect to see Ahriman's Anger at least once in this final battle with the Hunter. Keep Elika back and dispel the influence with your sword.

After you finally drain the Hunter's health, Elika can free him of his curse. She gently approaches the Hunter, who is crumpled on the ground, shamed in his defeat. She lays a hand on his shoulder and mercifully strips him of the corruption that has plagued his soul for centuries. The Hunter's spirit passes with peace and the Ruined Citadel is completely purged of Ahriman's threat.

Use the red power plates around the arena to escape the Hunter's Lair and return to the entrance. The sun breaks over the wounded sky as the Prince and Elika marvel at their accomplishment. But this is only one small victory on the path to forcing Ahriman back to the underworld.

The Vale

From the temple of the Tree of Life, the sight of hot air balloons swaying in the wind reveals the location of the Vale. Once the center of science and discovery for the Ahura people, the Vale is now desolate and crumbling. The region is overseen by the Alchemist, a genius whose quest for knowledge lead him to a very dark place. Now that the corruption of Ahriman has overtaken the Vale, the Alchemist returns to his old laboratories to rekindle his research. But no longer does he hunger for scientific truth. The Alchemist now thirsts for discoveries in the fields of pain and suffering.

What's Unleashed

When you visit the Vale, you have the potential to unlock a handful of changes to the dynamic world. One of the four traps is triggered by your presence, and fighting the Alchemist releases a new Ahriman's Influence for the other Corrupted to assume in their fights against you.

The Alchemist

The Alchemist is a significant figure in the history of the Ahura. This wizened scientist proves that vast intelligence does not protect the human spirit from corruption. In fact, it was the Alchemist's unwavering search for knowledge that allowed him to be tricked by Ahriman into giving up his very life. Fooled by Ahriman, the Alchemist now serves the whims of the dark god. His skills at invention are redirected toward nefarious purposes.

What finally undid the Alchemist was his search for the cure for death. And that knowledge is what powers his special move. The Alchemist draws energy from the corruption, regenerating health unless you attack him and stop the process. No other Corrupted has this skill, save for the Mourning King, who inherits it as soon as the Alchemist uses it for the first time.

The Alchemist also unlocks a new Ahriman's Influence: Ahriman's Fury. When the Alchemist calls upon this state change, he is enveloped in black. No attack except Elika's magic can dispel the effects of the influence. If you try to attack with the sword, you only injure yourself. You must start a combo with Elika's magic to scrape the veil of darkness from the Alchemist and then lead into the rest of your combo.

NOTE

As soon as the Alchemist uses Ahriman's Fury the first time, any other Corrupted or soldier can use the state change.

CAUTION

If for any reason you do not have Elika with you when Ahriman's Fury is called upon, you must just keep your distance and either wait out the state change or hope that Elika joins the fight soon.

The Traps

When you visit the Heaven's Stair area of the Vale and try to use the elevator room, the Alchemist releases the gas trap. This trap fills a chamber with tiny particles of corruption that seep through your skin and clog your airways if you remain in its presence for too long. Think of it as a time limit. If you remain in the affected chamber too long, you fail and Elika must rescue you. If you happen to perish due to the gas while in the middle of an acrobatic sequence, Elika brings you back to life at the last patch of solid ground. Unlocking the gas trap at Heaven's Stair releases the trap in the following areas:

The Windmills, Martyr's Tower, King's Gate, Machinery Ground, Heaven's Stair, the Cauldron, Spire of Dreams, Royal Gardens, Queen's Tower -- plus the routes between King's Gate, the Cauldron, & Temple, the routes between the Cauldron, the Cavern, & Temple, and the routes between the Cavern, City Gate, & Temple.

The Cauldron

RETURN OF THE PRINCE
MOVES IN MYSTERIOUS WAYS
DYNAMIC WORLD
DESERT
RUINED CITADEL
THE VALE
ROYAL PALACE
CITY OF LIGHT
TREE OF LIFE
SECRETS

The Cauldron is the gateway into the Vale. The area is not unlike a sinkhole, but one that is currently filled almost to the brim with corruption. To push into the Vale, the Prince and Elika must defeat the Alchemist and drain the Cauldron. Once the fertile ground is rescued, the pair must then continue their fight against the Alchemist until his reign of terror over the Vale has been extinguished.

Corrupt Approach

When approaching the Vale from the desert, you can either take the middle path or the left path. If you approach from the left path, break to the right when the route forks. Coming from the middle path, veer to the left at the fork. The paths are carved through a canyon. Use the vines to reach the tall ledges that overlook a series of fissures in the canyon walls.

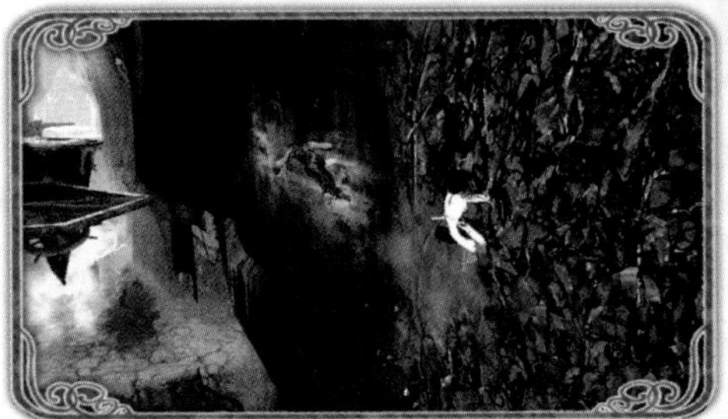

Wall run out to the scaffolding and the fissures and use then them cross the deep canyons. The vine patches are the key to closing in on the entrance to the Vale. When you reach the wooden platforms, you are near the Cauldron.

When you initially step into the Cauldron, the corruption is low. But since the path in front of you is blocked by a thick puddle of corruption, you must instead jump to the vines creeping over the wooden wall to the left. Climb to the top of the wall via the vines.

Within the Cauldron

When you reach the top of the wall, the corruption bubbles and pops at the bottom of the Cauldron. Before your eyes, it rises until the majority of the Cauldron is submerged. Your travel options are now severely limited, but at least there is a direct route to the fertile ground still available.

Jump from the top of the wall to a slide. You slip toward the corruption at an alarming rate. Jump at the bottom of the slide to grab the next wall. Scramble up it.

From the ledge, jump out to the post and then skip over to the next wooden platform that hovers just above the corruption. There are two broken columns just beyond the platform. Jump to the first one and swing around it.

Roof along the ceiling quickly to reach the second column. Position yourself so your back is to the brass ring at the end of the ceiling and then roof over to it. Press the gauntlet button when you reach the ring and hoist yourself up to the ledge over the two columns.

TIP

Having trouble with the timing of the rings? Just think of the rings as the word "and." Use it to link together two moves, like halves of a sentence. So, you cross the roof with the jump button *and* then scramble up the other side.

Jump across the next series of wooden platforms. You need to reach the post in the distance on the far side of the Cauldron.

Wall run under the post to grab it. Pull yourself up so that you're standing on top of the post.

Jump from the post to the next ledge. Then jump down to the slide. At the bottom of the slide, wall run to the fertile ground.

The Alchemist

When you reach the fertile ground, you catch your first glimpse of the Alchemist. He's on a balcony overlooking the fertile ground. He's performing some sort of experiment, and he pays little attention as you call out to him. Suddenly, the Alchemist vanishes from the balcony. But before you get too cocky and think healing the Cauldron will be a cakewalk, the Alchemist reappears. And he's right on top of you.

NOTE

If you have not yet defeated any of the Corrupted in their lairs yet—or have defeated just one of three—the Alchemist is not terribly aggressive. It's unlikely you will see Ahriman's Fury in this first encounter, or the Alchemist's regeneration technique.

Keep up your guard as you approach the Alchemist. He does not lunge like the Hunter or Concubine, telegraphing his punches. Instead, the Alchemist's basic move is a magic attack unleashed simply by raising and flicking his wrist. It's a fast move and tough to deflect until you have a good idea of what to look for.

When the Alchemist raises one arm and starts to flick his wrist, you have a chance to deflect. This attack can turn into a series of moves, so if you're unsure of when to retaliate, hold guard until the Alchemist finishes blasting.

After the Alchemist finishes an attack, begin a combo with your sword. If you see the Alchemist backing up to the wall, use an acrobatic move to keep him from being pressed into a corner. If you push the Alchemist up to the wall, the combo ends and you switch into a struggle.

The Alchemist's struggle: He grabs your sword arm with a dark tendril. Repeatedly tap the sword button to break free of his grip.

Whenever you spot an opening, close the distance and launch into a combo. Call on Elika's magic to push the Alchemist around like punching bag.

RETURN OF THE PRINCE
MOVES IN MYSTERIOUS WAYS
DYNAMIC WORLD
DESERT
RUINED CITADEL
THE VALE
ROYAL PALACE
CITY OF LIGHT
TREE OF LIFE
SECRETS

Unless you are repeatedly attacked while injured and fail Elika's save, your first battle with the Alchemist is short-lived. The scientist retreats into the Vale to fight another day. While the Alchemist regroups, purify the area and collect the released Light Seeds.

Healed

There are three routes leading away from the Cauldron. The northern path leads to the Vale. The western path returns to the fork divided between the desert and the Ruined Citadel while the eastern route leads to the Royal Palace.

The Cauldron

As the corruption drains from the Cauldron, many Light Seeds are revealed. Four Light Seeds are right around the fertile ground. They lead to the central tower in the middle of the column, which can be safely descended via the long panel of vines.

From the bottom of the tower, you can wall run around and collect more Light Seeds. The door to the northern route is near the bottom of the vines. Three Light Seeds are near the exit. Two are grabbed by wall running to and away from the vines. The third is directly above the vines.

Return to the top of the vine-covered wall you scaled at the beginning of the Cauldron.

Follow the path back around the Cauldron as if you were zeroing in on the fertile ground again. Run across the posts and rip down the slide to pick up a Light Seed on the next vine-covered wall.

Follow the path around the outer edge of the Cauldron. Jump across the two posts and scale the next wall. When you slip down the slide just beyond the wall you pick up a Light Seed. There is another one directly in front of you on the vines, as well as one just around the corner to the right.

Use the columns here to pick up three Light Seeds.

Use the ring at the edge of the columns to scramble farther up the Cauldron. Then cross the platforms to grab the Light Seed on the post. Another Light Seed is at the end of the slide to the left of the post; the slide drops you back on the fertile ground.

Green Power Plate

There are five Light Seeds in the alcove high above the Cauldron. With the Breath of Ormazd, you can reach the alcove and collect the Light Seeds. Once you have all five, grip fall down the divot in the ledge to grab the vines below and return safely to the main route around the Cauldron.

North Path

The northern path out of the Cauldron leads to the Vale. Wall run to the scaffolding on the left side of the tunnel. Follow the red planks along the tunnel and then jump to the opposite side and wall run to the next bits of scaffolding.

Run along the scratches and then jump to the adjacent wall. As you sprint to the vines, you grab a Light Seed.

RETURN OF THE PRINCE
MOVES IN MYSTERIOUS WAYS
DYNAMIC WORLD
DESERT
RUINED CITADEL
THE VALE
ROYAL PALACE
CITY OF LIGHT
TREE OF LIFE
SECRETS

Crawl up the vines and scramble to the top of the platform. This is the crossroads between the Cauldron and the Construction Yard, so unless the Construction Yard is already healed, expect a soldier here. After combating the soldier (drive it to the ledge for an instant kill), wall run to the Light Seed to the right.

West Path

Turn to the right as you exit the Cauldron and peer down the west route. There is a Light Seed on the wall above the wooden platform. Hop up on the railing and then jump to the wall beneath the Light Seed. Wall run up the cave to grab the prize.

Follow the vines along the cave to pick up an additional two Light Seeds.

Rush the fissures on the right side of the cavern to snag another Light Seed.

Hang off the ledge after the fissures to pick up two additional Light Seeds. Grip fall through the Light Seeds and grab the scaffolding to keep from falling into the abyss below.

Climb the vines just before the fork in the route that breaks toward the Ruined Citadel. There's one more Light Seed at the top of the vines.

East Path

Wall run away from the entrance to the Cauldron to pick up the first visible Light Seed. Grab the vines on the opposite side of the Light Seed to safely reach the nearby rocks. Jump out and wall run through the next two Light Seeds and then bounce to the opposite side of the cavern. Use Elika for a cooperative jump. Complete the wall run on the left side of the cave with the rings.

There's a Light Seed just below the ledge.

Wall run out to the vines to grab the next Light Seed.

Continue along the eastern path to pick up the last two Light Seeds on this route. One Light Seed is on the vines that hang down the left side of the route. The next Light Seed is on a ledge overlooking the fork in the road that either leads back to the Vale or continues on to the Royal Palace.

Construction Yard

The great ships—both air and sea—of the Ahuras were once constructed at these shipyards, but now the machinery is dormant. Corruption spreads across the yards, sliming what's left of the tools and implements. The Alchemist is here, plotting and planning for your arrival. Do not disappoint him.

Corrupt

Approach

There are three ways to reach the Construction Yard. Each route is a brisk series of jumps and wall runs. The goal is the same, though: Reach the southern tip of the abandoned shipyard, which marked with the glowing green power plate. This power plate is the launch to a tricky platform puzzle farther north, in the heart of the Construction Yard.

Wall run out to the green power plate. Tap Elika's magic as you reach the power plate.

When you stomp to the second power plate, you rotate to the left to crawl along the wall horizontally. Steer along the curved path.

Use the third power plate to ascend up the side of the wooden panels and reach a series of four platforms.

The Puzzle

When you clamber to the surface, the fertile ground rises into view, buoyed by a hot air balloon. The fertile ground is too far away to jump to directly. Instead, you must climb on top of the four platforms above you and use the cranks to rotate them. Once you have adjusted the platforms properly to create a bridge to the fertile ground, you can heal the area and start seeking out Light Seeds.

Wall run up this surface. Use the two rings for leverage.

Jump out from the post to reach the first of the four platforms. Each platform has a crank that rotates either all four platforms, or spins the entire mechanism so that all four platforms move in unison. Each platform has at least one post sticking out of it. The platforms are too far apart to jump to without using posts to close the gap. You must eventually rotate the platform to the right of the first platform so its extended post reaches all the way out to the fertile ground.

Rotate the first platform so you can jump to the platform to the north with just the two posts.

Rotate the platform to spin its posts so you can jump to the platform currently closest to the fertile ground. Make sure the extended post is facing to the east.

This platform spins the entire mechanism. Spin all of the platforms so the one with the extended post is now closest to the fertile ground, like this.

Now, jump to this platform and rotate the platforms so the extended post is pointed to the west.

Return to this platform and rotate the crank so the extended post is facing east again. (What's you done is create a network to actually reach the platform with the extended post.)

Rotate this crank so you can now jump to the platform with the extended post, which is still closest to the fertile ground.

RETURN OF THE PRINCE
MOVES IN MYSTERIOUS WAYS
DYNAMIC WORLD
DESERT
RUINED CITADEL
THE VALE
ROYAL PALACE
CITY OF LIGHT
TREE OF LIFE
SECRETS

Rotate the platform so the extended post is within jumping distance. Leap to that platform.

Finally, spin the crank so the extended post is pointed back to the fertile ground. Now you can jump to the sacred ground and heal the Construction Yard.

Not so fast, says the Alchemist.

The Alchemist

The Alchemist is again hesitant to land the first attack, but keep your guard up. Your strategy is the same this time—keep savaging the Alchemist with extended combos. Watch for his arm to rise, signaling the start of his attacks. Just as his hand flicks out, deflect the attack and then launch into a combo that calls upon Elika's magic.

NOTE

THERE ARE SEVERAL COLUMNS IN THIS ARENA THAT END COMBOS IF YOU SLAM THE ALCHEMIST INTO THEM.

There is a trick for defeating the Alchemist within a minute of the battle opener. Weaken the Alchemist with a long combo. As you conclude the combo, the Alchemist gives off blue sparks. When you see those sparks, back the Alchemist up to the edge of the arena and launch into an attack.

As expected, you enter a struggle.

If you win the struggle, though, you knock the Alchemist off the fertile ground and into the corruption below.

With the Alchemist in full retreat, Elika can heal the Construction Yard. Stand in the blue beacon and repeatedly tap the magic button to complete the purge and return light to this corner of the Vale.

HEALED

(SEE MAP ON NEXT PAGE)

There are three paths leading into the Construction Yard: The short route to the south, and then the two jumping routes to the east and west of the area.

CONSTRUCTION YARD

The easiest batch of Light Seeds to collect in the Construction Yard leads you away from the fertile ground and beneath the rotating platforms. After passing beneath the platforms, climb back up the wall with the rings. There is a Light Seed between the rings and one immediately behind you on the roof of the building.

Hang over the back side of the wall to grab another Light Seed.

Now, jump out to the rotating platforms to continue collecting.

Jump from post to post to pick up the three Light Seeds on the rotating platforms. The cranks work, so use them if you need to spin the platforms and adjust the posts.

Two Light Seeds are on an orphaned ledge to the east of the rotating platforms. You can only reach these Light Seeds via the extended post, so spin the platforms so that the extended post is next to the Light Seeds. Then, cross to that platform and spin the crank to move the extended post toward the Light Seeds. Jump from the post with Elika's help to capture the Light Seeds.

Use the green power plates to climb the building without fear of falling and pick up a Light Seed.

RETURN OF THE PRINCE
MOVES IN MYSTERIOUS WAYS
DYNAMIC WORLD
DESERT
RUINED CITADEL
THE VALE
ROYAL PALACE
CITY OF LIGHT
TREE OF LIFE
SECRETS

To Machinery Ground

x5

To Reservoir

South Path

x6

Legend

- Light Seed
- Breath of Ormazd Power Plate
- Wings of Ormazd Power Plate

Yellow Power Plate

A yellow power plate is next to the fertile ground. If you have the Wings of Ormazd, you can use this power plate to pick up the hidden Light Seeds in the Construction Yard.

As you zoom under the Construction Yard, steer into the Light Seeds. Watch out for the pillars as you swing beneath the rotating platforms.

The Wings of Ormazd carry you through a hole in the wall with the green power plates. Just as you pass through the hole, veer to the left to pick up another Light Seed before the flight ends back at the fertile ground.

South Path

Wall run to the red scaffolding and follow it down the south route back toward the Cauldron. At the end of the scaffolding, wall run out and jump to the adjacent wall to pick up another Light Seed. Be sure to wall run to the next red board before you fall. Continue following the scaffolding until you reach the edge of the Cauldron. There is a Light Seed right on the edge of the passage.

Lower yourself down to grab these two Light Seeds.

East Path

Run to the edge of the post overlooking the east route. Jump out to the flagpoles to grab a Light Seed and the flip over to the solid post. Turn to the vertical post and wall run up it to collect another Light Seed.

Wall run across the wooden planks to pick up a Light Seed. Jump at the end of the wall to swing around a flagpole and land on a platform.

Jump to the cliffs and wall run out to the next Light Seed. Just as you end the wall run, jump over to the wooden planks to the left. Wall run along those and then bounce back over to the cliffs so you can wall run to the vines.

Look up from the vines. Two Light Seeds are directly above you. Clamber up to the ring and wall run to the Light Seeds. Grip fall back down to the vines.

Wall run to the next set of vines. From the vines, wall run to the pair of rings. There is a Light Seed between the two rings. This run ends at the crossroads between the Construction Yard and the Machinery Ground. If the Machinery Ground is still corrupt, a soldier waits for you there.

Climb up the vines so you can grab the Light Seed on the high wall leading back to the Construction Yard. Wall run to the right of the top patch of vines and then jump out to the planks. Pick up the Light Seed as you wall run and then jump out to the next set of vines.

West Path

Jump to the wooden planks on the left and start wall running. Jump away from the wall and use the flagpole (with its own Light Seed) as a springboard to the wood panels to the right. Wall run to the vines.

Climb to the top of the vines. Scramble up to the top of the ledge to pick up two Light Seeds. Then grip fall back to the vines.

RETURN OF THE PRINCE
MOVES IN MYSTERIOUS WAYS
DYNAMIC WORLD
DESERT
RUINED CITADEL
THE VALE
ROYAL PALACE
CITY OF LIGHT
TREE OF LIFE
SECRETS

Grip fall down from the vines and grab the Light Seed near the ring.

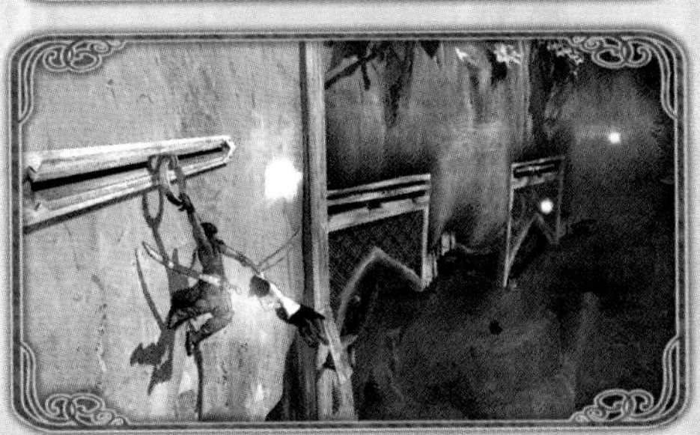

Jump out to the poles. You need Elika to reach the second pole. From there, jump to the cliff. Wall run to the right and snag a Light Seed. Slide along the ring slot and then wall run farther right to grab another Light Seed. Sliding that ring releases a series of platforms.

Jump across the two platforms (lower yourself over edge of the second one to grab a Light Seed) and then wall run to pick up the last Light Seed along this path.

Machinery Ground

The Alchemist lurks in the Machinery Ground, a former playground of cranes and gears. Boats that were once built here have been dismantled and left for scrap. The Prince and Elika must find the Alchemist's hiding spot in the Machinery Ground and push him farther back into the Vale. But the Alchemist has learned from previous encounters with the pair. This time, he is not going down without a fight.

Corrupt

Approach

There are three ways to enter the Machinery Ground. If you're coming from the Construction Yard, use the series of flagpoles jutting out of the cliffs to literally swing from pillar to post.

Rush along the wall and use the slotted ring to release a set of posts closer to the entrance of the Machinery Ground. Use those posts to link to another series of flagpoles and reach solid ground.

If you are approaching the Machinery Ground from Heaven's Stair, use the series of slides leading away from the crossroads (and the soldier battle). Jump out to the flagpoles and swing to the walkway leading toward the cliff side.

Wall run across the wooden planks. Jump down to the broken ship so that you can close in on the Machinery Ground.

Either path leads to the broken ship. Jump from the bow to the pair of flagpoles. Walk the railing that lines the patch of corruption and then wall run along the cliff. Link to the ring and then wall run to the vines. Follow these to the right. This is where you enter the area if you came from the Ruined Citadel. And this is where you will dive deep into the Machinery Ground.

Wall run out to the red power plate. Use Elika's magic to soar to the next power plate.

Wall run along the base of the platform, using the ring to keep up your momentum en route to the red power plate.

The Step of Ormazd launches you to another red power plate. Scramble up to it and activate it with Elika to bounce across the Machinery Ground.

Alchemist

When you land after launching away from the third red power plate, the Alchemist appears. He's confident in this fight, due in no small part to the pulsing corruption that lines the arena. If backed into this corruption, he simply sinks into it and then magically reappears behind you. Because this gives him a tactical advantage, try to position as much of the fight as possible in the center of the arena.

Deflect the Alchemist's regular attacks to keep him on his heels.

Return of the Prince
Moves in Mysterious Ways
Dynamic World
Desert
Ruined Citadel
The Vale
Royal Palace
City of Light
Tree of Life
Secrets

There it is—the Alchemist's regeneration move. When you spot blue magic curling away from the Alchemist's gaunt form, he is healing himself. You must strike soon to interrupt this technique, otherwise the Alchemist will undo any progress you might make against him.

TIP

While regenerating, the Alchemist will back away. You must charge him to interrupt the move.

CAUTION

The Alchemist will regenerate with his back to the corruption. That way, if you strike him into the poison, he will just reappear behind you, ready to push you into the muck.

When the Alchemist backs up to the corruption, start with an acrobatic move to launch over the Corrupted and push him back to the middle of the arena. Continue your combo to chisel away his health.

Just as the pair is about to defeat the Alchemist, he unleashes a special corruption attack against the Prince. The Alchemist covers the Prince in corruption, the same kind of black poison that claimed the Corrupted and is twisting Elika's father into an unrecognizable form. Elika thinks she can reverse the corruption, but she must reach the fertile ground to do so.

The Corrupted Prince

Now that the Prince is corrupted, the corners of his vision blur and darken. You must ascend the Machinery Ground to reach the fertile soil atop a giant broken ship. Start by running to the ring on the wall next to the Alchemist's arena. Scurry up the wall via the ring and climb on top of the post.

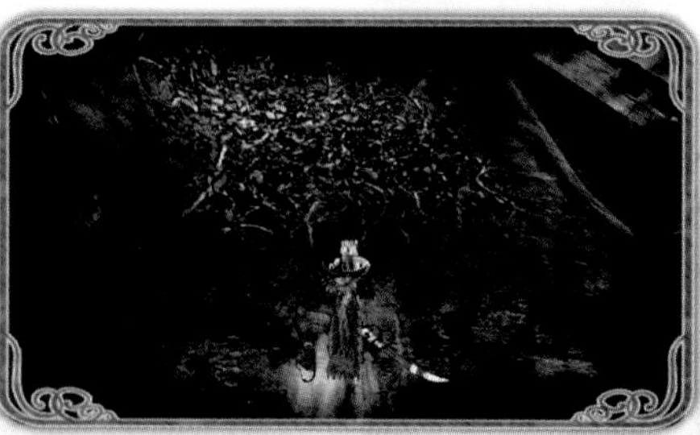

Jump to the wall and use the rings to reach a patch of vines.

Wall run to the left of the vines, using the ring to connect to another wall run. When you drop down to the ledge, wait for the gear to open and then leap through the hole.

After jumping through the hole in the gear, wall run across the two rings and then leap to the flagpole.

Jump across the posts and then swing around another flagpole.

Slide along the slotted ring and wall run just as the gear sticking out of the wall shifts. You grab a patch of vines.

Climb the rings above the vines and then wall run to the right. Pass through the hole in the gear to reach a stable ledge.

Jump across to the column and then roof along the rings. When you reach the ring at the end of the roofing sequence, scramble up the wall directly above it. There are vines above you to grab onto right away.

Wall run to the right, following the wall as it curves. After linking another wall run with the ring, jump away from the wall to grab another column and start roofing along a series of rings.

RETURN OF THE PRINCE
MOVES IN MYSTERIOUS WAYS
DYNAMIC WORLD
DESERT
RUINED CITADEL
THE VALE
ROYAL PALACE
CITY OF LIGHT
TREE OF LIFE
SECRETS

Jump from the roof to the flagpole. Double-jump from the flagpole to the wall and then grip fall down to the ring.

Roof over to the column and then drop down to the solid ledge. You're almost there.

Wall run out to the ring. As the ring slides along its slot, the spinning gear stops and you can wall run right through the holes. Use the ring on the other side of the gear to link up to a vertical fissure. Slide down the fissure to reach a post.

Jump to the wooden ledge and then wall run along the scratches. There's a ring at the corner of the broken ship. Swing around to the other side of the ship and then wall run to the vines. Climb the vines to the right and then slide along another slotted ring to shut down the nearby gear.

Wall run through the hole in the frozen gear and then bounce across a series of posts.

Jump from the posts to a crack in the wall. Grip fall down to the ring below.

Roof along the rings to come up on the other side. Now, climb to the top of the structure to reach the fertile ground.

There it is—the fertile ground and your salvation. Hurry to the blue beacon and purify the fertile ground with Elika's magic. Not only is the corruption blasted out of the Machinery Ground, but it's forced out of your body, too. Now that you've been healed along with the land, it's time to seek out Light Seeds so you can soon unlock another of Ormazd's magics.

Healed

There are three routes leading away from the Machinery Ground: north, south, and west. The west route directs you to the Ruined Citadel, home of the Hunter.

Machinery Ground

Once the area is healed, pick up your first Light Seed on the bow of the ship near the fertile ground. The view is pretty spectacular from up here, so soak up the splendor before setting about the task of pocketing Light Seeds.

Follow the three Light Seeds to the red power plate.

The red power plate bounces you to another plate. Wall run to the plate to return to the entrance of the Machinery

x6
To West Path
To Heaven's Stair
To Construction Yard

Legend
Light Seed
Hand of Ormazd Power Plate
Step of Ormazd Power Plate

Ground. From down here, you have several choices. You can either explore the Machinery Ground to collect its prizes, or venture out along the three paths to gather up their Light Seeds.

If you want to push into the Machinery Ground or access the west path, cross the flagpoles to the north, collecting a Light Seed. Swing down to the railing and then wall run to the vines. There is a Light Seed above the vines.

Use the red power plate to vault through the air and down to the next red power plate. Slide along the ring and into the plate to bound up to another power plate. Finally, scramble up to the power plate and drop down to the platform where you battled with the Alchemist.

Blue Power Plate

If you have the Hand of Ormazd, you can capture the five Light Seeds hanging in the air above the platform. Wall run out to the blue power plate on the cliff.

This plate arcs you through the air and through a line of Light Seeds and up to another blue power plate. Use this plate to pick up another two Light Seeds before dropping back down to the fight platform.

Hang off the side of the platform overlooking the blue power plate. Slide down the line of scratch marks to a ring.

RETURN OF THE PRINCE
MOVES IN MYSTERIOUS WAYS
DYNAMIC WORLD
DESERT
RUINED CITADEL
THE VALE
ROYAL PALACE
CITY OF LIGHT
TREE OF LIFE
SECRETS

Roof beneath the platform to reach two Light Seeds. Use the red power plate to return to the fork in the road between the Construction Yard and Heaven's Stair.

Follow the same path up to the fertile ground as before to pick up a series of Light Seeds. The lack of corruption actually makes movement easier. When you reach the frozen gears, slow down and look out to the right.

Two Light Seeds are on those cranes.

To reach those cranes, stop on the post directly across from them. Face the wall and climb up the two rings. At the top of the second ring, kick away from the wall and use Elika's cooperative jump to hurl you out to the closest crane. Double-jump to the next crane to collect both Light Seeds.

Continue moving up the broken ship to reach the fertile ground, picking up the Light Seeds along the way.

South Path

The route back to the Construction Yard is lined with Light Seeds. Jump across the series of flagpoles to reach the series of posts unlocked by sliding the ring. Look to the cliff and then glance up. A Light Seed is directly above you, just north of the ring. Scramble up the wall and vault beyond the ring to grab the Light Seed.

Jump from the posts to the cliff with Elika's help. Wall run through the Light Seed and then slide along the ring. When the ring reaches the other end of the slot, wall run through the next Light Seed. Jump away from the wall to reach a pair of posts. Scurry up to the Light Seed above the posts.

North Path

Jump out to the flagpole to start moving toward Heaven's Stair and collect another set of Light Seeds. Jump from pole to post and then wall run along the wooden planks. Use the ring to link two wall runs and then leap out to a sturdy post.

You are now positioned to make a fast loop around a series of slides to pick up a handful of Light Seeds. Jump out to the next pole and then swing around it to grab a Light Seed. Bolt across the platform on the other side of the pole to reach the slides.

Steer toward the Light Seeds as you race down the slides.

If Heaven's Stair has not been healed, you must contend with a soldier at the crossroads. Watch for it to use any of Ahriman's Influences that have been triggered by previous Corrupted battles.

RETURN OF THE PRINCE
MOVES IN MYSTERIOUS WAYS
DYNAMIC WORLD
DESERT
RUINED CITADEL
THE VALE
ROYAL PALACE
CITY OF LIGHT
TREE OF LIFE
SECRETS

Jump to the slides heading back toward the Machinery Ground. Steer to the left to pick up a Light Seed and then jump out to the vines. Grip fall through the vines to a lower patch of tendrils that's not easily visible. Climb around to the back side of the wall via the vines to pick up more Light Seeds. Now, complete the slides to grab the last light Seed on this route and return to the Machinery Grounds.

West Path

Cooperatively jump across the massive gap between the Machinery Ground and the west path that leads to the Ruined Citadel. Scurry up the wall to grab the first Light Seed along this short route and then walk to the edge of the platform to peer down the tunnel.

Call on Elika for another double jump to the next rock ledge. Pick up the Light Seed on the ledge and then look to the left. There are three visible Light Seeds. Jump ahead to the next platform to pick up the easy grab. The two off to the right are nabbed by double-jumping away from the platform and wall running up the side of the tunnel.

Wall run out to grab the last Light Seed on this route.

Reservoir

The Ahura water supply was stored at this site. A massive basin set into the cliffs was fed water by a long tube, then stored for days when the rains did not come. Ahriman has poisoned the Reservoir with corruption, giving the Alchemist yet another stronghold in the Vale. The Prince and Elika must cleanse the Reservoir so that one day, when the Ahuras rise again, this resource can be safely used.

Corrupt Approach

If you approach the Reservoir from the south, you must climb along patches of vines that grow on the cliffs. Bounce from the vines to the large wooden panels and wall run (link via those rings!) before bounding back to the cliffs.

Complete the approach on the Reservoir by running along the walls, darting from one fissure to the next.

If you are coming from the north, Use the rings under the planks to roof over to the cliffs. Jump from the column at the end of the planks to the rocks and then wall run to the vines for support. From the vines, continue to the right until you reach a vertical fissure in the rocks you can grab.

Follow the fissures in the wall to a slide. The slide leads to some vines. Climb the vines to reach the entrance of the Reservoir.

Power Plates

To reach the Reservoir, you must use a series of red power plates that are strategically placed around the site. As you bound from plate to plate, you are often dropped just next to a plate, so you must scramble along the walls to reach the plate before gravity pushes you down. To start the trip, wall run out to the red power plate at the end of the wooden planks overlooking the Reservoir. This sends you flying across the site to another wooden plank with a red power plate.

This plate blasts you across the Reservoir to a solid ledge. Wall run up to the red power plate.

You're launched into a crumbling water tube. Slide down the canvas and wall run out to the next red power plate. This shoots you directly to the next power plate, so be ready with Elika's magic.

The next power plate launches you over the Reservoir and to a wooden plank. Wall run to the power plate.

Climb up the wall to reach another solid ledge. Now, wall run to the next power plate to the left.

You're launched under an arc of free-flowing corruption. The ride ends at a slide. Jump to the wall at the bottom of the slide and run to the power plate.

Blast over to a series of slides. Race down the slides, cooperatively jumping across them. At the bottom of the second slide, jump out and scramble up to the red power plate.

Bounce away from the red power plate on the wall and drop into a tube that feeds directly into the basin.

Alchemist

The tube deposits the Prince and Elika into the basin. The fertile ground is down here, but so is the Alchemist. The basin is full of corruption. It lines the arena, making it a small one with dangerous edges. The Alchemist wants to be backed into the corruption so he can shrink down into it and then reappear behind you. You must use acrobatic combos that keep pushing the Alchemist back to the center of the arena and then juggle him into the air with magic.

The Alchemist relies strongly on Ahriman's Influences, especially Ahriman's Fury. Watch for those state changes and use the appropriate counter.

CAUTION

Be careful with Elika here. Because Ahriman's Fury requires Elika, if you accidentally injure her by using her against an inappropriate influence, you just have to dodge and wait out the Rage.

Keep the Alchemist in the center of the arena by switching back and forth around him via acrobatic moves.

The Alchemist can attack from distances now with a corruption blast. When the Alchemist's arms flick up together, he's releasing the attack. Deflect the attack to launch into your own counter.

Return of the Prince
Moves in Mysterious Ways
Dynamic World
Desert
Ruined Citadel
The Vale
Royal Palace
City of Light
Tree of Life
Secrets

TIP

Keep your guard up during the battle when not directly engaging the Alchemist.

Toss the Alchemist sky-high with the gauntlet attack.

Dispel the regeneration technique with a sword attack.

When the Alchemist is almost finished, get aggressive. Empty that health meter before the Alchemist has a chance to employ his regeneration move. Hammer the Alchemist with a fast series of sword attacks to banish him from the Reservoir. Now, cleanse the fertile ground so he may never return here.

Healed

There are three routes leading away from the Reservoir: north, south, and east. The east route connects the Vale to the Royal Palace. You must explore all of these routes as well as retrace your flight paths around the Reservoir to collect all the Light Seeds.

Reservoir

You must use the red power plates on the walls to escape the basin. There are four Light Seeds next to the power plates that surround the basin, so as you bounce around the scene, you collect the treasures. The red power plate network finally launches you out of the basin, depositing you right back at the entrance of the Reservoir.

Start back across the system of power plates to collect Light Seeds. When you reach the first solid ledge, a yellow power

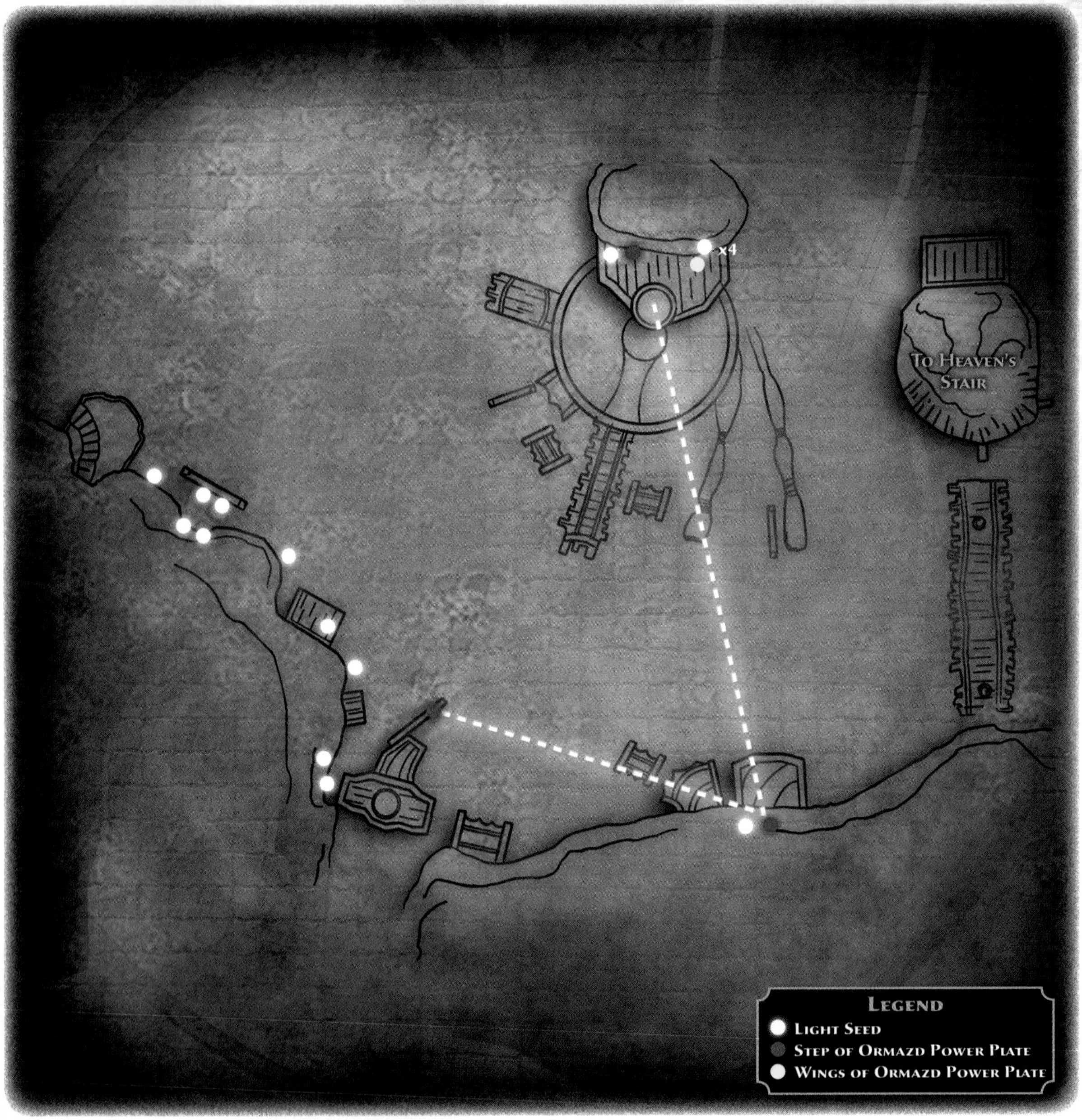

x4

To Heaven's Stair

Legend

Light Seed

Step of Ormazd Power Plate

Wings of Ormazd Power Plate

plate that was hidden behind corruption is now visible. If you have the Wings of Ormazd, you can activate this power plate and blast off to collect some hard-to-reach Light Seeds.

Follow the sequence of red power plates all the way back to the basin to collect Light Seeds. Once

you drop into the basin, use the power plates to return to the Reservoir entrance and explore the paths leading away from the area to gather more Light Seeds.

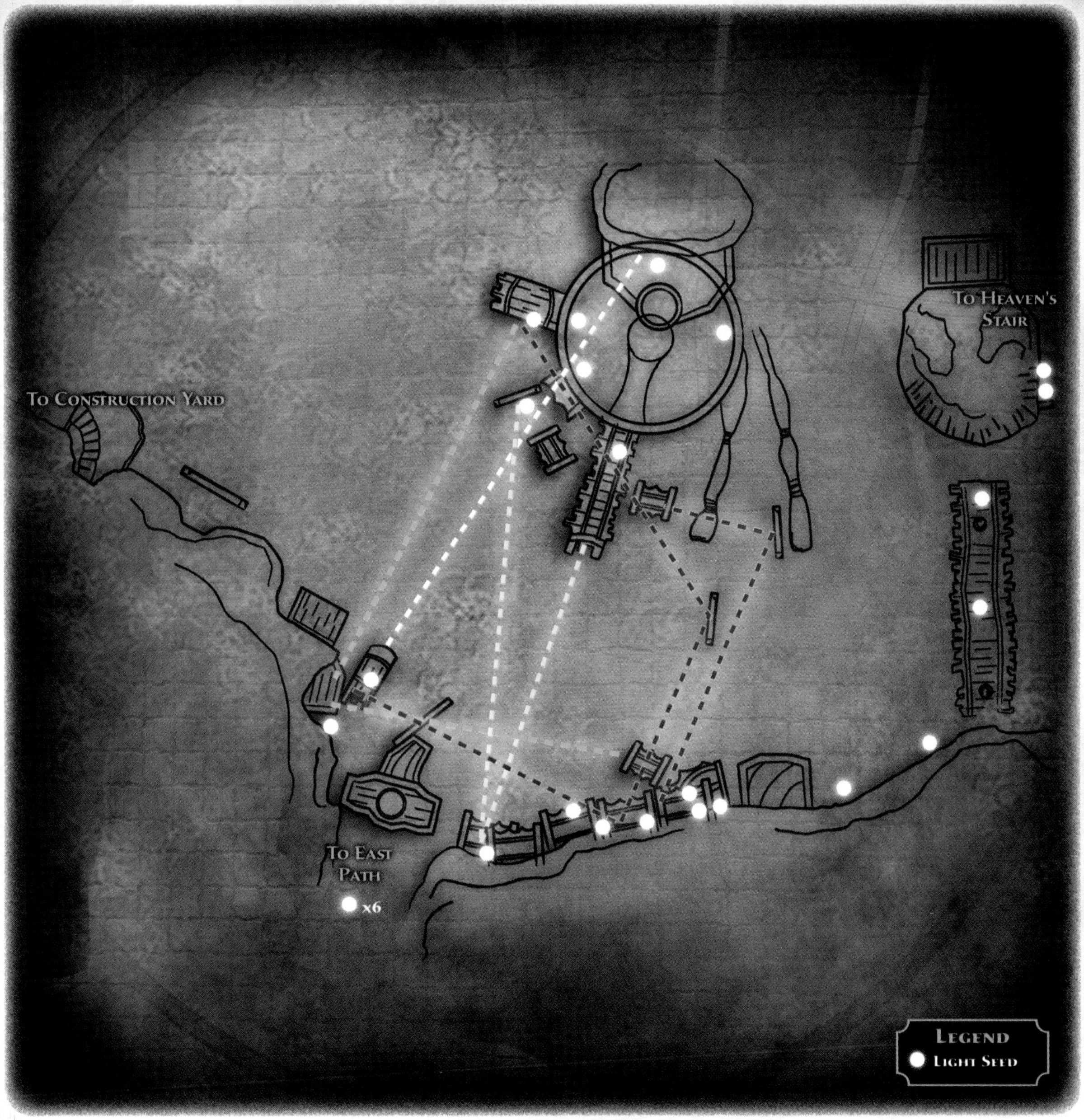

To Heaven's Stair

To Construction Yard

To East Path

x6

Legend

Light Seed

Yellow Power Plate

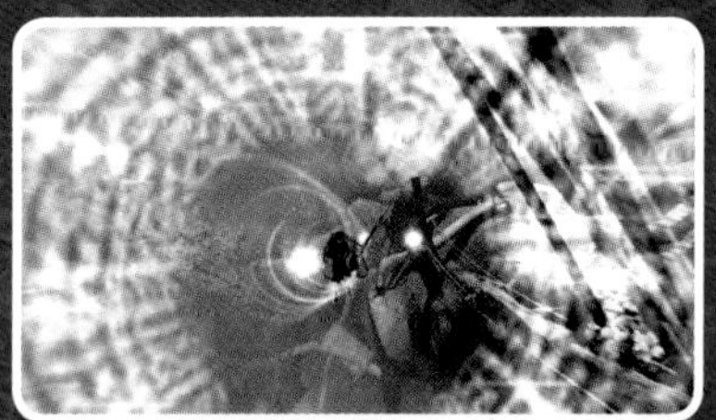

The yellow power plate launches you on a soaring flight path around the Reservoir. As you zoom through the air, steer into the Light Seeds. Dart left to right to pick up the first trio of Light Seeds.

Your flight path then leads between posts and pillars, so veer around them. The flight ends by shooting you straight up to collect two more Light Seeds. The Wings of Ormazd then gently drop you back down right in front of the yellow power plate.

North Path

Strike out for Heaven's Stair by heading to the left of the Reservoir entrance. Wall run out to the fissures. Once settled on the first fissure, look up. Wall run up to the Light Seed directly above you and then grip fall back to the fissure.

Wall run out to the vines at the edge of the cliff to pick up another Light Seed.

As you round the corner, you see two more Light Seeds. One is directly on your path to the north. The other, however, is under the wooden platform. Grip fall from the vines to the fissure below and then wall run to the vines under the platform. After capturing the Light Seed retrace your steps back up to the main path.

When you round the vines at the next corner, you see Light Seeds both high and low on the wooden planks. To get the low Light Seed, grip fall to the vines below and then wall run to the right. Jump out to the wood panel and wall run along it. On the way back, take the high route.

There are two Light Seeds in the alcove across from the vines on the wood planks. Wall run to the vines and then stop and kick away from the vines and into the alcove. Grip fall through the two Light Seeds and then jump back to the panel. You need Elika's help to complete both jumps.

South Path

Skate down the canvas awnings to pick up three Light Seeds. Veer left and right on the slides to capture the treasures. At the bottom of the third slide, jump down to the wooden ledge.

Wall run to the vines to collect two Light Seeds. From the vines, wall run to the edge of the rocks and then jump to reach a column. Roof along the rings between the columns to pick up two more Light Seeds. Once you reach the second column, kick away to land on the crossroads.

Hang down the north side of the crossroads and grip fall down to two Light Seeds.

Return to the other side of the columns and then follow the fissures and slides back to the entrance of the Reservoir to collect more Light Seeds.

East Path

The path to the Royal Palace is lined with Light Seeds, but you must scale some tricky rocks to reach them. Double-jump out to the first rock in the narrow canyon. From here, you can see the edges of Light Seeds in the distance. Cooperatively jump out to the lower rock.

There is a Light Seed on the next rock—it's only a hop away. But to gather the two Light Seeds on the wall, you must jump out over the abyss. Grip fall into the Light Seeds and then immediately kick back to the rock.

Scramble back to the start of the path and then cooperatively jump with Elika to the high rock. Jump across the network of rocks to pick up another Light Seed.

Wall run out to the next rock and grab the Light Seed. Then, grip fall to the rock below. The last Light Seed on the path is down there.

Heaven's Stair

Heaven's Stair is a huge tower that looms high above the Vale. It is the direct gateway to the Obser-vatory, which is the highest point in the entire kingdom. From here, the Alchemist was once able to look out across the stars and imagine new worlds. But the stars cannot be seen through the mist of corruption that hangs over the Vale.

Corrupt Approach

If you are coming at the Heaven's Stair from the east, use the columns and rings to reach a vine-covered cliff. Scurry across the vines and then leap out to another series of columns. There is a wooden panel that runs alongside the columns that you can use to cross the gap between the columns and reach the base of Heaven's Stair.

From the crossroads to the west, use the slides to reach a series of columns. Connect the two slides to the right with the vines on the wooden wall. When crossing between the columns, use the rings on the ceiling to roof. Once you reach the last column, hop down to the entrance to Heaven's Stair.

Ascension

The green power plates on the face of Heaven's Stair are your key inside. Wall run up to the first power plate and use Elika's magic. This sends you stomping up to the next power plate in the sequence. Use magic at this plate to change course. Now you run horizontally around the exterior of Heaven's Stair.

The circum-ference of Heaven's Stair is quite a trip. While climbing against gravity, steer left and right to dodge gears, holes, and broken planks. If you bump into any obstacle, you're sent back down to the bottom of Heaven's Stair and must start over.

Tap the magic button when you reach the next green power plate. Now you climb back up the side of the tower and inside a small chamber.

As soon as you enter the chamber, a soldier appears out of the corruption and challenges you.

RETURN OF THE PRINCE
MOVES IN MYSTERIOUS WAYS
DYNAMIC WORLD
DESERT
RUINED CITADEL
THE VALE
ROYAL PALACE
CITY OF LIGHT
TREE OF LIFE
SECRETS

The soldier is a quick kill if you push it up to the wall and strike with fast sword attack. Getting it into that position is the tricky part. This soldier calls upon any of the Ahriman's Influences you've encountered up to this point, which certainly include Ahriman's Fury. When you see the soldier encased in black tendrils, call on Elika to dispel the effects of the influence and then continue into a combo.

After the soldier is down, jump outside the chamber and leap to the next green power plate.

The power plate sends you romping along a trail of boards and planks all lashed together. The path is narrow and zigzags. Steer with the curves as the path winds around Heaven's Stair and leads you up to the next floor of the tower.

The Gas

As soon as you set foot in this chamber, the elevator on the far side of the room locks. You must unlock it if you want to reach the top of the tower. Elika suggests you try the green power plates to ascend the room and figure out a way to open the door on the elevator. Follow her advice and stomp up one of the green power plates.

NOTE

Pick any of the four power plates—it doesn't matter which one you try first.

Climb along the rings and columns to reach the ledges above the elevator.

Uh-oh. When you reach the ledge above the elevator, corruption gas hisses through the vent in the center of the room. This is the trap for the Vale, and now that you've triggered it here, it will appear elsewhere in corrupted areas. The gas hovers in the bottom half of this room. Any time you must cross to a different green power plate on the bottom floor, you must run or else be overcome by the gas.

To remove the gas and open the elevator, you must slide the four slotted rings in this room. There is one ring per green power plate. Sliding along the ring unlocks a gear. When all four gears are unlocked, the door to the elevator swings open.

Follow the scratches on the walls. When you slide across the ring, the nearby gear flips up and is unlocked.

Grip fall from the vertical slit between the gears to reach the floor and run to another green power plate.

TIP

Keep track of which power plates you have already used. Each power plate leads to one slotted ring switch.

Waste no time when running to a new green power plate when the gas is still active.

When the door opens, use the crank to raise the elevator.

At the top of the elevator shaft, jump out to the nearby column and then leap to the short wall. Scramble up to reach a balcony that overlooks the Vale. A green power plate is there to your right.

Romp and stomp along the winding path as you ascend the tower's exterior. Steer with the path. If you bump into a dead end or any obstacle, you return to the balcony next to the elevator. The path leads directly to the Alchemist.

The Alchemist

The Alchemist is determined to keep you from reaching the top of his Observatory. He challenges you on the roof of Heaven's Stair. It's a large, round arena with a few pillars but no open edges and only a small path of corruption against the large black door. You can keep the Alchemist away from it.

In fact, it's a great arena for combos since you can really juggle the Alchemist with alternating magic and lift moves in the center of the sizeable room.

The Alchemist cycles through any revealed influences, especially Ahriman's Fury during this battle. Be ready to counter with the appropriate attack.

If the Alchemist backs you into a wall, be ready for the resulting struggle.

If you are ever injured, keep your guard up. Should the Alchemist land a second successful attack while you are hurt, he goes in for a lethal attack.

As long as you prevent the Alchemist from regenerating his health via his special technique and guard against incoming attacks, handling him in this arena is totally manageable. Just keep the Corrupted close to the center of the room and launch him into the air so you can pound him every time he starts to come back down.

Healed

There are two paths that lead away from Heaven's Stair: west and east. The Observatory, the Alchemist's lair, is directly north of Heaven's Stair.

Heaven's Stair

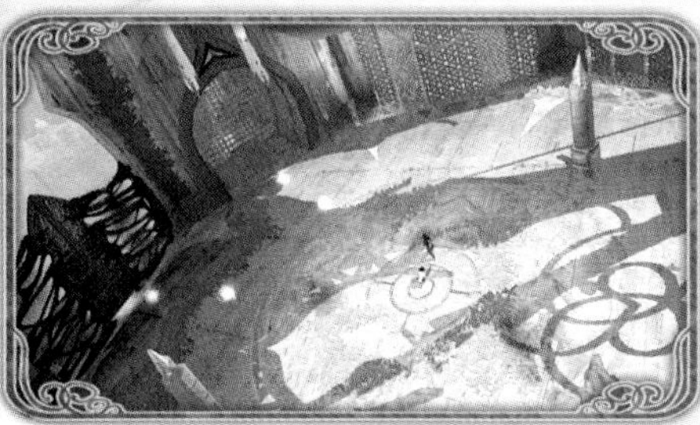

There are four Light Seeds around the fertile ground at the top of Heaven's Stair. Two of them lead to the large black gate that opens only when you've purified all four areas of the Vale. The other two Light Seeds lead to a large gate.

Pull the ring next to the gate. The gate falls, revealing a way down from the tower.

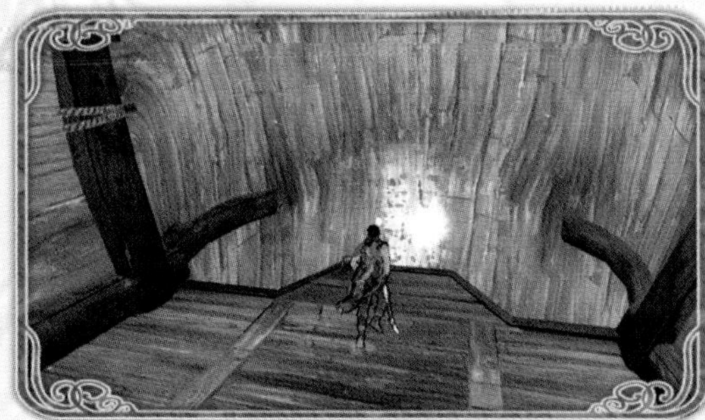

Jump out to the Light Seed in the shaft and then grip fall down.

RETURN OF THE PRINCE
MOVES IN MYSTERIOUS WAYS
DYNAMIC WORLD
DESERT
RUINED CITADEL
THE VALE
ROYAL PALACE
CITY OF LIGHT
TREE OF LIFE
SECRETS

To Reservoir
A
x6
To Machinery Ground
Legend
Light Seed
Breath of Ormazd Power Plate

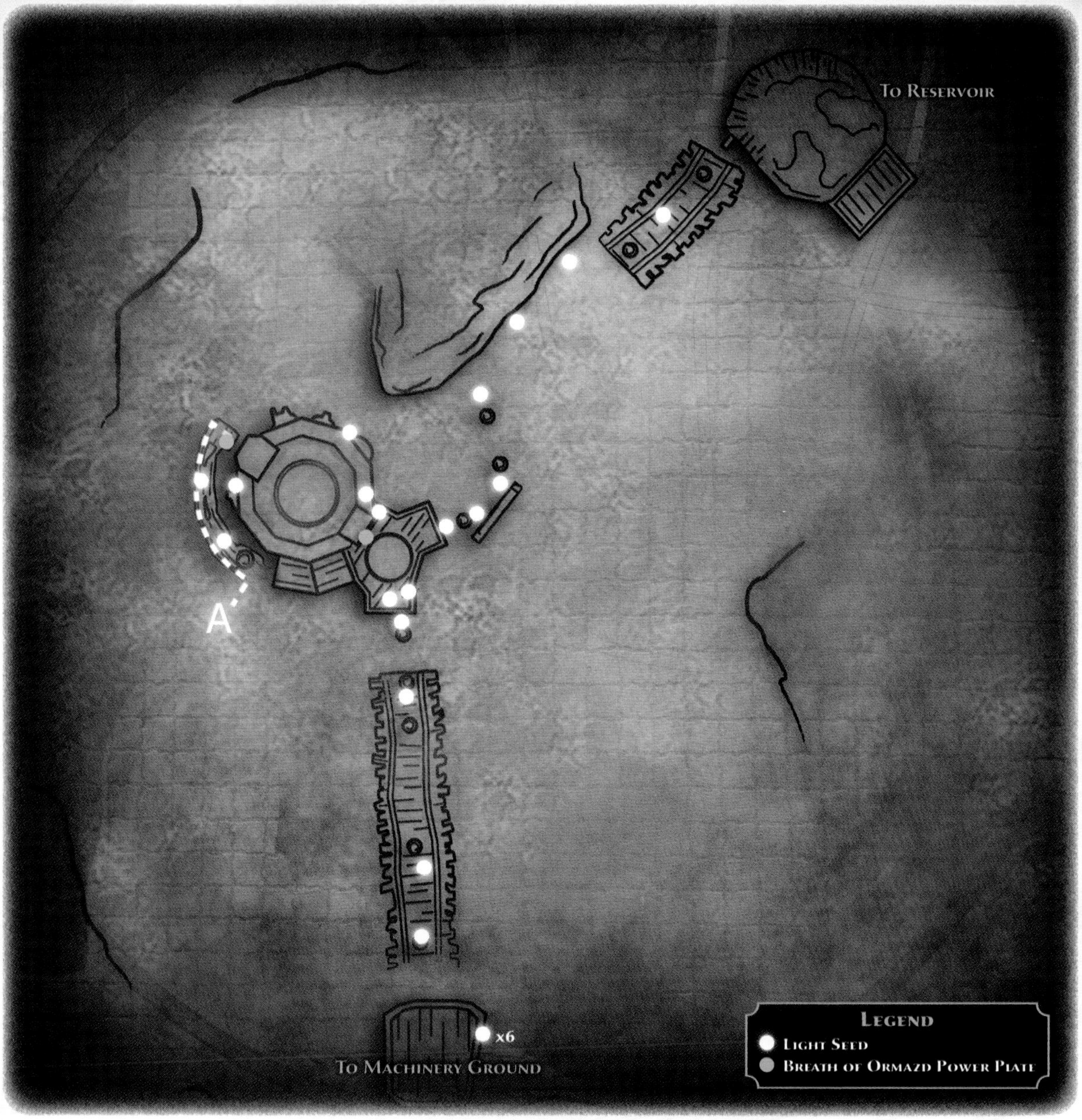

Dodge the wooden panels in the shaft as you grip fall, steering toward the Light Seed at the very bottom. This deposits you right outside the base of the tower.

Jump to the column with the sharp tip poking out above the platform outside Heaven's Gate. Slide down the column to pick up a Light Seed. At the bottom, swivel around the column to put your back to two more Light Seeds. Kick away from the column to grab the Light Seeds and land on another small pillar. Now, return to the platform.

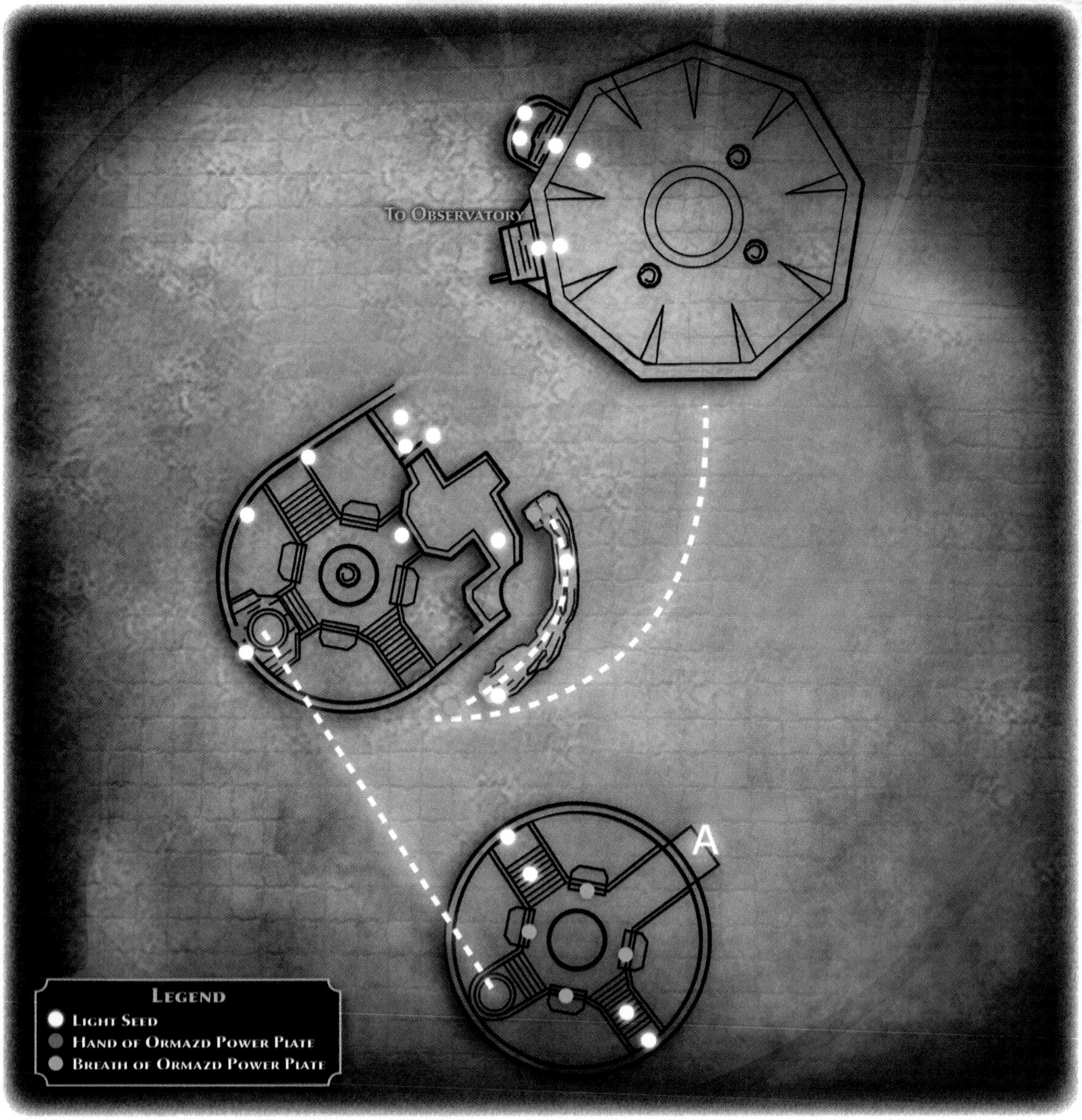

To Observatory

A

Legend
- Light Seed
- Hand of Ormazd Power Plate
- Breath of Ormazd Power Plate

Grab the two Light Seeds just to the right of the green power plate on the side of the tower.

Climb the side of the tower via the power plates. Steer into the Light Seeds.

A handful of Light Seeds is inside the gas room. Pick up the two Light Seeds tucked under the stairs. Then, use the green power plates to reach the slotted rings. Return to the slits between the gears and then grip fall into two more Light Seeds.

Use the elevator to rise to the next floor. Jump out to the column to pick up the Light Seed.

RETURN OF THE PRINCE
MOVES IN MYSTERIOUS WAYS
DYNAMIC WORLD
DESERT
RUINED CITADEL
THE VALE
ROYAL PALACE
CITY OF LIGHT
TREE OF LIFE
SECRETS

Blue Power Plate

Wall run to the blue power plate on the left side of the room (if you're outside looking in) and then activate it with Elika's magic. This arcs you to the power plate above the elevator and into a Light Seed. Wall run to the power plate to curve around the opposite side of the room.

When the Hand of Ormazd drops you against the wall, wall run to the rings to pick up two more Light Seeds. When you drop down to the ledge, pick up three Light Seeds. The first is out in the open. The other two are tucked in the corner, off to the right.

Exit the chamber above the elevator. Pick up the Light Seed on the landing and then jump out to the green power plate that rockets you to the top of Heaven's Stair.

Pick up two more Light Seeds on the winding path up to the roof.

West Path

From the entrance to Heaven's Stair, jump out to the columns leading back to the Machinery Ground. Roof along the rings between the columns to pick up a Light Seed. Cooperatively jump with Elika between the last two columns right before the crossroads to pick up another Light Seed.

Jump out to the loop of slides. Steer into the Light Seeds on the canvas slides as you slip down them. There are four Light Seeds on the slides, one per slide.

When you reach the crossroads, hang up the northwest side of the platform and grip fall to some vines to grab a pair of Light Seeds.

East Path

Start from the entrance to Heaven's Stair. Jump to the closest column and then run along the wooden plank. This sets you on a path for the crossroads between Heaven's Stair and the Reservoir. Wall run along the plank to gather two Light Seeds and then leap out to another series of columns.

Jump to the cliff and then wall run to the vines. Three Light Seeds are on the side of the cliff, each accessible via wall runs. Use the vine patches to avoid slipping off the cliff.

Roof out to the crossroads to gather the last Light Seed along this path.

The Observatory

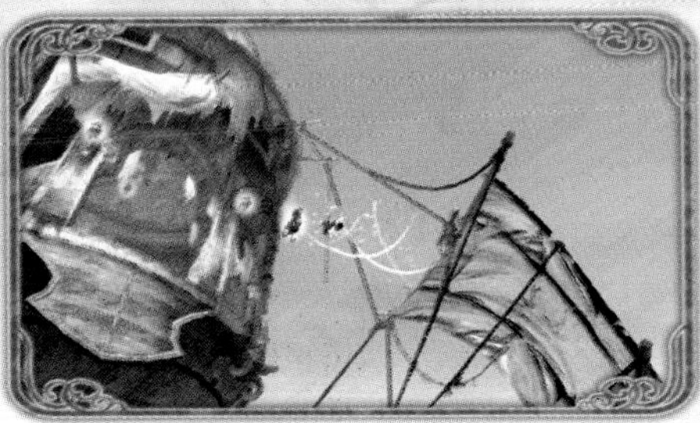

Now that the four areas of the Vale have been liberated from Ahriman's corruption, it's time for the Prince and Elika to challenge the Alchemist to one final fight. Outsmarting the Alchemist will not be easy. But if the Prince and Elika put their heads together, they may have just enough wits about them to stay one step ahead of Ahriman's mad scientist.

The Approach

After passing through the black gate, you spy a green power plate on a wooden structure. This is the launching pad for a wild ride up a series of hot air balloons that float above the Vale. The green power plate sends you running for a red power plate on the side of the structure.

Two red power plates bounce you up the Alchemist's balloons. When you reach the red power plate on the bottom balloon, tap the magic button to vault through the air again and land near a green power plate.

Use rings to link wall scrambles up to the power plates on the balloons.

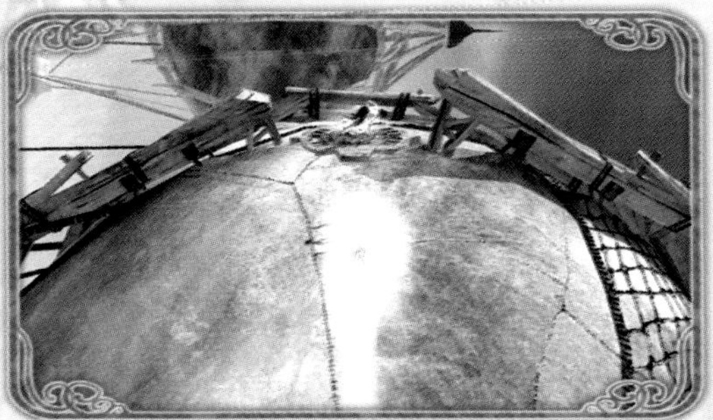

Follow the plates on the balloons to reach the bottom floor of the Observatory.

Wall run to the left and use the ring on the corner to swing around to a green power plate. The green power plate sends you stomping along the walls of the Observatory. Dodge the creeping corruption and wall fixtures on your way to a red power plate.

Keep alternating between red and green plates to climb the inside of the Observatory. When a red plate bounces you across the room, keep the button held down and press in the direction of the plate (or a ring to connect two wall runs) to wall run to the next available power plate.

RETURN OF THE PRINCE
MOVES IN MYSTERIOUS WAYS
DYNAMIC WORLD
DESERT
RUINED CITADEL
THE VALE
ROYAL PALACE
CITY OF LIGHT
TREE OF LIFE
SECRETS

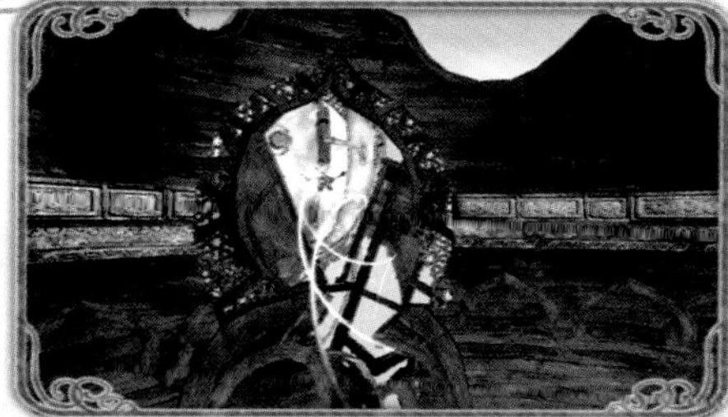

Soon, you are launched out of the Observatory and back to a balloon.

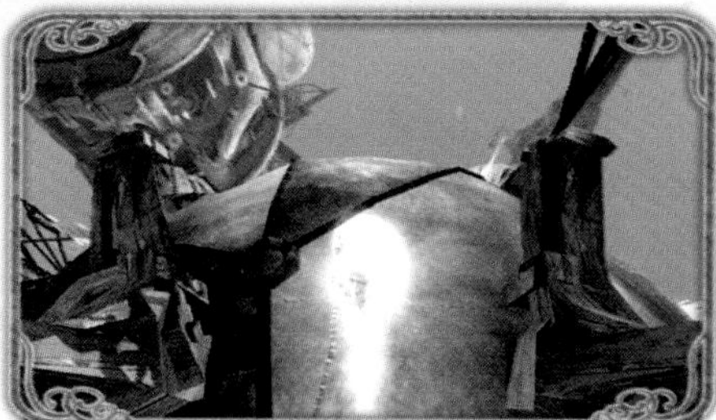

Activate the green power plate to run around the circumference of the balloon.

The red power plate on top of the balloon launches you to the top room of the Observatory where the Alchemist awaits you.

Final Showdown

The Alchemist rises from the floor of the chamber, cloaked in corruption. This Corrupted is a being of vast intelligence—he knows he has been cornered and you have the advantage here with Elika. But the Alchemist has nothing to lose at this point, not even his life, which was forfeit centuries ago. And so this man of science will now fight like a man of war.

Immediately start the battle with an acrobatic move to keep the Alchemist centered in the small arena. With a successful start like this, you can then launch the Alchemist into the air with the gauntlet and keep him bobbing around with Elika's magic attacks.

Half of the arena wall is lined with corruption. The Alchemist tries to stick to that side of the room. You must push him away from it.

Watch for the blue curls that indicate the regeneration technique. When you see them, close in immediately and attack so the Alchemist cannot recover too much strength.

Watch for throwing the Alchemist into the wall. It does little damage to the Corrupted and he recovers from it right away. In fact, he returns the favor with a struggle. If you fail the struggle, Elika must save you, giving the Alchemist a few seconds to recover his health.

Use the gauntlet when you have the Alchemist in the dead center of the room. It launches him straight up, making him easy prey to a long combo.

RETURN OF THE PRINCE
MOVES IN MYSTERIOUS WAYS
DYNAMIC WORLD
DESERT
RUINED CITADEL
THE VALE
ROYAL PALACE
CITY OF LIGHT
TREE OF LIFE
SECRETS

Keep the Alchemist reeling with your combos.

TIP

ABG. Always Be Guarding. When not attacking, have your defenses up because the Alchemist is both fast and aggressive in this final fight.

Observe This

After zeroing out the Alchemist's health bar, he vanishes back into the floor. Elika didn't purify him, so he's still alive somewhere in the Observatory. After the Alchemist disappears, the room shifts, revealing a red power plate.

The red power plate launches you to a small platform. When you land, a solider leaps into action. Slice up the soldier, pushing it toward one of the edges for a quick kill. Watch for state changes, though, as these soldiers can assume unlocked Ahriman's Influences.

After eliminating the soldier, use the next red power plates to bounce you around the planetary models hanging from the ceiling.

The third red power plate blasts you out of the Observatory and to a platform held aloft by balloons. Another soldier is waiting for you out there.

Hammer the soldier with your sword attacks. When the brute is done for, wall run up to the next red power plate.

After soaring through the air, you drop down on a very small platform on top of the Observatory. It is lined with corruption on all sides. This is the perfect spot for the Alchemist to make his last stand—so he does, with fire and fury in all of his attacks. Stay on guard and try not to push the Alchemist into the corruption!

The Alchemist has only a quarter of his strength for this last stand.

Use acrobatics to maneuver between the Alchemist and the corruption. With his back to the arena's center, launch into a combo. Keep the Alchemist in the middle of the platform to neutralize any of his advantages.

Grab the Alchemist with your gauntlet and shove him skyward. As he rises, send Elika up to finish the job with a flurry of magic attacks. The Alchemist flops to the ground in failure. As he dissolves back into the corruption, Elika leans down and places her hand on the Alchemist, releasing him from his torment. Eternal life is not worth such a cost.

Short Trip Down

As the Prince and Elika try to catch their breath, the platform atop the Observatory slips from its foundations. The platform slides off the tower and sends the pair flying toward the balloons. The Prince and Elika land on a small platform amongst the magnificent hot air balloons. Now they must use the power plates on the balloons to safely descend from the Observatory.

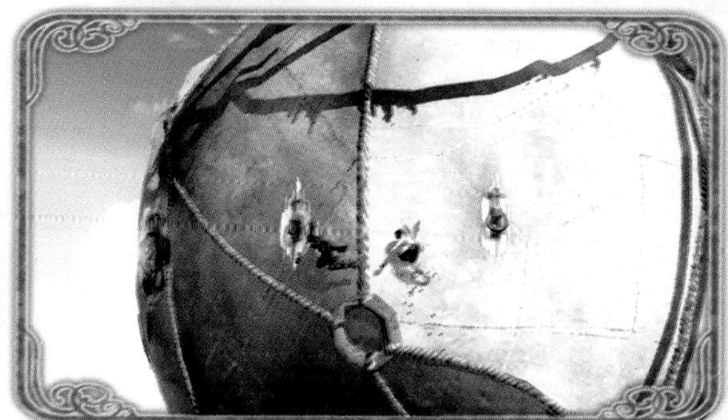

Wall run across the colorful balloons the reach the necessary power plates.

Follow the paths around the balloons without crashing into moorings.

Finally, the Prince and Elika reach the bottom of the Observatory. A brilliant sun shines over the Vale, casting the skies in a blue the Prince has never seen before in his life. His spirits are up—defeating the Alchemist was quite a feat. But Elika does not share in all of his exuberance. What burden is she carrying that she chooses to shoulder alone?

Royal Palace

RETURN OF THE PRINCE
MOVES IN MYSTERIOUS WAYS
DYNAMIC WORLD
DESERT
RUINED CITADEL
THE VALE
ROYAL PALACE
CITY OF LIGHT
TREE OF LIFE
SECRETS

The Royal Palace was once home to the Ahura royal lineage. Unfortunately, time and fate have not favored the royal family. Once-lively halls are now deathly still. Lush gardens are choked by weeds. But it is not too late to restore the Royal Palace to its former glory. If the Prince and Elika can purify the fertile ground in the regions and push the corrosive power of the Concubine out of the palace, perhaps one day joy can return the Ahura capitol. Maybe the royal line will return to claim the throne and lead the Ahuras out of decline and into a renaissance period of peace and prosperity.

What's Unleashed

As with the other regions in the world, visiting the Royal Garden unlocks both a special trap and one of Ahriman's Influences. So, before striking out into the Royal Gardens and purifying the Royal Palace, make sure you're ready to handles these new dynamics.

The Concubine

The Concubine is the Corrupted that haunts the Royal Palace, poisoning the region with the sad sin of jealousy. The Prince and Elika must engage the Concubine five times before they can finally confront her in her lair. The Concubine does her best to twist the budding trust between the Prince and Elika. If the Concubine will never again know love, then she will prevent these two from developing it also. To do this, she will sow the seeds of doubt between the pair.

The Concubine's tactic is to separate the Prince and Elika physically. During many encounters, she will use her powers to hold Elika, preventing her from participating in battle. The Prince must then rely on fighting techniques that do not involve Elika's magic. Acrobatic and lift combos can be harnessed, but anything using magic cannot until the Concubine's hold over Elika is severed.

Standing against the Concubine also unlocks one of Ahriman's Influences: Patience. This state change can only be dispelled by a gauntlet attack. Once the Concubine unleashes Ahriman's Influence, it can be used by all other Corrupted, the Mourning King, and even some of the soldiers that guard the crossroads between the areas. So, if you think you can handle Ahriman's Patience, then strike hard against the Concubine. Just be ready to use that gauntlet again on other foes.

NOTE

The only Corrupted that will not assume Ahriman's Patience is the Warrior. This Corrupted is just too large to be affected by the gauntlet. But lest you think the Warrior is some sort of pushover, he has his own special state change that poses its own special set of problems.

The Traps

Upon exploring the Coronation Hall, the Concubine releases the swarm trap. This trap is a small storm of corruption particles that coalesce into a frenzied grouping. This swarm then chases the Prince for a few seconds. If the Prince stops moving, the swarm catches up and attacks. Elika must then step in and save the Prince. If the Prince was in the middle of an acrobatic sequence, such as running along walls between column jumps, the Prince is then returned to the last piece of solid ground he stood upon. The sequence must then be tried again, and performed faster, to keep the swarm from targeting the Prince.

Unlocking the swarm in the Coronation Hall releases the trap in the following areas:

Martyr's Tower, Marshalling Ground, Sun Temple, King's Gate, Machinery Ground, Heaven's Stair, the Observatory, Construction Yard, Reservoir, Spire of Dreams, Coronation Hall, Royal Spire, the Cavern, Tower of Ormazd, Tower of Ahriman, City Gate -- plus the routes between the Cauldron, the Cavern, & Temple and the routes between the Cavern, City Gate, & Temple.

The Cavern

Before the Prince and Elika can enter the Royal Palace region and seek out the fertile ground needed to heal the region, they must pass through the Cavern. This gateway area was once a magnificent temple that is now in ruin. Lonely columns hang from the ceiling. Poles long since stripped of their banners jut from the walls. And in the center of it all is a beautiful staging ground that must have once hosted some impressive ceremonies. But now, it only echoes with the cackle of the Concubine.

Corrupt

Approach

There are two ways to reach the Cavern. If you take the eastern path from the desert, make a left when the route forks. The way into the Cavern is short, but not without peril.

A series of broken columns leads deeper into the Cavern. The columns jut out of deep pits, surrounded by the throbbing corruption unleashed by the return of Ahriman. Keep to the columns and avoid the walls poisoned by this corruption.

Leap out to the first column. Now, scramble to the opposite side of the column. Press the jump button to kick away from the column. (Remember, the direction your back is toward is the direction you jump.)

Elika follows closely behind as you climb the columns and jump away from the encroaching corruption.

Leap from one column to the next by facing away from your target and pressing jump.

The next column is too far away to jump to without assistance. You must use a cooperative jump with Elika to bridge the chasm. Leap into the air and then call upon Elika to use her magic to defy gravity and complete the jump.

There is no column to help you across this abyss. Wall run to the two rings on the right side of the corridor. Use the gauntlet button to grab the rings and link the wall runs. Just before you lose your momentum, kick away to propel yourself to the ledge on the chasm's opposite side.

The corruption is spreading. Jump out to the next column and beware of the writhing hatred on the walls.

Climb the exposed wooden fixtures to reach the interior of the temple.

The fertile ground is at the center of the temple. You can see it from your ledge—you're just a few jumps away. But the ruins are less forgiving now. Little of the floor remains, so you jump at your own peril. To close in on the center of the temple, leap out to the column hanging from the ceiling.

There is a brass ring in the ceiling just beyond the column. It's almost within reach, but you have to jump to it to grab it. Scramble around so your back faces the ring, climb high on the column, and then kick away. When you grab the ring, you can now perform the roofing maneuver. You kick free of the ring and roll in the air, pushing off the ceiling with your feet and propelling yourself into the next column.

Jump from the column to the pair of poles sticking out of the temple wall. Jump when your body is starting to extend to wheel through the air and grab the next pole.

You're almost there. Jump out to the next set of columns, which extend over the center of the temple. On the second column, jump down.

Now, if you approach the Cavern from the middle path leading away from the desert, make a right turn at the fork. From here, follow the series of columns along the route since there is no floor.

RETURN OF THE PRINCE
MOVES IN MYSTERIOUS WAYS
DYNAMIC WORLD
DESERT
RUINED CITADEL
THE VALE
ROYAL PALACE
CITY OF LIGHT
TREE OF LIFE
SECRETS

The columns stretch pretty far down the cave. Since the walls are throbbing with corruption, you must stick to the columns until you can finally see clean patches on the cave walls. Be on the lookout for scratches in the walls as indicators of where to wall run—they are always a perfect guide. When the scratches vanish and you're nowhere near solid ground, kick away and jump to a column.

Soon, you arrive at a tall wall. There are two lines of scaffolding crossing the wall. Scramble up the wall, grabbing the wooden planks before gravity kicks in and pulls you back down. Pull yourself up at the top of the wall.

You can see the fertile ground from this vantage point, too. But you must find a way down to it, and it's a long way down.

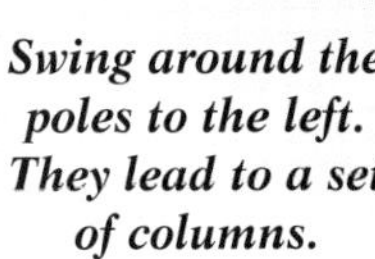

Swing around the poles to the left. They lead to a set of columns.

Jump between the two columns to reach a solid ledge that overlooks the fertile ground.

Well, there's no easy way down to the fertile ground, but that trio of columns in front of you can at least get you closer to it. Jump out to the first column. Rotate around the column and then kick over to the next one. Just as you close in on the column, it disappears. You crash down to the fertile ground. That's when you realize you are not alone.

The Concubine

Elika is seized by a dark tendril. The Concubine looks down on you from above, taunting your dilemma. How will you ever manage to make it up to the Concubine without Elika's help? This is the trickery of the Concubine—to prevent you from working with Elika and improving your symbiotic relationship. Without Elika's magic to complete those cooperative jumps, how can you hope to ever reach the Concubine?

Start your push toward the Concubine by running to the end of the post on the opposite side of the fertile ground from Elika.

TIP

Since there are multiple posts jutting out of the platform, make sure you start with the one that points directly to a column and a tall wall with no rings.

At the top of the column, jump on the tall ledge threatened by corruption.

The Concubine doesn't move as you clamber to the top of the ledge. She stands defiantly even as you jump to the top of the wall to the right and then launch yourself onto the next platform.

Neither does the Concubine move when you leap to the pair of poles and launch through the air, easily jumping from one to the next. Does she not understand that's she's just thirty seconds away from tasting cold steel?

Wall run from the second pole and then jump down to the Concubine.

Close in on the Concubine when you land. She turns to face you, but as soon as you unsheathe your blade and run her through, she vanishes. It was just an illusion.

RETURN OF THE PRINCE
MOVES IN MYSTERIOUS WAYS
DYNAMIC WORLD
DESERT
RUINED CITADEL
THE VALE
ROYAL PALACE
CITY OF LIGHT
TREE OF LIFE
SECRETS

The Concubine reappears on the opposite side of the chamber, mocking you. You must now jump down from this ledge onto the fertile ground and find another route to reach her new location. Or is she also a mirage? Only one way to find out.

Return to the post you first used to reach the Concubine's illusion and scramble to the ledge atop it. However, instead of heading to the posts to the right, jump down to the slides on your left.

Ride the two slides down to the bottom of the Concubine's ledge. Leap from the second tilted platform to the ledge and wall run up it.

Again, the Concubine disappears when you flash your steel.

Return to the fertile ground (and the writhing Elika) and then run to the post to the right. This post leads to a short column. It's not high enough to scale the wall next to it, so instead, you must jump out and use the ring to link a wall run to the top of the wall.

From the top of the wall, jump down to the nearby slide and ride it to the pair of flagpoles. Jump to the flagpoles and swing around them to reach another slide. The slide speeds you down to the bottom of the ledge with the Concubine. Jump out and wall run up to the Concubine.

As expected, the harridan blinks out of sight as soon as you slice her with your sword.

The Concubine reappears, but this time she does so next to Elika. The Concubine taunts you, and even though her mouth is covered with a veil, you just know her lips are curled into a disdainful smile. Her words drip with treachery. Jump down to the Concubine to begin your first battle. As soon as you land, the Concubine releases Elika from her grip to concentrate solely on you.

Your clash with the Concubine begins immediately. Approach her with your guard up. The Concubine is fast, so deflecting her attacks requires lightning reflexes. Test her out while guarding to get a feel for her speed. While guarding, you can push toward the center of the fertile ground and keep the battle away from the edges of the arena.

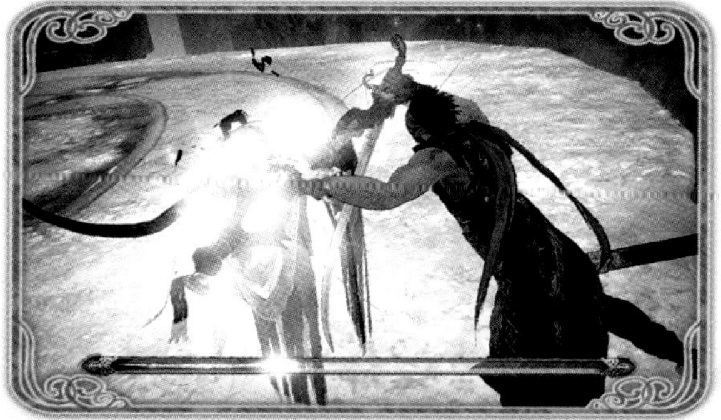

If the Concubine manages to push you against the edge of the arena, you enter a struggle. Tap the sword button repeatedly to win the struggle and nudge the fight back toward the center.

CAUTION

IF YOU LOSE A STRUGGLE, THE CONCUBINE KNOCKS YOU OFF THE EDGE. WHILE ELIKA SAVES YOU, THE CONCUBINE EARNS BACK HEALTH.

Use extended combos to bring down the Concubine's health. If you are nearing an edge, start with an acrobatic move to guide the battle back to the middle. Mix up sword attacks with Elika's magic to draw out the combo and keep the Concubine from getting in an attack of her own.

If the Concubine attacks you successfully while you are injured, she goes for a lethal attack. Press the button as it flashes on-screen to save yourself. Otherwise, Elika must rescue you and the Concubine regroups.

When the Concubine is almost finished, she turns mean. She attacks aggressively, so keep your guard up. Guarding against her massive staff lets you survive a string of attacks until you see the perfect opening.

TIP

WATCH FOR THE CONCUBINE TO SWEEP THE STAFF ACROSS THE GROUND BEFORE ATTACKING. THAT SIGNALS HER LAST ATTACK IN THE STRING. ONCE SHE RETURNS TO A STANDING POSITION, STRIKE BACK.

Once the Concubine is defeated (she is down but hardly out—you'll see her five more times), it's time to heal the fertile ground. As soon as Elika works her magic on the sacred soil, color returns to the Cavern and Light Seeds are spread across the area.

Healed

After purifying the area, you must explore three paths as well as the main body of the Cavern to pick up the Light Seeds.

The Cavern

As Elika composes herself, the Cavern fills with the sparkle of Light Seeds. Two of them are immediately available from the platform with the fertile ground. The rest stretch out along the paths leading into the Cavern and the ruins that surround the fertile ground.

Begin the hunt at the post to the right. There is a Light Seed on the post, as well as in the space between the nearby column and wall. Jump out to the wall and grab the Light Seed before jumping back to the column. Climb the column and jump to the ledge.

Use the rings atop the ledge to grab another Light Seed. Climb to the top of the wall.

From this point, you are at a crossroads. You can either keep collecting Light Seeds inside the Cavern or start down the eastern path. The east path heads away from the Cavern and is marked with a long column that is hanging from the ceiling.

Roof along the rings in the eastern corner of the Cavern to grab another Light Seed. At the end of the rings, use the column to jump over to solid ground. From there, you can either strike out to the north or continue weaving around the Cavern to pick up more Light Seeds.

See that yellow power plate on the wall? If you have the Hand of Ormazd, you can collect some extra Light Seeds.

RETURN OF THE PRINCE
MOVES IN MYSTERIOUS WAYS
DYNAMIC WORLD
DESERT
RUINED CITADEL
THE VALE
ROYAL PALACE
CITY OF LIGHT
TREE OF LIFE
SECRETS

Yellow Power Plate

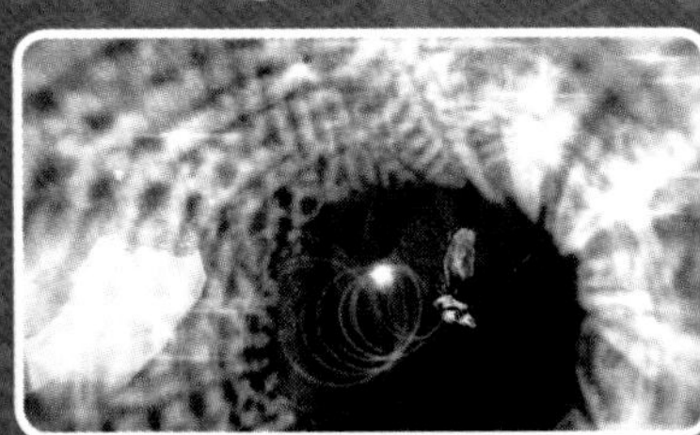

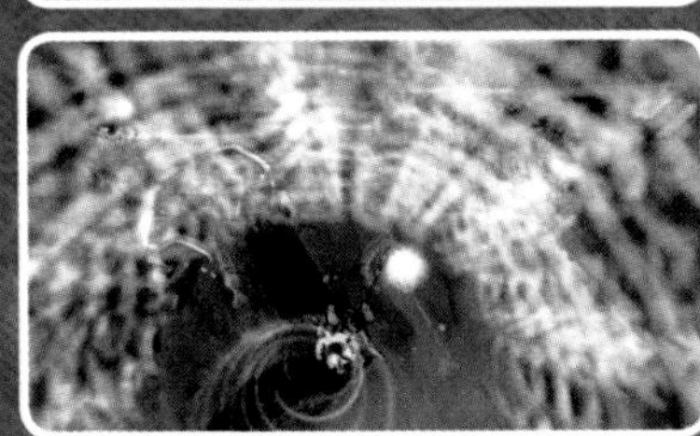

Once you have unlocked the Hand of Ormazd, you can launch from the yellow power plate on the Cavern wall and fetch a quartet of Light Seeds inside the Cavern. Steer around the stalagmites to grab a Light Seed. As you zoom around the rest of the room, veer into the other three Light Seeds to grab them. If you miss any of the Light Seeds, just scramble up to the yellow power plate again and give the Cavern another whirl.

Jump out to the center of the Cavern via to columns to pick up another set of Light Seeds.

From the yellow power plate, follow the columns to the west. There is a Light Seed at the top of the column. Then, double-jump away to the next column to reach a set of poles. Swing around the pole to reach the exit to the west path leading away from the Cavern. From here, you can venture away from the Cavern and slide down the wall to grab a Light Seed.

The Light Seed is just below you. Use the rings to safely descend.

Grip fall down the wall to the right to grab another pair of Light Seeds.

To get back on track from here, double-jump to the slide that drops you back to the fertile ground. Use the post to the right of the slide to jump back to a column and ascend the wall via the rings.

Jump to the tilted platform to the left. Stay to the center of the slide to breeze right through a Light Seed. At the bottom of the slide, jump to a pair of poles with a Light Seed. Swing around them to land on another slide. Again, stay to the center of the slide to pick up a Light Seed.

From the fertile ground, head out to the post pointing toward the wall without a ring. From the top of the wall, you can jump to a set of poles and then wall run out to another Light Seed. (You closed in on first of the Concubine's illusions out here.) Return to the wall via the post again and then head in the opposite direction.

Follow the slides to pick up two more Light Seeds. A third is on a nearby post.

IF YOU SEE A BUNCH OF LIGHT SEEDS HANGING OUT IN THE MIDDLE OF THE AIR, DON'T WORRY—YOU CAN FETCH THOSE WHEN YOU HAVE THE HAND OF ORMAZD POWER.

East Path

When you leave the main room of the Cavern, you see two Light Seeds on the second column pointing straight down into the abyss. Jump out to the first column, swing around to its backside, and then jump again. Use Elika's magic for a co-op jump to the second column. Then, jump to the Light Seeds and grip fall through the pair. Jump back to the column.

Slide to the bottom of the column and jump to the series of rock ledges that extends away from the Cavern. There are Light Seeds visible from the ground. Link your wall runs with the rings on the left side of the corridor to pick up another prize.

Keep tracking away from the Cavern. As you enter the long corridor with little floor, use wall runs and columns to cross the gaps. Grab the Light Seed along the wall as well as the one at the end of the corridor. Now, backtrack to the Cavern to continue collecting Light Seeds.

West Path

Slide down the wall just beyond the Cavern to pick up one Light Seed. After grabbing it, jump with Elika out to the column fragment hanging from the ceiling. Jump from the column and wall run into the next Light Seed and grab onto a fissure.

Follow the scaffolding in the fissure down the tunnel wall. At the end of the fissure, wall run to the right. Two Light Seeds are visible farther down the corridor. Use the column between the two Light Seeds to reach the treasures.

Continue down the path. As you round the corner, two more Light Seeds appear in the distance. One is at the edge of a solid platform. The next is farther down the corridor. Use the columns to reach the far Light Seed. Now, return to the Cavern to keep grabbing Light Seeds or move to another area.

North Path

Return of the Prince
Moves in Mysterious Ways
Dynamic World
Desert
Ruined Citadel
The Vale
Royal Palace
City of Light
Tree of Life
Secrets

Use the series of columns to cross the abyss to the north of the Cavern. At the second column, jump out and wall run along the slanted wall to pick up a Light Seed.

Jump across the next two columns and scramble up the tall wall (which is helpfully lined with brass rings) to pick up another Light Seed and reach a good vantage point. From up there, you can see the crossroads between the Cavern and the Royal Gardens.

From the ledge above the rings, look down the narrow alcove. There are two Light Seeds all the way at the bottom of the alcove.

If the Royal Gardens have not been healed, there is a soldier at the crossroads. Now, depending on whether you've fought any of the Corrupted, this soldier may know a few more techniques than basic sword strikes. Use Elika's magic in combos that back the soldier up to the edge of the platform and then run him through with your sword for a quick kill.

TIP

THE EARLIER IN YOUR ADVENTURE THAT YOU CLEANSE THE GATEWAY AREAS, LIKE THE CAVERN OR CAULDRON, THE FEWER SPECIAL POWERS YOU MUST CONTEND WITH WHILE FIGHTING THE SOLDIERS. REMEMBER, THE MORE BATTLES YOU WIN, THE HARDER FUTURE SOLDIERS WILL FIGHT BACK.

You must loop back toward the Cavern to collect the rest of the Light Seeds on the north path. Cooperatively jump out to the slide. At the bottom, wall run through the next Light Seed. Jump over to the slide and then wall run through the rest of the path to grab another Light Seed.

TIP

HAVE ENOUGH LIGHT SEEDS TO UNLOCK ONE OF ELIKA'S NEW MAGIC POWERS? DON'T DELAY—RUSH BACK TO THE TEMPLE OF THE TREE OF LIFE AND EARN A NEW TECHNIQUE!

ROYAL GARDENS

Once the pride of the kingdom, the Royal Gardens are now little more than a weed patch. Beautiful fountains that once entertained the populous with stunning sprays of water are now gummed up with corruption. Elika remembers when this was a place of great happiness—her mother loved these gardens more than any other place in the kingdom. But those days are long gone. Perhaps if Elika can redeem the gardens, she can at least feel closer to her mother.

CORRUPT

APPROACH

There are three ways into the Royal gardens. If you're coming from the south, the Cavern, follow the bleached column fragments along the tunnel walls. If you're coming from the east or west, follow the beams. You must use the columns along the edges of the gardens to close in on the yellow power plate that launches you into the Royal Gardens. If you have released any traps, watch out for them on the walls.

WATERWORKS

The yellow power plate directly ahead of you is your way into the heart of the Royal Gardens. Ease down to the wall that leads out to the power plate. Wall run out to the power plate and use Elika's magic to launch the two of you through the air. Ormazd's magic blasts you over the gardens and to a pair of narrow walls.

Wall run between the two walls, jumping from one side to the other to keep your momentum going. There is another yellow power plate at the end of the left wall. Activate it to zoom over the gardens, straight to another yellow power plate.

Hold the magic button as you fly so you can wall run to the left as soon as you land.

RETURN OF THE PRINCE
MOVES IN MYSTERIOUS WAYS
DYNAMIC WORLD
DESERT
RUINED CITADEL
THE VALE
ROYAL PALACE
CITY OF LIGHT
TREE OF LIFE
SECRETS

CAUTION

Did you visit the City of Light? If so, then you're seeing the results of unlocking the tendrils. Remember, triggering traps makes traveling the world much trickier.

The yellow power plate drops you down to the lower level of the Royal Gardens.

At the bottom of the gardens, Elika points out a yellow power plate on the back wall. That power plate is your ticket to the large, ornate platform directly above you. However, there is no way to reach the plate unless you somehow raise the ground beneath it. Turning on the water that fed the garden would raise the platform, but there's no water here anymore. However, there is plenty of corruption. You must fill the reservoirs on each side of the plate to raise the platform. But to fill those reservoirs, you must adjust the channels on each side of the gardens.

Turn the cranks (four on each side) to adjust the channels. Each channel has at least two grates that allow corruption to flow through it. You must create a path for the corruption from the pool at the top of the garden all the way down to the reservoir. Each crank controls a different set of channels. Some cranks control the same channels.

Let's start with the left side of the chamber:

Turn this crank until these three channels are full of corruption.

Drop down to this crank and turn it until the corruption flows farther up the gardens.

Turn this crank until the corruption flows into the next channel.

Turn this crank so you adjust the channel you just filled. You want to shut the channel off.

Return to this crank and turn it.

The channels click into place and the corruption flows all the way down into the reservoir.

CAUTION

Be careful around those channels. If you step into one that's full of corruption, Elika must save you.

Now, let's move to the right side of the room and fill that reservoir. It's a bit tougher than the previous side.

Turn this crank to spin the channel that leads to the reservoir. Spin it so the grates are in place to feed the corruption into the reservoir.

Turn this crank to fill these two pools.

Turn this crank so the channels around it look like this.

Turn this crank up here to fill these channels.

Now, turn this crank to complete the route for the corruption to pass through to the reservoir.

TIP

Having problems with the channels? Teleport to a healed patch of fertile ground to totally reset the channels. Come back and try again with a fresh look at the puzzle.

Filling the second reservoir raises the platform beneath the yellow power plate Elika pointed out. Now it's time to face down the Concubine.

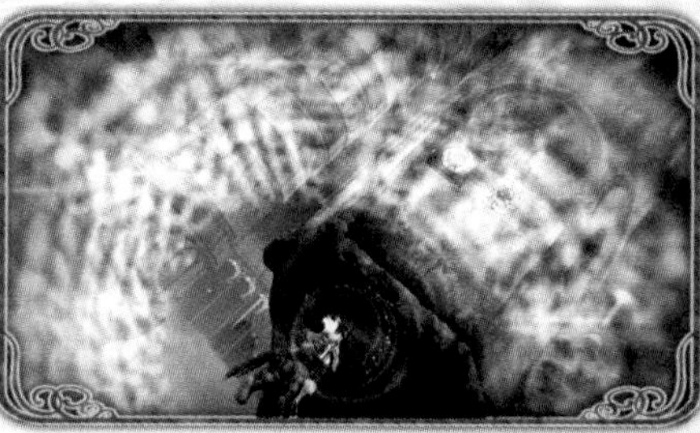

Jump with Elika across the corruption-filled reservoir. You cannot make it alone. On the other side, wall run up to the yellow power plate and activate it with Elika's magic. You curl through the air over the channels and land on a platform high above the gardens.

The Concubine

The Concubine again strikes Elika so you cannot use her at the beginning of the battle. Slip into the guard position and wait out the Concubine's first set of attacks while Elika recovers. Once she pulls herself off the ground and comes to your side, it's time to meet the Concubine's aggression with your own.

CAUTION

The arena is partially lined with corruption. Do not back the Concubine up into it. Corruption is beneficial to your enemies, allowing them to be absorbed and then warp into an advantageous position behind you.

Due to the corruption around the arena, it's in your best interests to keep the Concubine close to the center of the platform. Use acrobatic attacks to prevent the Concubine from edging you toward the corruption. If she nudges you into it, Elika must save you and the Concubine regains her health.

The Concubine can effectively counterattack, so if you're injured, don't try anything too bold. If the Concubine counterattacks effectively, you push press the on-screen buttons to deflect each of her twirling moves. If you fail any of these inputs, the Concubine gets the drop on you and goes for a lethal attack.

Missing the lethal attack lets the Concubine recover lost strength, so be ready to press the flashing button!

Keep the Concubine out of the corruption.

RETURN OF THE PRINCE
MOVES IN MYSTERIOUS WAYS
DYNAMIC WORLD
DESERT
RUINED CITADEL
THE VALE
ROYAL PALACE
CITY OF LIGHT
TREE OF LIFE
SECRETS

NOTE

The Concubine will use any Ahriman Influence unlocked by other Corrupted, so watch out for those special attacks.

Unless you eliminate the Concubine right away with a series of sweet combos that keep her from reaching the corruption, the witch will likely reveal Ahriman's Patience in this battle. When you see the witch turn dark and yellow sparks pop from her torso, you know it's time for a gauntlet attack.

Let the Concubine attack. Deflect and then immediately reply with your gauntlet. Throwing her into the air dissipates the influence. Now you can hammer away with any kind of combo.

CAUTION

Watch out for the pillars in this arena. If the Concubine slams you into one and then lands another attack, you're immediately injured.

As soon as the Concubine is defeated, have Elika heal the land. The garden returns to life—not quite to full bloom, but another season of care should turn this place into a small paradise. Now it's time to collect Light Seeds.

Healed

There are three paths leading in and out of the Royal Gardens: east, west, and south. There are Light Seeds along these three routes in addition to those inside the restored Royal Gardens.

Royal Gardens

After healing the area, pick up the four Light Seeds available right on the platform with the fertile ground.

Use the columns flanking the gardens to pick up the Light Seeds above the restored fountains. Jump

from the balconies out to the columns on each side of the area to collect Light Seeds and boost your total.

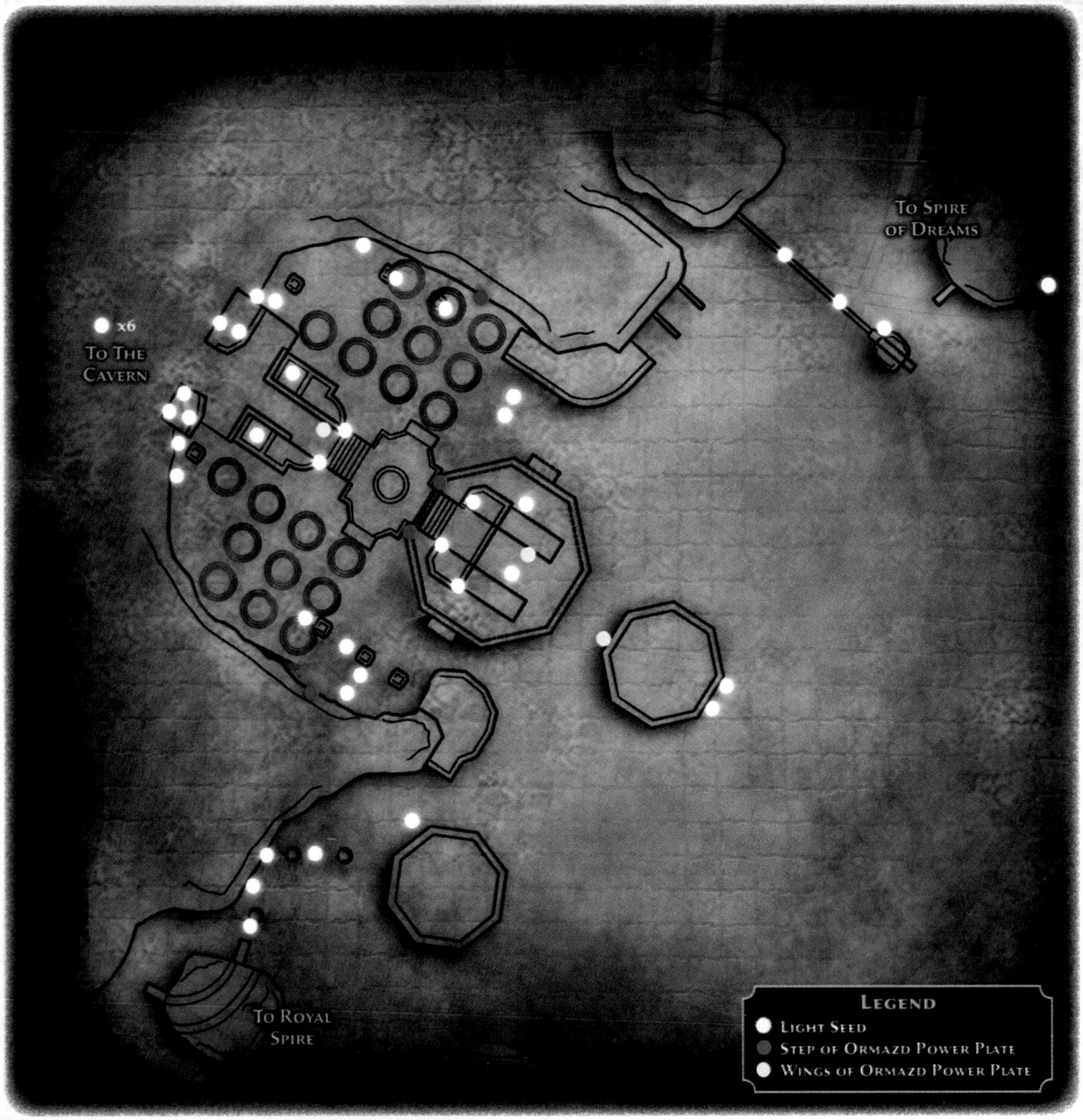

To Spire of Dreams

x6

To The Cavern

To Royal Spire

Legend

Light Seed

Step of Ormazd Power Plate

Wings of Ormazd Power Plate

Red Power Plate

If you have unlocked the Step of Ormazd, you can collect the hard-to-reach Light Seeds in the Royal Garden. Climb the vines on the west side of the garden (if you are looking toward the fertile ground) to reach the power plate.

This power plate launches you to another red power plate below the fertile ground.

You are then blasted up to a small platform above the gardens that holds two Light Seeds. Now, repeat this on the east side of the garden.

Access the red power plate against the wall by using the fissures next to the columns. Bounce across the garden to a high ledge with three Light Seeds. To get down from either ledge, just use grip fall to land softly.

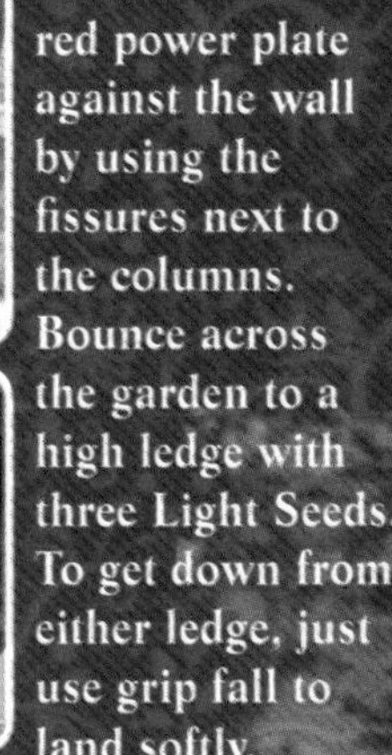

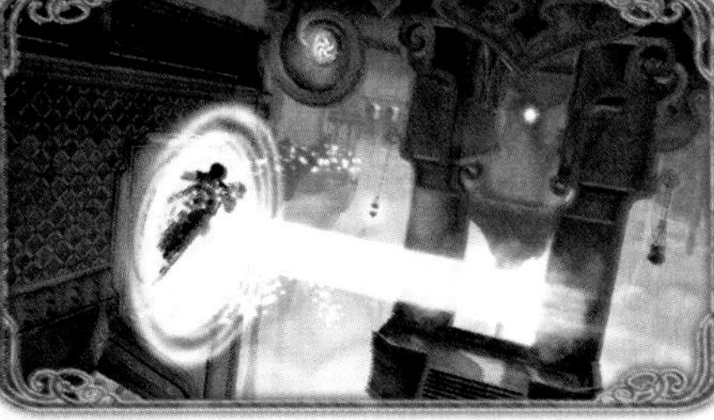

Use the yellow power plate to rocket to the Light Seed in the distance.

Hang from the edge of the former corruption pools to grab Light Seeds that hang just over the edge.

RETURN OF THE PRINCE
MOVES IN MYSTERIOUS WAYS
DYNAMIC WORLD
DESERT
RUINED CITADEL
THE VALE
ROYAL PALACE
CITY OF LIGHT
TREE OF LIFE
SECRETS

Pick up the Light Seeds in the reservoirs.

TIP

Getting these Light Seeds is pretty tricky. Use the column to the right of the ledge. Wall run up the column and then kick away to grab the lattice on the ledge. Scramble to the top of the lattice. When you pull yourself up, you can nab the two Light Seeds.

West Path

The balcony to the left of the fertile ground leads out to the western path away from the Royal Gardens. Jump from the balcony to the two flagpoles. Swing from the second flagpole to the nearby wall. (This requires a double jump with Elika.) Wall run along the wall and then jump out to a post.

Follow the beam to collect two Light Seeds.

Wall run along the base of the tower to grab another Light Seed. Jump to the flagpole before you fall.

Turn around on the flagpole. The change in view reveals two Light Seeds on the ledge behind the tower. Edge to the left on the flagpole and then jump out to the tower. Wall run to the ledge.

Unless you healed the Royal Spire to the west, a soldier waits at the crossroads between the two areas. Because you have now encountered the Concubine and seen Ahriman's Patience, it is entirely possible this soldier—and any you encounter after it—will call upon that special power. The crossroads are small, though, so with a good acrobatic combo, you can push the soldier to the edge of the arena and finish it with a sword drive.

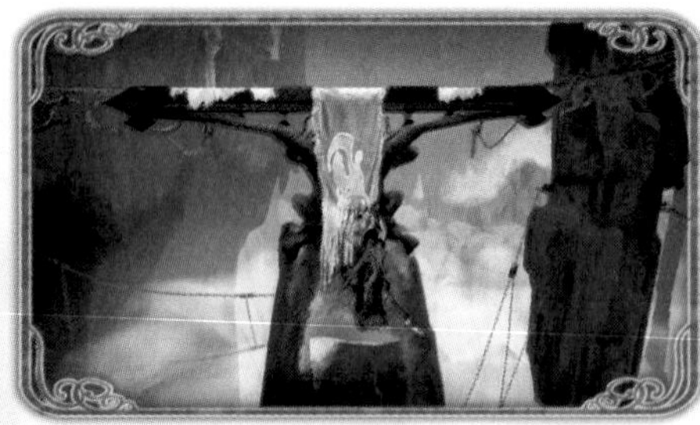

Cooperatively jump out to the tattered banner to the west and climb up to the post.

Jump to the nearby wall. Wall run and hop to the adjacent wall to pick up the last Light Seed on the west path.

East Path

From the balcony that overlooks the eastern path out of the Royal Gardens, wall run through the visible Light Seed. Leap the column just beyond the wall, using a little help from Elika to close the gap.

There is a Light Seed between the two columns. From the second column, jump to the rock wall and wall run to the vines, passing through the Light Seed.

Climb straight up the vines. Look up. There are two Light Seeds directly above you. Wall run up to the top patch of vines to grab the Light Seeds.

Drop back down the vines and wall run to the column to the east. Jump out to the column and swivel to pick up the last Light Seed along this path. You do not need to jump out to the crossroads. But it's always fun to test out some new combos on the waiting soldier.

South Path

Step away from the Royal Gardens and back toward the Cavern to locate another batch of Light Seeds. There is a loop to be made here via slides and wall runs. Start by wall running to the slides on the left and steering into the Light Seeds as your sandals find no purchase.

From the column at the bottom of the slides, swing around to look into the dark corner off to the left. Jump to the ledge with the two Light Seeds and then bounce back to the column. Then leap to another tilted platform. This races you down to the crossroads between the two areas. From the crossroads, tack to the right. A post sticking out

of the platform points to a tall wall. Jump to the wall (with Elika) and use the rings to reach the ledge above it. A Light Seed is found at the top of the rings.

RETURN OF THE PRINCE
MOVES IN MYSTERIOUS WAYS
DYNAMIC WORLD
DESERT
RUINED CITADEL
THE VALE
ROYAL PALACE
CITY OF LIGHT
TREE OF LIFE
SECRETS

Jump from the post at the top of the wall and use the columns as links between a series of wall runs. The last Light Seed along this path is to your right as you wall run back to the entrance to the Royal Gardens.

Royal Spire

The majestic Royal Spire rises high above the Ahura palace. But its powerful presence against the skyline disguises a rotting interior. A victim of neglect as the royal line declined, the Royal Spire is now more of a playground for corruption than a sign of regality. The Prince and Elika must ascend the spire and confront the Concubine at the top. Banishing the Concubine is the only way to reach the fertile ground and push the shadows out of the Royal Spire.

Corrupt Approach

Entering the Royal Spire from any of the possible paths requires deftly jumping from column to column. If you are coming from the Royal Gardens, use the system of vines and columns to navigate along the cliffs. (If you have triggered the tremors, you must time your jumps when the rolling corruption moves out of the way.)

If you are coming from the Coronation Hall, use the network of columns hanging from the ceiling of the decorated hall. There is no floor, so you have to stick to the ceiling via the rings. Roof across the gaps between the columns, and then jump down to enter the bottom floor of the Royal Spire.

Ascend the Tower

To begin climbing the interior of the tower, you must jump to the blue power plate in the center of the chamber. It's on an axle, rhythmically rotating. When the blue power plate slides into view, wall run up to it and use Elika's magic to start your flight.

You land on the wall just below another blue power plate. Hold the button and press up to scramble to the plate before you slide off the wall. This power plate launches you to a column farther up the spire.

Jump to the wall and skitter along it to the next power plate.

This power plate zips you up to a column. Jump away from the column and wall run along the tower. At the end of the run, jump out to the next column.

CAUTION

Time these moves right! If you miss a jump and fall, Elika saves you—but it sends you all the way back to the central axle with the first blue power plate.

Jump away from the column with Elika's help and then wall run to another blue power plate. This blasts you up to a ledge.

The ledge overlooks the axle in the middle of the tower. There is a blue power plate on a flap attached to the axle. The flap swings toward you every few seconds. When the flap starts to move, jump out to it. Use Elika to complete your jump and then run up to the power plate. Activate it with Elika's magic.

The Hand of Ormazd magic lifts you to another blue power plate, but the trajectory is too short. Scramble up the wall to access the plate and use Elika's magic to blast up to another solid ledge. The magic isn't enough to quite get you there, so when the screen starts to turn gray, call on Elika to fling you all the way to the ledge.

Wall run across the clockwork gears to reach the next blue power plate.

At the top of the bounce, use Elika to complete the arc and land on a column.

Jump from the column with Elika's help and wall run to another blue power plate.

Another lift from Ormazd that isn't strong enough. Use Elika to reach the wall and run to the next power plate. Continue using Elika to complete your magical leaps as you wind your way up the tower.

When you reach the balcony after the series of blue power plates, look to the center of the tower. That elevator is your way to the top of the Royal Spire. Jump to it and use the crank with Elika. The elevator rises, delivering you into the waiting fingers of the Concubine.

The Concubine

When the elevator reaches the top of the Royal Spire, the Concubine immediate puts the screws to Elika. Elika doubles over in pain. You must complete the first part of this battle without Elika's magic to extend your combos, so you must stick to sword, gauntlet, and acrobatic attacks. After a few moments, Elika regains her strength and enters the battle.

As before, the Concubine is no shrinking violet. She launches attacks right away, so unless you are confident about being able to deflect an incoming strike from her magical staff, just use the guard button.

The Concubine will always try to push you out from the center of the arena. She wants to struggle with you at the edge of the arena because if she wins and you fail the save, she earns back her health.

Return of the Prince
Moves in Mysterious Ways
Dynamic World
Desert
Ruined Citadel
The Vale
Royal Palace
City of Light
Tree of Life
Secrets

When Elika is in play again, use acrobatics to get the Concubine's back to the center of the arena. Then launch into an extended combo that keeps the Concubine reeling. Start with an acrobatic and then segue into Elika's magic. Keep the combo moving with sword and gauntlet moves so that the Concubine cannot ever react to stop the combo.

Watch for Ahriman's Patience. When you see the Concubine emit the yellow sparks, keep Elika back. If Elika attacks when the Concubine uses Ahriman's Patience, you lose your companion while she recovers from the crushing blow.

NOTE

The longer the fight rages, the more often the Concubine relies on state changes. If you've defeated other Corrupted, the Concubine calls on their influences to keep you on your toes.

CAUTION

DON'T PUSH THE CONCUBINE TO THE EDGE OF THE ARENA. SHE SIMPLY TELEPORTS BEHIND YOU, WHICH IS DEFINITELY NOT ADVANTAGEOUS FOR YOU.

Defeating the Concubine and healing the fertile ground is good news, to be sure. But the Concubine's attempts at sowing doubt are taking hold. Just what game is this succubus playing at here?

HEALED

There are three paths that feed into the Royal Spire: south, north, and east. You must explore all of these routes to gather the Light Seeds in this area.

ROYAL SPIRE

The elevator was a one-way trip. The only way off the spire is down its outside. Follow the trail of Light Seeds to the edge of the spire. Hang over the edge and look down.

A trail of scratches leads down the spire. Apparently, You're not the first person to be stuck up here. Use grip fall to take the express route down. Slide into the Light Seeds as you descend.

CAUTION

THE LONGER YOU GRIP FALL, THE FASTER YOU GO. AND THERE ARE NO BRAKES WHEN GRAVITY IS CONCERNED.

As you slide down the spire, take note of the green power plates. If you have unlocked the Breath of Ormazd, you can climb back up the tower later to grab additional Light Seeds.

Inside the spire, wall run around the bottom floor and use columns to pick up a trail of Light Seeds.

GREEN POWER PLATE

There is a green power plate on the face of the spire, just above the doorway that leads back inside. Use the green power plate to stomp up the side of the spire. Steer away from the second green power plate (for now) and toward the Light Seed above. After gaining the Light Seed, purposefully bump into a wall to return to the bottom of the tower.

Now, head back up the tower via the green power plate. This time, veer to the left to use the next green power plate. This sends you on a horizontal path around the tower. Keep to the left to dodge an outcropping and then follow the next power plate back up the tower.

Green Power Plate (continued)

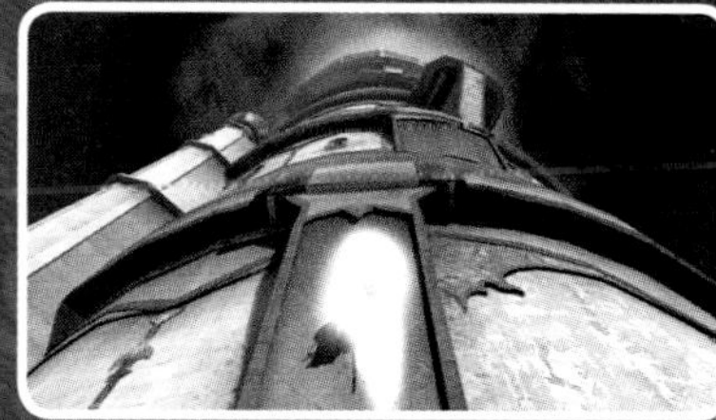

The power plates lead up to the back side of the spire. Steer to the right to climb the smooth path beneath a balcony. There are five Light Seeds on the balcony. Once you have them, use the green power plate above the balcony to finish your climb up the spire. Grip fall back down.

Hang down the ledge in front of the green power plate. Let yourself fall. There are two Light Seeds on a small platform just below. Use the ring on the wall behind the Light Seeds to scramble back up.

Use the blue power plate on the base of the central axle to launch yourself back up the interior of the spire. You need to wind your way back through the spire to collect the Light Seeds. Without traps or corruption patches, traveling through the spire is a touch easier. Follow the same path as before, using Elika to complete arcs that fall a bit short.

Hang from the elevator at the top of the spire to spot a Light Seed below you.

RETURN OF THE PRINCE
MOVES IN MYSTERIOUS WAYS
DYNAMIC WORLD
DESERT
RUINED CITADEL
THE VALE
ROYAL PALACE
CITY OF LIGHT
TREE OF LIFE
SECRETS

Use grip fall to reach the Light Seed.

Grip fall down the interior of the spire to grab a Light Seed tucked beneath some clockwork gears. Slide against the side of the gears so you grab a fissure before landing on solid ground at the bottom of the spire. Climb along the fissure to pick up the Light Seed.

South Path

A handful of Light Seeds are on the path leading back to the Royal Garden. Jump from the post at the base of the spire to the rock wall. Wall run to the vine patches to pick up two Light Seeds.

As you climb to right along the far patch of vines, you see four Light Seeds. Two are tucked in a dark alcove. The other two are an easy grab along the next wall run. Just use the nearby column as a springboard to grab those Light Seeds.

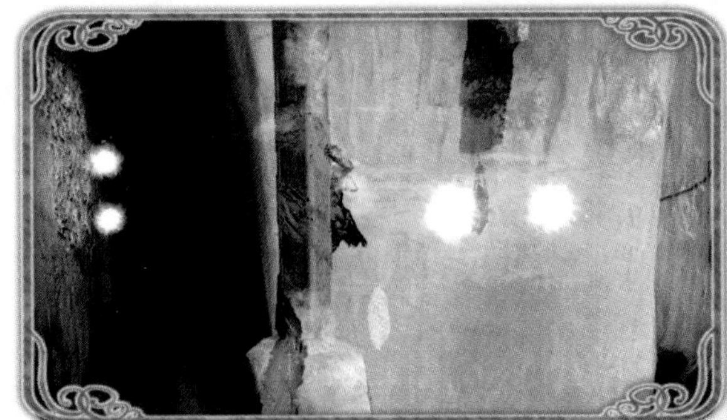

To capture the Light Seeds in the alcove, rotate around the column so that your back is toward them. Jump to the wall and wall run to the vines. Now you can pick up the Light Seeds.

East Path

Step through the exit of the spire to the east—as if you were about to make a break for the City of Light. Jump down to the rock outcropping below you. Hang off the side of rocks and then slide down to the Light Seed. Jump off the wall to get back up to solid ground.

Continue east. Jump from one rock to the next, picking up the visible Light Seeds.

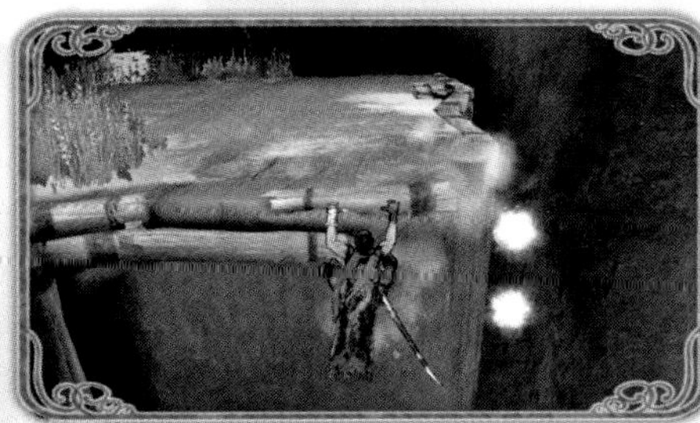

When you reach the midpoint of the path, look over the edge of the rocks to spot two more Light Seeds. Hang over the ledge and drop down to the lower level. Then, jump out to the wall and wall run straight up to collect the pair. Jump away from the wall to land on the rocks and then either return to the Royal Spire or move on to your next targeted fertile ground.

North Path

The corridor that leads to the Coronation Hall hosts six Light Seeds. Four are immediately visible from the spire door. Jump to the wall and wall run out so you can reach the closest column. Then, use roofing to move from ring to ring and pick up the Light Seeds along the ceiling.

Tap the gauntlet button in time with the rings to smoothly travel along the roof and collect the Light Seeds.

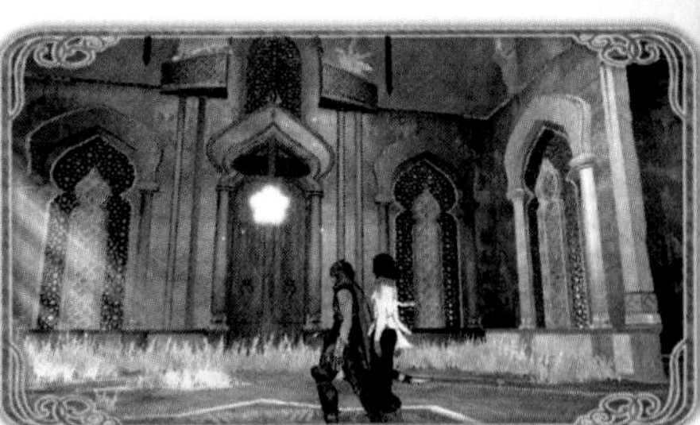

The fifth and sixth Light Seeds are at the crossroads, guarded by a soldier, if the Coronation hall has not been cleansed. After defeating the monster, collect the two Light Seeds and then move on to your next destination.

RETURN OF THE PRINCE
MOVES IN MYSTERIOUS WAYS
DYNAMIC WORLD
DESERT
RUINED CITADEL
THE VALE
ROYAL PALACE
CITY OF LIGHT
TREE OF LIFE
SECRETS

Spire of Dreams

The Spire of Dreams, sister tower to the Royal Spire, rises high over the kingdom. Somewhere at the top of the tower, the Concubine waits. She broods. She plots. Elika and the Prince must ascend the Spire of Dreams and banish the Concubine from its borders so the tower is not shrouded in permanent nightmare.

Corrupt

Approach

If you approach the Spire of Dreams from the Royal Garden, use the length of chain leading away from the crossroads to reach a gloomy tower. Wall run along the face of the tower and jump betwixt a pair of white columns to reach an entrance of the Spire of Dreams.

Should you approach the Spire of Dreams from the Coronation Hall to the north, you must pass down a corridor with no floor. Use the columns to survive the passage. Wall run between each column until you reach the Spire of Dreams.

CAUTION

Did you release the tremors? If so, those pesky traps are stirring in this corridor. Time your jumps just as the balls roll out of range.

Climb the Spire

Unless you took the direct route into the Spire of Dreams from the Vale, scramble around the tower interior via the flagpoles to reach the solid ledge next to the blue power plate. Run out to the power plate and use Elika's magic. The arc slams you into the wall too short of the next power plate.

Wall run to the ring and use it to link another wall run to the blue power plate.

Continue your spiralling path around the interior of the spire. Use the two rings on the wall to reach the next power plate.

The power plate bounces you up to an elevator. Use the crank with Elika to raise the elevator.

When the elevator locks into position, Elika is seized again by corruption. The Concubine is about. You spot a glimpse of her pink robes in the shadows of the spire. To free Elika, you must reach the Concubine, but without the benefit of Elika's strength. There will be no double jumps.

The Concubine appears in front you. You know it's an illusion, but humor the witch. Carve the mirage.

After the Concubine disappears, wall run along the right of the elevator. Link with the rings to keep wall running and then jump out to the column.

Roof between the two columns via the ring. Jump from the second column to the ledge with the Concubine. Slash her doppelgänger.

Continue wall running around the spire to catch up with the Concubine. She's waiting at the ledge next to the elevator again.

When you land, rush to the Concubine and dispatch the illusion with your sword. Doing so frees Elika from the Concubine's grip. With your companion back at your side—really, what would you do without her?—it's time to move up the spire.

Return to the column after the short roofing sequence. Jump away from the column but use Elika's magic to launch you to the wall. Wall run to the two rings.

You're back on solid ground. When Elika catches up, wall run to the next blue power plate. Use the ring to link your wall runs. Keep wall running around the tower interior to access the system of blue power plates.

Use the flagpoles to keep moving up the spire. After jumping from the second pole, call on Elika to help you reach the next power plate.

Continue following the poles as you circle the spire, inching ever upward.

Finally, you reach a fissure in the wall. Clamber along it to access the next elevator.

The elevator shoots you straight up to the top floor of the Spire of Dreams. The Concubine is waiting for you. She has no traps planned for your welcome. The moment you reach the top floor, the elevator drops away and the Concubine launches into her first attack. Be ready for it by holding the guard button.

The Concubine

Without a center to this arena, you are forced push the Concubine around the rooftop. Keep away from either edge—the outer edge or the empty elevator shaft—so the Concubine cannot engage you in a potential struggle. If you do end up with your back to the open air, use an acrobatic attack to change places with the Concubine.

NOTE

Elika joins you for this entire fight—the Concubine has separated you enough for this area.

RETURN OF THE PRINCE
MOVES IN MYSTERIOUS WAYS
DYNAMIC WORLD
DESERT
RUINED CITADEL
THE VALE
ROYAL PALACE
CITY OF LIGHT
TREE OF LIFE
SECRETS

The Concubine wastes no time before employing Ahriman's Patience. Use the gauntlet to dispel the effect.

After using the gauntlet to strip away Ahriman's Influence, keep the Concubine in the air with Elika's magic and more gauntlet or acrobatic attacks.

TIP

Juggle the Concubine along the "lap" at the top of the tower. Keep switching back and forth with acrobatics and magic to prevent the Concubine from landing and mounting a counterattack.

The Concubine always attacks while utilizing Ahriman's Patience. Move in and hold guard when you see the state change. As soon as you see the Concubine start to move her staff, get ready to deflect. As the staff swings wide, hit the sword to knock it aside. The Concubine is momentarily defenseless. Hit the gauntlet to launch the Concubine into the air and rip away the influence. Use this move as the springboard for a combo.

The Concubine spins when she attacks. Use that spin as a marker. As the twirl begins, hit guard and be ready to deflect when the staff comes flying around.

Sometimes, though, nothing gets the job done better than a well-executed, basic four-hit sword combo.

After the Concubine is down, let Elika purify the area. Green spreads from the fertile ground, restoring color to the Spire of Dreams. Now, it's time to gather up some Light Seeds.

Healed

There are three paths that leads into the Spire of Dreams: north, south, and west. The west path leads to the Vale. You must trek through all three path to collect all the Light Seeds.

Spire of Dreams

There are two Light Seeds on a small balcony that at first seems not easy to reach. However, if you hang off the side of the spire, you spot a post several feet down. Drop to the post and then drop farther down to a series of flagpoles. Swing around the poles to reach the balcony with the two Light Seeds.

Next, use the trio of Light Seeds on the roof as a guide. After collecting them, hang over the side of the roof and look down. A series of scratch marks points the way. There are Light Seeds on the side of the tower you can pick up as you grip fall to the bottom. While grip falling, though, you see green power plates and a few out-of-reach Light Seeds.

Green Power Plates

Use the green power plate at the base of the Spire of Dreams to start your vertical march. The plate sends you straight to a second green power plate that, when activated, changes you trajectory. Now you move horizontally, around the circumference of the tower. Dodge the fixtures as you stomp until you reach the third green power plate.

This green power plate resumes your ascent. Shoot up the side of the spire, following the path to the bottom of a balcony. Use the curved path to access the balcony, which holds five Light Seeds. After collecting your bounty, make use of the nearby green power plate to reach the roof.

RETURN OF THE PRINCE
MOVES IN MYSTERIOUS WAYS
DYNAMIC WORLD
DESERT
RUINED CITADEL
THE VALE
ROYAL PALACE
CITY OF LIGHT
TREE OF LIFE
SECRETS

Back at the bottom of the spire, hang off the ledge below the green power plate. Two Light Seeds are below you. Drop down to the prizes. Then, use the ring on the wall to clamber up back up.

Enter the tower and circle the base to collect several Light Seeds. Swing on the flagpoles and hop across the posts to bank the treasures. After making a lap around the base of the tower, use the blue power plates to begin your ascent.

Use the elevator to keep moving up the tower, following the same path as your first visit through the spire.

Pick up the Light Seeds on the platforms that jut out of the spire walls.

Keep moving from one blue power plate to the next, grabbing the Light Seeds that hang in the air.

Use the fissure at the top of the spire interior to access the second elevator. However, do not use the crank to move the elevator. Instead, pick up the Light Seed on the ledge leading to the elevator and then step onto the platform. Jump out to the Light Seed between the four red banners with Elika's help. After getting the Light Seed, bounce off the wall to return to the elevator.

South Path

Start at the green power plate on the base of the spire. Launch away from the Spire of Dreams via the two columns and bag the Light Seed on the first solid platform. Jump from the post pointing south to the small tower. Use Elika's help to complete the jump. Wall run along the tower to grab another Light Seed.

Jump away from the wall to a chain the leads back toward the Royal Gardens. Two Light Seeds wait at the far end of the chain. Once you reach those Light Seeds, look to the north. There is a platform with two more Light Seeds. Lower yourself down to the post pointing to the Light Seeds and use Elika to double-jump to the platform.

West Path

Leave the Spire of Dreams and move toward the Vale via the corridor to the west. Several Light Seeds await collection along this path. The first is accessible to the right. When you jump out to the Light Seed, you can see two more on rock platforms in the distance. Double jump with Elika to reach the platforms and collect the Light Seeds.

When you reach the mid-point of the path, double back and take the high road by wall running between a narrow series of rocks. There are two Light Seeds to the left as you return to the Spire of Dreams. Jump out to the wall and scramble up it to grab the prizes. Then kick away from the wall to get back on the path to the Spire of Dreams.

North Path

The corridor that leads to the Coronation Hall is littered with Light Seeds. Wall run along the left wall to pick up a pair, and then bounce to the columns in the middle of the hall. Continue switching between wall running and jumping to the columns to reach the crossroads and pick up the rest of the Light Seeds along this path.

Coronation Hall

The opulent Coronation Hall, once the site of grand celebrations when stewardship of the Ahura passed from one generation to the next, was already in disrepair before the release of Ahriman. The royal line of the Ahuras was in decay. There would be no passing of the crown. But if the Prince and Elika can drive Ahriman out of the Royal Palace, perhaps hope will return to the world and the Ahuras will unite under a new leader.

CAUTION

Are you sure you want to release the swarm trap now? Because as soon as the Concubine lets it loose, it infects the entire world.

Corrupt

Approach

The two approaches to the Coronation Hall are corridors—neither of which has a floor. If coming at the Coronation Hall from the west, you must use the rings on the walls to link runs between the sparse columns. Jump from the walls to the columns to move down the corridor and zero in on the Coronation Hall.

The eastern approach on the Coronation Hall is another exercise in roofing. Leap out to the first column and then clamber along the roof via the system of rings. Time those gauntlet button presses as you see the Prince reach out so that he never loses his hold.

At the end of the corridor, wall run to a corner swing to swing around to the Coronation Hall entrance.

Escape the Swarm

The fertile ground is just inside the entrance to the Coronation Hall. The Concubine is nowhere in sight. All you need to do is use the yellow power plate on the wall to fly around the Coronation Hall and drop down near the sacred ground. This is almost too easy.

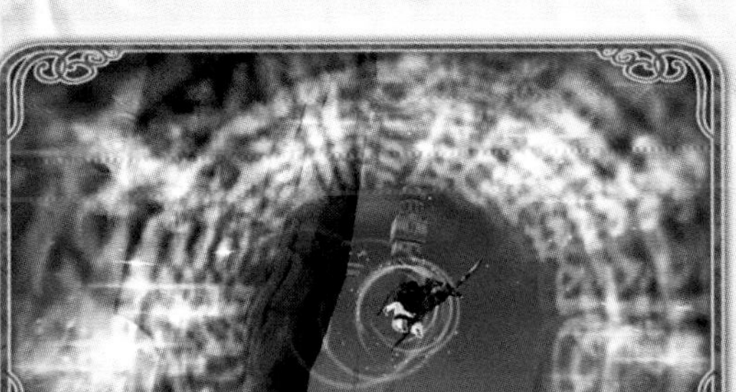

Dodge the rocks as you fly through the air on the Wings of Ormazd.

RETURN OF THE PRINCE
MOVES IN MYSTERIOUS WAYS
DYNAMIC WORLD
DESERT
RUINED CITADEL
THE VALE
ROYAL PALACE
CITY OF LIGHT
TREE OF LIFE
SECRETS

When you land, though, the Concubine does finally show herself. The Concubine lashes out with dark tendrils, trapping Elika in an iron grip. You must chase down the Concubine on your own, without the benefit of Elika's magic.

Jump over the rivulet of corruption and close in on the Concubine as she mocks you from the fertile ground. As expected, brandishing your sword makes the harpy vanish. As she disappears, though, a locked gate rises. You must follow the path to catch up to the real Concubine and free Elika from her grip.

The Concubine's illusion appears again in the new corridor. Slash it to open the next gate.

The gate opens into a long corridor with a slanted, broken floor. You must slide down the corridor, jumping over the gaps. Keep to the center of the platforms—the corruption on the walls is ravenous. It reaches for your innocent flesh as you skate through the hall on your sandals.

Use the columns to cross the wider gaps in the floor.

The Concubine appears again at the bottom of the slides. Slice the illusion.

Elika catches up to you, somehow free of the Concubine's trap. You can now call on her help to keep moving up the Coronation Hall. Start at the ring on the wall and pull yourself up to the ledge. Use the slotted ring to travel across the wall. The ring lowers a cage from the ceiling just in time for you to jump and grab onto it.

The Concubine appears again—the real Concubine. She holds out her skeletal fist and slowly opens it. Her gift is deadly. It's the swarm trap. The swarm buzzes like angry hornets. You must now rush through the Coronation Hall to keep one step ahead of this unflagging trap.

NOTE

From this point forward, the swarm trap is now active.

With the swarm nipping at your heels, jump to the flagpoles and keep moving around the interior of the tower.

Wall run along the tower interior. Jump out to the columns before you lose purchase on the wall.

Jump across the columns and then back to the wall. Rush through the series of rings as the swarm continues its pursuit.

Return of the Prince
Moves in Mysterious Ways
Dynamic World
Desert
Ruined Citadel
The Vale
Royal Palace
City of Light
Tree of Life
Secrets

Jump from the slotted ring to the tall column. Shimmy up the column to keep ahead of the swarm. When you reach the top of the column, you're back at the fertile ground. As you jump to the fertile ground, the swarm dissipates. But now you have an even bigger problem.

The Concubine

The Concubine strikes as you reach the fertile ground. The arena is a small square, which really limits your movement. Two sides of the area are edges that the Concubine can warp away from, with just a small patch of corruption. The other two edges are lined with walls that immediately put you into a struggle with the Concubine. The cleanest path to victory is to use acrobatics to keep the Concubine as close to the center of the arena as possible for the main duration of the fight.

Depending on when you challenge the Concubine in relation to your engaging the other Corrupted affects how aggressive she is. If you have already destroyed any of the other three Corrupted, expect the Concubine to make a major push at the start of this fight. Keep you guard up and draw her to the center of the arena. Wait for your opening. An unforced error is the worst way to start a fight.

Watch for Ahriman's Influences. The Concubine is not shy about state changes. She will always call upon Ahriman's Patience, as well as other influences unleashed from any previous Corrupted encounters.

The Concubine is adept at counterattacks. If she nails you while you're injured, you'll be on your back. Be ready for the on-screen button so she cannot reclaim any lost health.

CAUTION

Always steer the battle away from that patch of corruption in the corner. If the Concubine is backed into it, she benefits.

Be ready for the Concubine's special attack. The witch tries to charm you with a magic spell. When you see that strand of pink extend from her arm and slither toward your face, roll away and put distance between you and the Concubine. If the Concubine's spell connects, your controls are temporarily reversed.

TIP

Keep your guard up at all times. The Concubine moves fast and attacks even faster. With your guard up, you are always ready to withstand her assaults.

The Concubine can also call on a special attack that wraps you in tendrils. When you see it, get ready to tap an on-screen button to wriggle free. If you fail, you're pinched and the Concubine heals.

Keep launching into lengthy combos when the Concubine unleashes Ahriman's Patience. It's a perfect opening to start a nice combo with the gauntlet move. With the Concubine in the air, you can juggle her between Elika's attacks and more acrobatic moves. When the Concubine is finally defeated, heal the fertile ground to purge the corruption from the Coronation Hall.

Healed

There are only two paths into the Coronation Hall. After banishing the corruption, retrace your steps to either the Spire of Dreams or the Royal Spire after collecting Light Seeds in the Coronation Hall to add to your still-growing collection.

Coronation Hall

The four Light Seeds sparkling in front of the yellow power plate are a pretty good sign to use Elika's magic and fly back to the entrance of the Coronation Hall. From the entrance, you can either delve back into the basement of the Coronation Hall to search for more Light Seeds or retrace your steps down the east and west approaches.

There is one Light Seed directly in front of the black gate that leads to the Concubine's lair.

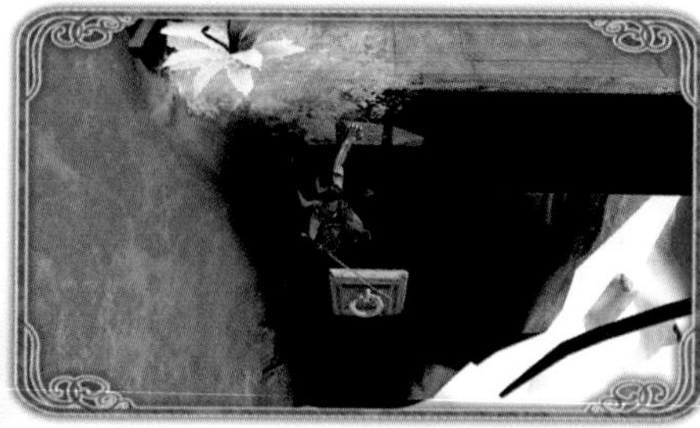

Drop down to the ring just below the ledge with the black gate. As you grip fall to the ring, jump away to reach a small balcony you cannot quite see from the Coronation Hall entrance. There are two Light Seeds down here. Use the ring to clamber back up to the ledge above.

Another Light Seed is on the ledge just outside the western exit of the Coronation Hall. This ledge also leads out to a red power plate.

Red Power Plate

Wall run out to the red power plate and use the Step of Ormazd to bound away from the rocks. The plate launches you just short of the red power plate in the distance, so use the ring to scramble up to the plate and rocket over to a hidden ledge.

There are five Light Seeds on this ledge. After collecting them, use the next series of red power plates to return to the entrance of the Coronation Hall.

From the ledge where you can see the red power plate, grip fall down a set of rings to reach a narrow platform. There are two

RETURN OF THE PRINCE
MOVES IN MYSTERIOUS WAYS
DYNAMIC WORLD
DESERT
RUINED CITADEL
THE VALE
ROYAL PALACE
CITY OF LIGHT
TREE OF LIFE
SECRETS

Light Seeds on a balcony directly across from this platform, accessible via two columns.

Return to the fertile ground via the yellow power plate next to the Coronation Hall entrance. Retrace your steps back down to the basement of the hall. Follow the slides all the way to the bottom of the Coronation Hall, picking up Light Seeds as you slip.

Follow the system of rings, wall runs, and columns you used to get back up to the fertile ground and fight the Concubine. There are several Light Seeds directly along this path. You'll pick them up as you climb back up.

East Path

Start from the eastern door of the Coronation Hall (there's a Light Seed right on the platform) and then wall run out to the ring at the corner of the stone cliff. Swing around the corner via the ring and wall run to the next ledge.

Grab the Light Seed on the ledge and use the nearby columns to reach the corridor with no floor.

Explore the roof along the top of the corridor to pick up four Light Seeds.

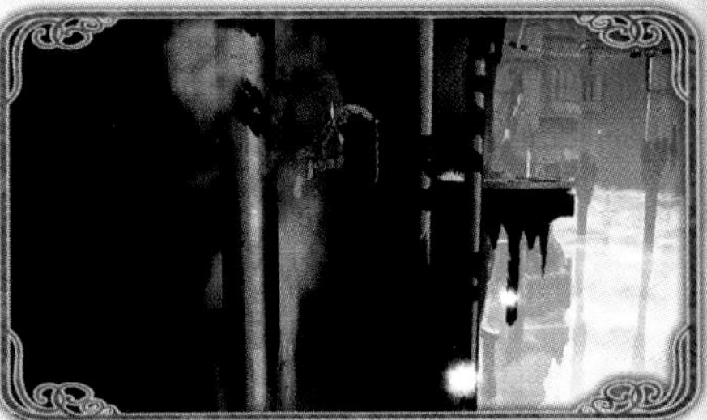

When you return to the Coronation Hall after collecting the Light Seeds in the corridor, look down. Two Light Seeds are at the base of the columns used to access the corridor. When you jump out to the columns, slide down and collect the out-of-the-way Light Seeds.

West Path

As you exit the western gate of the Coronation hall, pick up the Light Seed on the platform. Follow the columns down the corridor to pick up more Light Seeds.

Tip

Once you reach the crossroads, turn around and look back to the Coronation Hall. There are two Light Seeds tucked in the corners of the room.

Concubine's Chambers

After purifying all four areas in the Royal Palace, the Prince and Elika can throw open the doors north of the Coronation Hall and make their final approach on the Concubine. The succubus is cornered—which makes her all the more dangerous. With nothing to lose and a heart squeezed so tight by aching jealousy, the Concubine will fight with everything she has. The Prince must be ready to counter every blow—especially those that come not from the Concubine's hands, but her poison lips.

The Approach

Start moving on the Concubine via the yellow power plate directly beyond the black gate. Jump through the air with Elika's help. When you land on the wall just short of the plate, scramble up and quickly use Elika's magic to take flight.

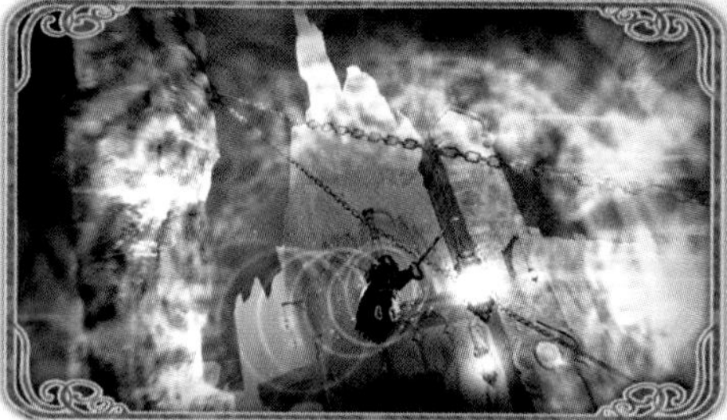

As you race through the air, veer around the giant rocks. If you crash into one, you and Elika are sent all the way back to the area's entrance.

The first leg of the flight ends just below another yellow power plate. Wall run up to it.

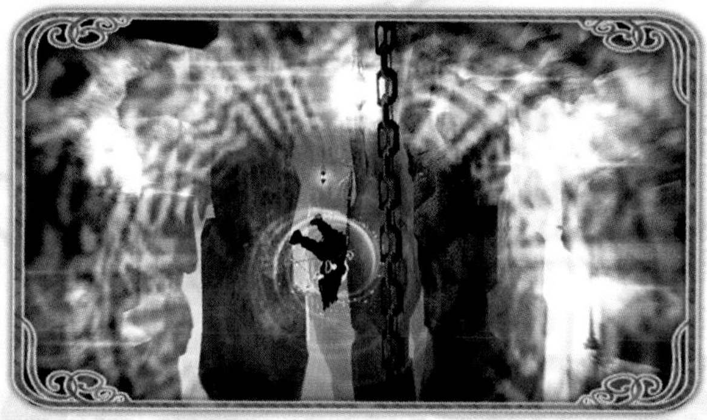

As you fly through the air, steer around the hanging chains and rock pillars.

You gingerly drop to solid ground. There is a blue power plate right in front of you. Scramble up to it. This arcs you to another plate. You land just short, so quickly wall run up to the next blue power plate and blast off across the sky.

You land under a yellow power plate. Wall run up to it and use Elika's magic to launch back into the heavens.

RETURN OF THE PRINCE
MOVES IN MYSTERIOUS WAYS
DYNAMIC WORLD
DESERT
RUINED CITADEL
THE VALE
ROYAL PALACE
CITY OF LIGHT
TREE OF LIFE
SECRETS

Dodge the rock archway as you fly to another blue power plate.

The blue power plate boosts you to a yellow power plate.

This final yellow power plate launches you to the Concubine's chambers and the final battle with the Corrupted.

Final Showdown

The Concubine is waiting for you. She's not alone. The chambers are full of Concubines. You know one of these is not an illusion, but there's just no telling which. Each looks like a perfect replica of the Concubine, so the only way to discover the real Concubine is to race to each mirage and cut it down with your sword.

They are all illusions? Where is the real Concubine?

Right behind you.

First Sequence

Mercifully, this circular area has no edges overlooking the void, nor any corruption. The arena is quite large, too, giving you a lot of room to stage extended combos and keep the Concubine juggled in the air by switching between gauntlet and acrobatic moves. Wait for the Concubine to attack and then deflect her incoming blow to create an opening.

When the Concubine tries Ahriman's Patience, you have a great opening to launch into a combo. Yank the Concubine off the ground with the gauntlet and then hammer her with a series of alternating sword and magic attacks.

TIP

If the Concubine uses Ahriman's Influence when her back is against the wall, move away. If you throw her into the wall, your combo ends prematurely and the Concubine gets a chance to attack.

When the Concubine loses a third of her health, she disappears.

Second Sequence

Where did the Concubine go? The witch leaves a little hint by opening a gate that leads out to a ledge. There is a blue power plate at the end of the ledge, so wall run out to it. This launches you to a yellow power plate. Follow the flight path to the next yellow power plate.

You land just shy of a blue power plate. Wall run out to it. The blue plate directs you to another yellow power plate. This magic of this power plate sends you flying straight into the Concubine's clutches. It's time to resume the fight.

The Concubine strikes Elika, knocking her out. You must fight the Concubine without your companion's help.

Since you do not have Elika's assistance during this part of the fight, erase any attempts to use magic moves in combos. Stick to the gauntlet, acrobatics, and the sword.

Trade blows with the Concubine, deflecting her attacks as you launch your own. Keep her busy this way until Elika can recover.

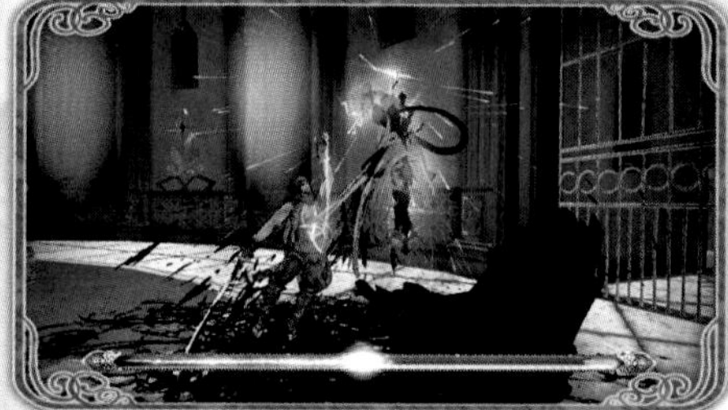

The Concubine continues to call upon Ahriman's Influence. If Elika is still hurt, back away and make sure the Concubine's back is not against the wall. Fling her into the air and then slam her to the ground with a hearty sword strike.

Third Sequence

After you eliminate the next third of the Concubine's health, she vanishes again. The Concubine opens another path back out of the tower. Run out to the blue power plate and use it to reach a yellow power plate.

The flight is not enough to reach the next blue power plate. Just as the screen turns gray, tap the magic button to make Elika throw you all the way to the wall with the power plate.

Wall run to the next blue power plate.

The blue power plate launches you to a yellow power plate. The Hand of Ormazd then carries you to all the way to the top of the tower.

The Concubine tries to further drive a wedge between you and your partner by creating a series of Elika illusions. Is the real Elika among them? Or is this another trick? You must cut down each Elika illusion to play out the Concubine's game. However, after slicing through every illusion, you're left on the roof all alone. Where is Elika?

It's now time for a test of faith and trust. You cannot see Elika. You just have to believe she is there. By proving your trust in Elika, she will reappear. The only way to truly show your faith in Elika is to leap off the edge of the tower. If Elika is still with you, she will save you.

And indeed she does.

RETURN OF THE PRINCE
MOVES IN MYSTERIOUS WAYS
DYNAMIC WORLD
DESERT
RUINED CITADEL
THE VALE
ROYAL PALACE
CITY OF LIGHT
TREE OF LIFE
SECRETS

Infuriated by the purity of the connection between you and Elika, the Concubine strikes. Her aggression is on overdrive, so guard well against her incoming flurry of attacks. She only has a third of her health left, so keep your guard up. If you are injured and the Concubine manages to land a lethal attack, she can regain a lot of that lost health, extending the battle.

Keep the Concubine in the center of the arena. She tries to draw you to the edge where she can push you off. Use acrobatics to roll around her and keep the action in the center.

Ahriman's Patience remains your best setup for an attack combo. When you can start with a gauntlet attack, a successful juggle will eliminate the remainder of the Concubine's health.

Beaten, the Concubine extends her hand to Elika. She welcomes her touch, freeing her of Ahriman's spell and setting her soul to rest. After Elika redeems the Concubine, the sun returns to the skies above the Royal Palace. Elika's strength is sapped. And even though you just showed her how much you trusted her, the Concubine's taunts still linger in your ears.

City of Light

The corruption of the once magnificent City of Light demands an answer from the Prince and Elika. The pair must rush to the defense of the religious center of the Ahura world, pushing back against the creeping darkness. By purifying all of the fertile grounds in the City of Light, the Prince and Elika gain the strength to challenge the Corrupted that dominates the region: The Warrior. The Warrior's past may be worthy of sympathy, but that is an unaffordable luxury in the face of so much destruction. The Warrior must be slain so the City of Light can again burn brightly and resurrect the fading hopes of the Ahuras.

What's Unleashed

When the Prince and Elika arrive in the City of Light, they risk unlocking two problematic features into the rest of the corrupted world. Not only is a new trap unleashed—the tendrils—but as soon as the Warrior exhibits his rage attack, that also spreads across to other your enemy encounters, such as the Mourning King.

The Warrior

Of all the Corrupted, the Warrior is the most tragic. A war wages within him, as Ahriman's corruption tries to snuff out the last flames of good inside the fallen king. But even though the Warrior is conflicted, that does not mean he will go easy on the Prince and Elika.

The Warrior's explosive special attack is Ahriman's Rage. The Warrior raises his hands to his head, trying to fight back against the power of the corruption. This internal struggles manifests itself physically, too. Cracks of corruption make the ground around the Warrior harmful to stand on. The air around the Warrior also fills with corruption gas. There is no way to counter this influence with a particular move, unlike Ahriman's Patience or Anger. Instead, you must fall back and let the attack run its course.

Because of the Warrior's size and his incredible armor plating, you can never defeat the Warrior through direct attacks. In all of your encounters with the Warrior, you must use the Corrupted's heft against him. Lure the Warrior to the edge of an arena, get him to enter into a struggle, and then push the Warrior into the darkness. But you must weaken the Warrior before you can heave him over an edge. And to do that, you must launch into an extended combo—starting with an acrobatic move—that uses Elika's magic. Once Elika swings on top of the Warrior and tugs at his mask with her magic, finish with your sword to weaken him. Now, you only have a few moments to lure the Warrior to the edge of an arena and push him to his demise.

Due to his huge size, you can never use your gauntlet against the Warrior. That limits your combo possibilities, so adjust your strategies accordingly. Concentrate instead on acrobatic and Elika combos.

The Traps

When you reach the City of Light, the area closest to the Warrior's Fortress, the Corrupted unlocks a new trap: tendrils. Affected walls are now infested with swirling pools of corruption. Every few seconds, tendrils explode from the pool and flail about. If you are trying to wall run across a surface with this trap and get clipped by a tendril as it pops out of the wall, you're grabbed and violently slammed into the wall. Elika rescues you, but you return to the last solid surface you stood on and must restart the acrobatic sequence. So, look at the tendrils like a timing game. When the tendrils disappear into the wall, start whatever acrobatic feat is needed to cross the surface. Unlocking the tendril trap in Coronation Hall releases the trap in the following areas: The Windmills, Martyr's Tower, Marshalling Ground, Sun Temple, King's Gate, Machinery Ground, Heaven's Stair, Construction Yard, Reservoir, the Cauldron, Royal Gardens, Royal Spire, Tower of Ormazd, Tower of Ahriman, Queen's Tower, City of Light, City Gate -- plus the routes between King's Gate, the Cauldron, & Temple, the routes between the Cauldron, the Cavern, & Temple, the routes between the Cavern, City Gate, & Temple, and the routes between Royal Spire & Tower of Ormazd.

City Gate

The City gate is the entrance to the City of Light. The Prince and Elika cannot venture into the city without first passing through this gauntlet and banishing the encroaching corruption. Once the City Gate has been purified, the pair must collect the revealed Light Seeds so Elika can learn Ormazd's magic and unlock the paths to the fertile grounds of the City of Light.

Corrupt

Approach

From the fork in the path leading away from the desert, look to the right. The grim, dark cave leads to the City Gate. Jump out to the tilted platform on the left side of the cave and slide to the solid ledge. Run straight ahead and jump out to the next series of sloped platforms. Slide down the slanted rocks to reach a pair of rings hammered into the stone wall of the cave.

Scramble up the two rings and pull yourself up to the ledge.

RETURN OF THE PRINCE
MOVES IN MYSTERIOUS WAYS
DYNAMIC WORLD
DESERT
RUINED CITADEL
THE VALE
ROYAL PALACE
CITY OF LIGHT
TREE OF LIFE
SECRETS

After sliding down the next ledge, step through the gates to look across the City Gate. There is a massive door in the distance, surrounded by ornate architecture that has fallen into ruins. Chains hold up bits and pieces of the crumbling kingdom. And in the center of the fallen scene is the fertile ground, illuminated by a blue beacon. However, the fertile ground is under the foot of the Warrior. The Corrupted is waiting patiently for your arrival. Do not disappoint him.

Jump out to the titled platform in front of you. As you slide toward the Warrior, a falling rock shatters the far end of the platform. Jump to the right to avoid sliding into the abyss.

Scramble up the vines on the wall with Elika. The path to the Warrior continues at the top of the wall.

More of the City Gate collapses as you pull yourself to the top of the wall. The archway ahead of you cracks and falls, leaving behind only a few pieces of exposed stonework and a single column. That column is your ticket to the Warrior now. Wall run to the vines on the right and then shunt over to the stable platform next to the column. Jump out to the column and swing around it. With your back to the next landing, kick away.

Jump across the next pair of columns. Elika is right behind you, following your movements. Slide down the second column in the pairing and then kick away to the next platform.

CAUTION

The walls are covered with corruption, so keep your distance when approaching the City Gate. Keep to the edges of the platforms.

The Warrior is only one jump away. Leap down to the fertile ground and challenge the Warrior to battle.

The Warrior

The Warrior is a hulking monster, covered in armor plating too thick to pierce with your blade. Instead, you must find a way to outsmart the behemoth and lure him to his own doom. The Warrior is by no means foolish, though. He will keep away from the edges, which he can sense you will use to defeat it. And to push back from the edges, the Warrior uses his superhuman strength in conjunction with fists the size of camels. You must block these incoming blows or suffer the consequences. Elika may be able to save your life just as the Warrior brings down one of his massive hands, but while you recover from such a beating, the Warrior regains any spent strength.

The Warrior starts on the attack. He brings his fists down on you right away, so be ready to deflect. If you don't trust your timing, just hold the guard button to withstand the torrent of blows. The Warrior has such momentum behind his attacks that he can swing four or five blows in rapid succession without taking a breath.

You must weaken the Warrior to heave it over the edge of the fertile ground landing. The only way to do this is to chain combos against the brute. Starting with a sword attack, though, will not get the job done. Instead, you must use the Warrior's great size to your advantage. Start an acrobatic combo by running toward the monster and using the dodge button.

TIP

If the Warrior backs you up to the edge and you are wounded, just use the dodge to slip between his legs and then retreat to the far side of the arena to recover.

The Warrior is too slow to keep up with your graceful moves. Now that you've slid between the Corrupted's legs and are behind him, chain together a combo that uses Elika's magic so she pounces on his back and attacks.

CAUTION

Never try a lift combo against the Warrior. He's too heavy for you to raise with your gauntlet. If you attempt it, the beast will just swat you away.

After completing the combo, blue sparks pop from between the Warrior's armor plates. His health meter shows no damage, but he's temporarily weakened. Now it's time to push the monster up to the edge.

Though the Warrior has been weakened, he does not stop swinging. The Warrior still throws those fists, requiring you to deflect each attack. If one of the blows connects, you're sent sprawling. He can then launch a lethal attack.

The only thing bigger than the Warrior's fists are his feet. While you're knocked to the ground, the Warrior stands over you and raises a giant foot. You have a split-second to tap the on-screen button to avoid the coming stomp. If you hit the button, you roll away and can fight back with a new combo. If you miss, though, Elika is forced to rescue you and the Warrior has a chance to recover his strength. The sparks vanish and you must attempt a new acrobatic combo to weaken him again.

While regular sword attacks do not damage the Warrior, they do push him back a few inches at a time. Use these to nudge the Warrior to the edge of the platform.

Return of the Prince
Moves in Mysterious Ways
Dynamic World
Desert
Ruined Citadel
The Vale
Royal Palace
City of Light
Tree of Life
Secrets

Once you back the weakened Warrior up to the edge of the platform, land at least some part of a combo that does not start with an acrobatic move. (If you try one, all you do is slide between the Warrior's legs and end up with your back against the edge—not exactly advantageous.) This triggers a struggle. You and Elika push against the Warrior's mammoth foot. Repeatedly tap the attack button to knock the Warrior off balance.

CAUTION

If you push the Warrior to the edge when he is not weak, you still enter the struggle, but you always lose—and take damage and he kicks you away.

After the Prince and Elika push the Warrior into the pit of corruption below, a wall of flame shoots into the air. It will take more than a tumble to defeat the Warrior—after all, the corruption is where he gets his power—but it does buy enough time to purify the fertile ground and heal the City Gate. Once the fertile ground has been claimed by Elika, the hunt for the Light Seeds begins.

Healed

There are two paths leading into the City Gate area—north and south. The Light Seeds are spread across the two paths, with the majority of the 45 concentrated in the immediate area around the fertile ground.

City Gate

A host of Light Seeds are practically right on top of the fertile ground. As soon as Elika recovers, collect the Light Seed above the City Gate by scrambling up the nearby wooden door.

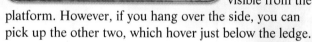

There six Light Seeds on the immediate platform. Pick up the three to the left of the wooden door. All three are on top of the platform. There are three more to the left (if you are facing away from the door), but only one is visible from the platform. However, if you hang over the side, you can pick up the other two, which hover just below the ledge.

Return to the left of the wooden door. Several Light Seeds lead away from the fertile ground. Slide down the tilted platform and then scramble up the wall to grab the Light Seed near the vine patch on the adjacent wall. Next, climb up the vines. Wall run through the Light Seed along the cavern wall and stop in the next vine patch.

Jump to the column and then rotate so your back is to the wall with the two Light Seeds. Kick away and grip fall down the wall to pick up the pair. Then jump back to the column before you slide off the wall entirely.

Roof between the next two columns to pick up another Light Seed.

Slide down the ramp beyond the columns, picking up the Light Seed in the center. There is a little loop you do here to grab a collection of Light Seeds that then points you toward the north path, away from the City Gate.

Use the wooden slide pointing away from the north path to keep collecting Light Seeds in the main area. There is a host of Light Seeds along the loop of slides

directly beyond the wooden slide. The middle of the loop positions you in front of the entrance to the south path, which leads back out to the desert.

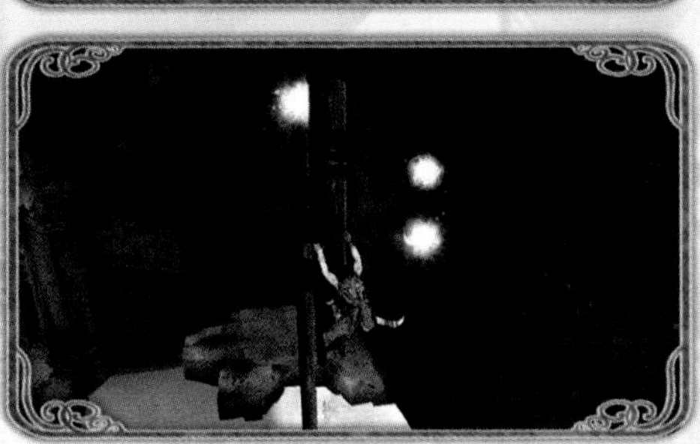

Retrace the steps that lead to the fertile ground and your bout with the Warrior to pick up five more Light Seeds. You must kick away from the columns and into the walls to pick up all of the Light Seeds. Just make sure you use the grip fall to keep from slipping off the wall as you slide into the Light Seeds.

North Path

From the fertile ground, head north and look down to cavern. There is a Light Seed on the wall to your right and you can see even deeper down the cavern. Wall run to the patch of vines to grab the first Light Seed. Wall run to the next collection of vines. Two Light Seeds are directly above you. Scramble up the wall and grab the Light Seeds, then grip fall back into the vines.

RETURN OF THE PRINCE
MOVES IN MYSTERIOUS WAYS
DYNAMIC WORLD
DESERT
RUINED CITADEL
THE VALE
ROYAL PALACE
CITY OF LIGHT
TREE OF LIFE
SECRETS

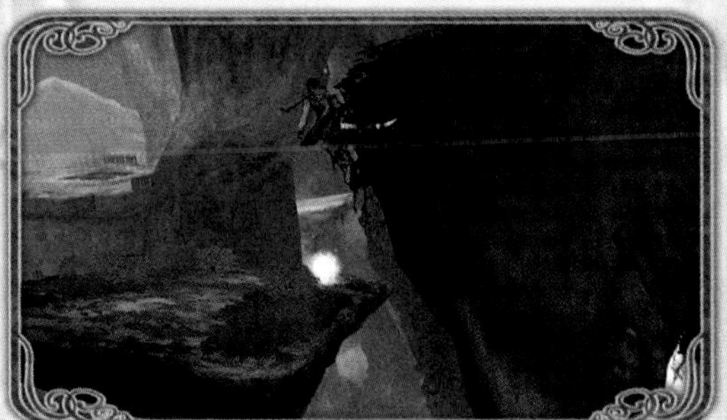

Wall run away from the vines and jump out to the tilted platform. Immediately steer to the right to pick up another Light Seed.

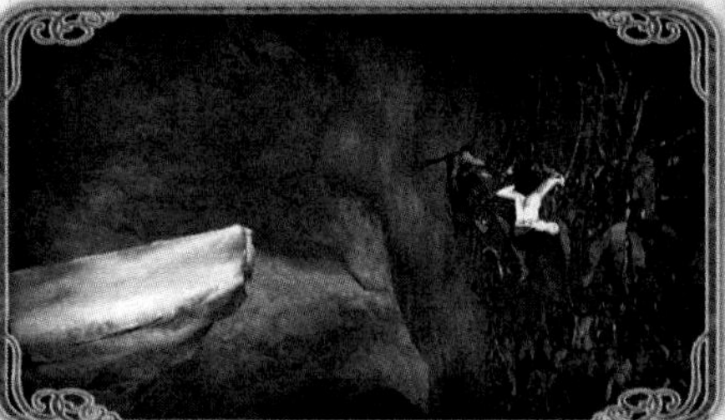

To collect all of the Light Seeds, you must double back to the fertile ground, so jump toward the wall at the end of your slide and then climb along the vines so you can kick into another tilted platform.

The slide leads to the crossroads between the City Gate and the Tower of Ahriman. Exchange blows with the solider, deflecting its attacks as you push it up to the edge of the landing. Rattle off a combo against the monster using Elika's magic to significantly chisel away its health bar as you push it to the edge. Attack the monster again at the edge to finish it off by plunging your blade into its chest.

After defeating the monster, turn back toward the City Gate. There are two slides. Jump out and rush down the first slide, positioning yourself in the center so you can grab the Light Seed. Jump off the second slide and wall run to the vines. Climb up the vines and then kick back to grab another Light Seed and slide back toward the City Gate.

Blue Power Plates

You must have the Hand of Ormazd in order to collect all of the Light Seeds in this area. Once the blue power plates are active, return here and finish your collection.

Climb the vine patch directly across from the fertile ground. Wall run out to the power plate and tap the magic button. You and Elika fly through the air and land on top of a second blue power plate. Tap the magic button to blast off from the power plate and access a ledge high above the City Gate that hosts a handful of Light Seeds.

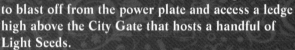

The arc of the plate flings you into the wall just below the ledge. Scramble up to grab the first Light Seed. Walk to the edge to pick up the second Light Seed. Then, hang off the edge and grip fall into the last three Light Seeds in this area.

South Path

Retrace your path toward the desert to collect more Light Seeds. Since you used slides to reach the City Gate and those are one-way streets, you must use the ring and fissure on the cavern's left side to return to the fork in the path. Wall run out to the ring and scramble over to the exposed woodwork in the fissure. Climb it and then wall run over to the platform high above the path. There is a Light Seed on the platform.

Cooperatively jump across the gap between the platform and the slide to the south. The slide whips you around a corner and points you right out into a huge gap. Jump with Elika to the next wooden slide and keep to the right so you pass right through the next Light Seed. At the end of this ramp, jump with Elika down to the rock landing.

Follow your steps back to the City Gate. At the rock near the bottom of the first slide, jump out to the right to collect two Light Seeds against the wall. Grip fall through the Light Seeds and then use Elika to jump back to the rock safely.

Tower of Ahriman

Piercing the skies above the City of Light, the Tower of Ahriman is a respectful monument to the god of darkness. The Prince and Elika must scale the tower, slipping both inside and outside its crumbling structure, to challenge the Warrior at the very top. Only after the Warrior has been defeated can Elika purify the tower and begin liberating the City of Light from Ahriman's clutches.

Corrupt

Approach

The crossroads between the City Gate and the Tower of Ahriman is guarded by one of Ahriman's soldiers. Unload into the soldier with a lengthy combo. Drive the soldier to the edge of the landing and then attack one last time to drive your sword into its heart.

The air is thick with corruption particles. You must hurry to the tower. Jump on the tilted platform to the north and slide toward the cavern wall. Jump out to the vines on the wall and then cross to the left.

Jump to the next slide. Jump away from the slide at the bottom and wall run to the next set of vines.

Wall run and then jump over to the slide. This rockets you to the base of the Tower of Ahriman.

Climb the Tower

Begin your ascent of the tower by climbing the ornate column in the center of the bottom chamber. At the top of the column, face away from the beam that ends in a brass ring. Roof over to the ring and then climb up the wall just above it. At the top of your possible wall scramble, kick away to land on the blue power plate on the opposite wall.

Your jump comes up a touch short, so you need to scramble up the opposite wall to reach the power plate.

RETURN OF THE PRINCE
MOVES IN MYSTERIOUS WAYS
DYNAMIC WORLD
DESERT
RUINED CITADEL
THE VALE
ROYAL PALACE
CITY OF LIGHT
TREE OF LIFE
SECRETS

You arc away from the power plate and land on a corner structure inside the tower. Grab the wooden scaffolding. Climb up the scaffolding to reach the top of the corner structure.

There is a large door on this floor of the tower. Walk to the left of the door and jump out to the exposed scaffolding. Climb the wall by jumping to the next set of boards.

Kick away from the wall and scramble up the opposite wall to reach a balcony overlooking the tower exterior.

LOOK FOR VISUAL CLUES IN THE WALLS OR BENEATH CORRUPTION FOR THE ORMAZD MAGIC NEEDED ON RETURN VISITS. ON THE BALCONY, FOR EXAMPLE, YOU CAN SEE A POWER PLATE PULSING BENEATH THE MUCK.

Outside the tower, use the vertical crack in the stonework to climb the wall. There is a metal plate above the crack with a horizontal slot in it. Run up the wall from the top of the crack to grab the plate.

Wall run from the plate to the small vertical crack in the center of the tower wall. There is nothing to grab at the top of this crack, so wall run to the right again. There is a stable platform on the far side of the tower wall with a ring mechanism nearby. Jump up and grab the ring. Your weight pulls it down. This lowers a metal plate directly above you.

Climb the vertical crack next to the ring to reach the plate above. Shimmy along the slot in the plate and then wall run to the left to reach more exposed scaffolding. Wall run from the far side of the scaffolding to reach another steady wooden platform.

Turn the crank on this platform to rotate a giant metal plate on the outside of the tower. There is a crease in the center of the metal plate that, when vertically oriented, can be used to keep ascending the outside of the tower. Wall run to the crease and then climb up it. Run up the wall above the plate to grab a few boards. Shimmy to the right and then wall run to a wooden platform.

Pull down the ring on the wooden platform to lower two more metal plates down the side of the tower. These plates have horizontal slots useful for crossing back to the other side of the tower. Climb up the vertical scaffolding next to the ring and then wall run across the two metal plates.

Turn the crank on the wooden platform until the two metal discs on the tower are oriented like this. The slots in the bottom disc should read like an L. Jump across the face of the tower to the outer platform. Call on Elika to complete the giant jump.

Turn this crank so the upper disc mirrors the position of the bottom disc. Then, grab the nearby ring to drop two metal plates in between the discs so you can climb the tower.

Cross back to the other crank. Wall run to the bottom disc and then crawl up it. Use the metal plate to link over to the upper disc. Crawl up the slot in that disc so you can wall run straight up to a long horizontal fissure.

At the right side of the fissure, wall run and then kick to the overhang. Wall run to the blue power plate at the far end of the overhang.

RETURN OF THE PRINCE
MOVES IN MYSTERIOUS WAYS
DYNAMIC WORLD
DESERT
RUINED CITADEL
THE VALE
ROYAL PALACE
CITY OF LIGHT
TREE OF LIFE
SECRETS

The blue power plate launches you to another decorated column. Climb up this column with Elika and then turn so your back is facing away from the top of the tower. The Warrior is waiting for you. As soon as you kick off the column, the Corrupted swings into action.

The Warrior

The Warrior atop the Tower of Ahriman is much stronger in this battle, capable of unleashing Ahriman's Rage to make you keep your distance. The goal is the same, though. Use a combo to weaken the Warrior. When you see the blue sparks emerge from between the armor plates, back the Warrior up to the edge of the roof and then push him off.

The Warrior may called upon Ahriman's Rage in this battle. When he's enveloped by the particles, step back and let the attack play itself out.

NOTE

If you do not push the weakened Warrior off the roof quickly, he often calls on the particle storm to repel your attacks as he heals himself.

The Warrior has learned a few new attacks that can only be deflected by timed button inputs. When you spot the Warrior raising both arms, he's about to slam his fists to the floor and cause a minor quake. If you don't react in time, you're knocked backward. While you get back to your feet, the Warrior closes in and readies a regular punch. If the Warrior was weak at the time, the pause in the fight gives him a chance to heal himself. You must then find an opening for another acrobatic combo.

Another new attack comes when the Warrior goes for a slow punch. If you counter just as his fist comes down, you deflect the blow as usual. However, you then grab the arm and climb on top of the Warrior. There are four button presses in this combo, all sword strikes. If timed correctly, you scramble around the Warrior's body, stabbing him in weak spots as he struggles to shake you loose. Hitting all four attacks in the sequence weakens the Warrior.

CAUTION

If you fail to repel any of the Warrior's big attacks and Elika has to save you, the Warrior returns to the center of the arena. You must then back him up to the edge all over again.

Just as in the first battle with the Warrior, inch him to the edge of the tower while he's weak. Repeatedly tap the attack button to push the Warrior off the tower.

After the Warrior falls from the tower, he sinks into the corruption below. It is not be the last time you will see him. He will be back. And he will be stronger. So you must ready yourself by purifying the fertile ground and collecting the Light Seeds to unlock Ormazd's magic and push deeper into Ahriman-controlled territory.

Healed

There are three paths breaking away from the Tower of Ahriman that you must explore in order to collect all 45 Light Seeds. Plus, you must be able to use red power plates to locate a handful of tough-to-find Light Seeds.

Tower

There are four Light Seeds on top of the Tower of Ahriman, easily collected after Elika rescues the fertile ground. After collecting the four Light Seeds, investigate the wood panel that magically rises near the broken wall of the tower roof.

Grip fall down the wood panel. Near the bottom, jump away from the panel. You land on a slide that rushes you toward a wooden wall. As you grip fall down that wall, you pass through your next Light Seed. At the bottom of the panel, jump away to land on another slide.

There's a gap in the middle of the slide. Jump over the gap and then leap to the next wood panel. Grip fall down the panel and then kick away to reach another slide. There is a Light Seed in the center of that slide.

Use grip fall to slide down the panel on the opposite side of the slide. It's a long panel with a Light Seed as a reward at the end of your descent.

Slide down the tilted platform and back to the left side of the tower face. Jump off the slide and grip fall down the wooden plank. You stop at a slot in the planks. Use the scaffolding on the right to reach the actual face of the tower and then grip fall down the stonework. Slide around the doorway so you safely land on the balcony below.

CAUTION

Time your jumps right because if you fall off one of the slides, you must start all the way back at the top of the tower.

The balcony circles the tower. There are two Light Seeds on the balcony, so make a lap.

A lone Light Seed is just inside this floor of the tower. If you look up, though, you see several Light Seeds on a series of red power plates. If you have the Step of Ormazd, you can use these plates and collect the Light Seeds. Climb the corner structure as if you were traveling back up to the top of the tower.

Red Power Plates

Remember when this power plate was covered by corruption? Now that the area is pure, you can jump to the power plate and bounce around the tower interior to collect five Light Seeds. Jump out to the first red power plate and use Elika's magic. The first plate launches you across the tower, but you land to the right of the next plate. Hold down the magic button and press the left control stick to the left so that you wall run to the plate. (There are two Light Seeds on the plate.)

Keep holding the magic button when you leave a power plate because you always land near the next power plate—not directly on top of it. When you complete a circle around the tower interior via the red power plates, you are five Light Seeds richer.

Step out on to the balcony next to the red power plate. There are Light Seeds on the tower face, so you must ascend back to the top. Climb up the metal plates and use the scaffolding to maintain your grip on the tower when not wall running from left to right and back again.

Round the tower and use the vertical slot in the large disc to ascend the side of the tower and grab another pair of Light Seeds. The two Light Seeds are on the metal plates above the disc, so you must use the scaffolding to reach them.

Climb along the two L-slots in the pair of metal discs to reach the last Light Seed on the tower exterior. Now that you are near the top, you must use the wooden panels to slide back down to the lower balcony.

Once back down on that middle balcony, step inside the tower and grip fall to the bottom floor to finish collecting all of the Light Seeds inside the tower.

Four Light Seeds are on the main floor of the tower, clustered around the ornate column. After collecting all of these Light Seeds, walk to the opposite side of the column from the three carvings of the Warrior on the wall. Hang over the edge and look down. There's a ring beneath you. Drop down and use a system of rings under the floor to cross the center of the tower and pick up a hidden Light Seed.

Climb the central column in the tower and return to the blue power plate. Jump over to the plate, but do not use it just yet. Instead, have Elika throw you to the opposite wall from the plate so you can scramble up and grab a Light Seed. Slide back down to the ring and return to column.

South Path

With the corruption gone, it's much easier to see your way through the southern path. Start by sliding down the tilted platform and then wall run across the patches of vines to pick up a Light Seed as you work your way back to the purified nexus between the City Gate and the Tower of Ahriman. (This is where you fought a soldier.) There are two Light Seeds at the very top of the vine collection between the rock walls at the bottom of the slide.

When you reach the landing, turn to the right (if you are facing south) and jump off the platform onto a slide. At the end of the slide, jump onto the wall and then run to the vines. Wall run to the right and hop off to another slide. This shoots you back to the base of the tower.

East Path

When you step out of the east side of the Tower of Ahriman, you can see all six Light Seeds on the east path. Jump to the slide on the left. Pick up the Light Seed in the center of the slide and then use the column to link to the next slide, which also hosts a Light Seed. Jump off that slide and then climb to the top of the column. There are two Light Seeds high in the air that you can get by kicking away from the column. After getting the Light Seeds, jump back to the column and then complete the loop of slides to end up back at the Tower of Ahriman.

West Path

Jump across the gap to the west to start hunting Light Seeds. There is one visible directly from the gap between two lines of exposed woodwork. You must use Elika to jump the distance between the platform and the wall with the woodwork, and then scramble up it to keep from falling.

Wall run to the right of the Light Seed and jump down to a curved slide. Stick to the right of the slide to grab another Light Seed and then jump to a wall run to bank another Light Seed.

Jump away from the wall to land on another set of slides. There is a Light Seed at the bottom of the slides, but unless you have already purified the Tower of Ormazd, a soldier is just waiting for you at the opposite landing.

RETURN OF THE PRINCE
MOVES IN MYSTERIOUS WAYS
DYNAMIC WORLD
DESERT
RUINED CITADEL
THE VALE
ROYAL PALACE
CITY OF LIGHT
TREE OF LIFE
SECRETS

Destroy the soldier with a lengthy combo that involves Elika's magic so that it's backed against the wall. Then keep attacking until you drive your sword into the soldier.

After defeating it, jump to the wall with the scratch mark leading straight up. There's scaffolding you can hold as you shimmy your way around the bend.

Follow the scaffolding up the wall and around the corner. Start running and then quickly jump away from the wall to land on a slide that leads straight to two Light Seeds. The only catch is a gap in the middle of the slide so wide it requires Elika's help to cross. These slides lead right back to the base of the Tower of Ahriman.

Tower of Ormazd

The Tower of Ormazd is the second of the two towers the Ahura people erected in honor of their gods. This giant structure reaches into the sky, like a hand extended in the hopes the wandering god will one day take it. The Warrior returns to keep the Prince from reaching the fertile ground on top of the tower. As he waits, the Warrior steels himself for yet another tough match against the Prince and Elika.

Corrupt

Approach

There are three ways to reach the Tower of Ormazd—from the Royal Palace to the west, or from the north or south within the City of Light. If you are coming from either the north or south, you must contend with a soldier at the nexus between the two areas. Use the appropriate counterattack to any influences and then lay into the soldier with a flurry of attack combos starting with either the sword or the gauntlet.

If you approach from the Tower of Ahriman, use the series of slides to reach the Tower of Ormazd. If you approach from the City of Light to the north, cross the system of poles to close in on the tower. If you come from the Royal Gardens, no soldier waits and you arrive directly in front of the tower.

The Warrior

Use the green power plate on the wall to climb straight up the wall. However, there is corruption directly above the power plate, so you must shift to the right to avoid the poison. Use the rounded corner to cross over to the wall to the right and shoot into the second story of the tower.

You shoot right into the Warrior.

There is no edge in this chamber to push the Warrior off, so you must instead find another way to trap him. Three of the corner structures in this chamber are cracked or broken. If you back the Warrior into one of these structures and somehow push him into it, his incredible weight will bring the entire structure crashing down. The falling stonework does far more damage to the Warrior than any of your puny sword attacks could.

> **TIP**
>
> The key to this battle is to line up the Warrior with the cracked structures. Any engagement with the Warrior when he's not lined up with one of the structures is pointless. You must use the dodge button to quickly shift around the arena and keep the Warrior always lined up with one of the three structures.

The Warrior undergoes several fits of Ahriman's Rage during this fight.

> **TIP**
>
> While retreating from the particles, use the time and space to move around the arena and line up the Warrior with one of the cracked structures.

RETURN OF THE PRINCE
MOVES IN MYSTERIOUS WAYS
DYNAMIC WORLD
DESERT
RUINED CITADEL
THE VALE
ROYAL PALACE
CITY OF LIGHT
TREE OF LIFE
SECRETS

Any time either you or the Warrior are backed up against a wall and an attack is initiated, you enter the struggle challenge. Tap the attack button repeatedly to at least escape it unscathed.

As before, you must weaken the Warrior to successfully overturn the brute. Start your attack combo with an acrobatic move and then continue to hammer him with Elika's magic and more sword slashes. (Keep avoiding use of the gauntlet!) After a string of successful hits, the Warrior shows his weakened state through the appearance of the blue sparks.

CAUTION

You have only about 20 seconds to get the Warrior backed into the structure before he shakes off the injury with an explosion of corruption.

Shove the Warrior into the structure to bring it down on his head. The Warrior tumbles, rattling him to the core as you watch a third of his health bar vanish.

Back away from the Warrior as he gets up and position yourself between the Warrior and another of the structures. Goad the Warrior to approach you. As he closes in, slide between his legs with the start of acrobatic combo and then launch into a chain that reduces him to his weakened state again.

After you send him crashing into the third stack of stone, the Warrior is wrapped in corruption and pulled into the floor. Ahriman rescues the Corrupted so he may fight another day. Now that the Corrupted has fled the area, you can concentrate on reaching the fertile ground at the tower's top.

The Tower

As soon as the Warrior vacates the tower (for now), use the two rings in the corner to start your ascent. At the top of the rings, kick back to the opposite wall and run up to the balcony. The balcony leads outside the tower, which is smothered in corruption.

Wall run through the safe patch on the wall and use the ring on the corner of the tower to link another wall run over a dangerous mass of corruption. There is a patch of vines in the middle of the tower face you must grab at the end of the wall run.

Crawl up the vines and look skyward. Use the ring above the vines to propel you and Elika into the hole in the side of the tower.

As you enter the tower, the stairs leading to the roof collapse. You must now wall run around the corruption, bouncing off the walls to reach the stair landings. A lone ring is in the center of a patch of corruption near a hole in the tower. Run and jump to the ring and then scramble straight up the wall. At the top of the wall run, jump back to grab the ledge directly behind you. After pulling yourself up, step out onto a balcony.

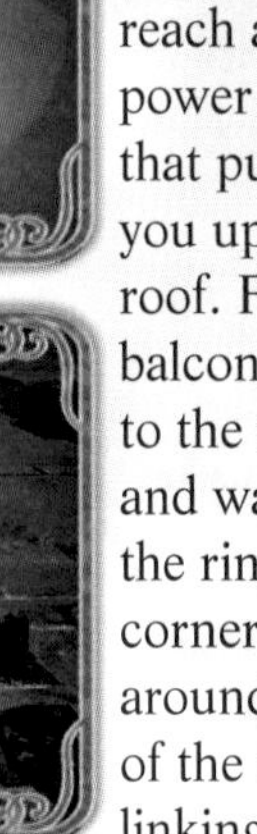

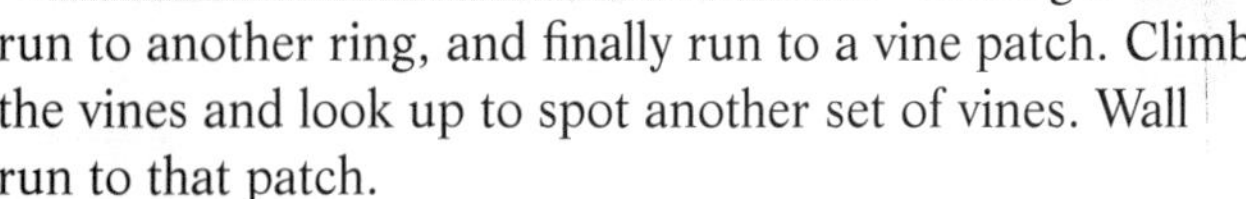

Now, you must circle the building almost twice to reach a green power plate that pushes you up to the roof. From the balcony, run to the right and wall run to the ring at the corner. Whip around the side of the tower, linking a wall run to another ring, and finally run to a vine patch. Climb the vines and look up to spot another set of vines. Wall run to that patch.

Use the two rings near the corner of the tower (to the right) to round the building and reach a broken balcony that's barely hanging on to the structure.

Wall run from the balcony to another ring and round the next corner. You immediately reach a patch of vines. Crawl up the vines until you spot another ring in the tower exterior.

Wall run from the ring to a pair of ornate wooden panels. Bounce from the tower to the two panels as you make a turn around the building.

Jump off the second panel to land on some more vines. From the right side of those vines, wall run out to a pair of rings. Use these two to complete another lap around the tower, lining you up with the green power plate. Use the green power plate to rush up the remainder of the tower to the rooftop and its fertile ground.

The Warrior is back. And he's angry.

The Warrior shakes the tower so much that the roof collapses. The fertile ground now drops to the middle floor of the tower. You must now ride a series of slides back down to the middle floor to reach the sacred ground. Start by jumping to the first slide and then keep bounding from one slanted platform to the next. When you reach a piece of surviving wall, jump out and wall run as far as you can before jumping back to another slide. When you spot the ring in the wall, use it. As you wall run away from the ring, use Elika's power to perform a super jump to the next slide.

The slide directs you back outside the tower. Jump off the slide and use the scaffolding to climb around the side of the building. When you reach the end of the scaffolding, look down. There are no obstacles between you and the balcony outside the middle floor of the tower, so use a grip fall to safely descend.

Once back on the ground, purify the fertile ground inside the tower to release the Light Seeds.

RETURN OF THE PRINCE
MOVES IN MYSTERIOUS WAYS
DYNAMIC WORLD
DESERT
RUINED CITADEL
THE VALE
ROYAL PALACE
CITY OF LIGHT
TREE OF LIFE
SECRETS

Healed

The Light Seeds in the Tower of Ormazd are spread across not only the tower itself, but also the three paths: north, west, and south. All four areas must be explored to capture all of the 45 Light Seeds.

Tower

Three Light Seeds on the floor near the fertile ground: Two are in the corners of the room, and the third is dangling in the hole in the floor. The hole leads down to the bottom floor of the tower where there are, indeed, more Light Seeds, but don't slide down there just yet. There are several more Light Seeds to gather on this floor.

Step out onto the balcony. Four Light Seeds are on the outer railing surrounding the tower. Jump on top of the railing and then hang down on the other side to pick up the Light Seeds.

Yellow Power Plate

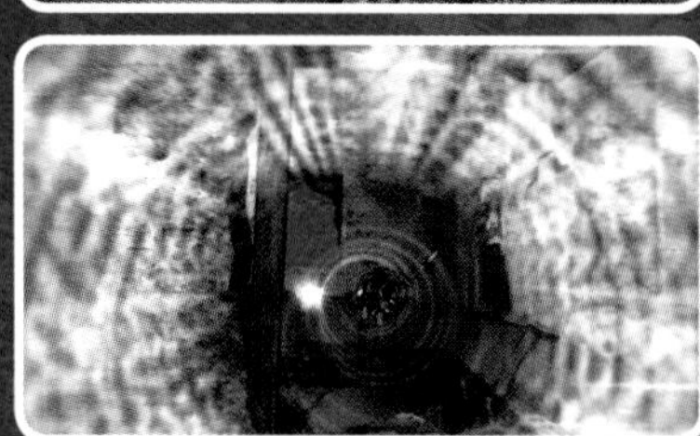

If you have activated the yellow power plates by earned the Wings of Ormazd magic, you can collect a series of Light Seeds otherwise unobtainable. Climb up the side of the tower interior via the ring on the wall and tap the magic button while on the plate. You and Elika zoom into the air, swirling around the Tower of Ormazd. Steer into the Light Seeds along the path of Ormazd. When you cross through the tower windows, dodge the walls so you aren't knocked back to earth. The trip deposits you back inside the tower, directly in front of the yellow power plate.

After capturing the Light Seeds on the balcony, climb the interior of the tower via the two rings on the wall. Wall jump backward to another balcony that spills outside. There is a Light Seed above the rings and another just outside the tower.

Before stepping outside, jump to the wall on the opposite side of the balcony and scramble up to the waiting Light Seed.

From the outside balcony, wall run to the left and use the system of rings and vines to circle the building and pick up a pair of Light Seeds.

After you collect the Light Seeds outside the Tower of Ormazd, return to the hole in floor and drop down the ledge. From the hole you can see that the bottom floor is littered with Light Seeds, so grip fall down by using the rounded corner to descend right over the green power plate you used to climb the tower when it was corrupted. There's a Light Seed on top of the green power plate, too.

Once you're on the bottom floor of the tower, collect the obvious Light Seeds on the ground.

West Path

After clearing the tower of Light Seeds, turn west and start down the path to the Royal Palace. A Light Seed waits just outside the tower. After collecting the Light Seed, use Elika to jump across the wide gap between the tower and the stone steps leading west. There is one more Light Seed at the top of the steps.

To capture the Light Seeds on the west path, you must jump across a series of rock outcroppings, Most can be reached with a single hop, but if the gap looks too wide, use Elika's help to cover the distance. You have to make a loop around this canyon to collect all of the Light Seeds, so don't worry about missing any on the high ledges to the right as you jump across the rocks.

When you reach the mid-point of the canyon, turn back to look east. From the highest rock, you can see the remaining Light Seeds along the path. Jump down the high rocks you could not access on your first trip through the canyon to clean up the rest of the Light Seeds.

To collect the two Light Seeds dangling off the right side of the canyon (when you are facing back toward the Tower of Ormazd), jump with Elika toward the wall and the scramble up it.

South Path

When you look out the southern side of the tower, you see not only a Light Seed on the immediate ledge, but also one in a small cave below the landing on the opposite side of the gap. To collect that Light Seed, grip fall down the ledge right in front of you and then kick away near the bottom. Use Elika's help with the jump. You land in the small cave and grab the Light Seed. Return to the tower the way you came.

Jump on the landing above the small cave. There is a ledge on the left side of the path, but it's not possible to jump to it because it's slanted toward you. Instead, jump to the column on your right and then leap to the platform just beyond it.

RETURN OF THE PRINCE
MOVES IN MYSTERIOUS WAYS
DYNAMIC WORLD
DESERT
RUINED CITADEL
THE VALE
ROYAL PALACE
CITY OF LIGHT
TREE OF LIFE
SECRETS

Complete the loop here. Jump from the platform to the column now on your right. Shimmy to the top of it and then turn so your back it toward the slides. Jump onto the slides and ride them through two Light Seeds. And the end of the bottom slide, do a double jump with Elika's help to get back to the tower.

North Path

Collect the Light Seed directly outside the northern tower exit. The path stretches over the water, so you must stick to the posts and poles jutting out of the architecture on the left. While standing on the first post, wall run straight up to grab the hanging Light Seed.

From the post, hop on the slide and ride it to the wall. Jump to the wall and run along it to the right, passing through a Light Seed. Just as you collect the Light Seed, use a double jump to land on another slide. At the end of the tilted slide, jump to the trio of poles and vault around each one, picking up a Light Seed.

If you haven't cleared the northern area, the City of Light, there is a soldier waiting for you on the far side of those poles. Smash it with an extended combo so you can get back to Light Seed collecting.

Wall run away from the crossroads to pick up a Light Seed. As you grab the Light Seed, jump with Elika's help to another trio of poles. On the middle pole, though, stop moving. Hang straight down and then release the pole with the grip fall button. You drop onto a post. Drop down one more post to pick up two Light Seeds. Jump back up the posts (use vertical wall runs) and then loop back to the tower via a slide.

Queen's Tower

The Queen's Tower is an essential part of the City of Light, the great place of worship for the Ahuras. But now the late queen's favorite place in the kingdom has been ruined by Ahriman's corruption. The Prince and Elika must find a way to the top of the tower to battle the Warrior and redeem the fertile ground before it's too late.

Corrupt Approach

There are two ways into the Queen's Tower. If you're coming from the Tower of Ahriman, the Queen's Tower is just a hop, jump, and another jump across a series of slides. The slide are broken apart due to the ravages of time, though, so you must use jump over the gaps or use wall runs.

However, if you approach the area from the north, at the City of Light, you must come at it from a series of rings dangling from a roof. The rings connect you to a pair of slides. The slides are too far apart to cross, even by a double jump with Elika. Use the column hanging from the wrecked ceiling to bridge the gap.

The Tower

Once inside the Queen's Tower, zero in on the green power plate. Jump to the wall beneath the power plate and scramble up to it. Use Elika's magic to fully activate the plate and start your ascent up the tower. The climb winds along a path of curved stone, but there are no obstacles in your way.

The next green power plate is on the opposite side of a river of corruption. Have Elika toss you over the poison to reach the plate safely.

The plate sends you stomping up the wall. Steer around the lamp in the middle of the ceiling en route to the next green power plate.

CAUTION

If you hit an obstacle while climbing, you're knocked free of the wall and sent back to the last patch of stable ground.

Keep moving along the network of green power plates. Tap the magic button every time you touch one so you continue climbing the walls and ceiling without interruption.

Watch out for more lamps hanging from the ceiling and fixtures sticking out of the walls.

Eventually, the power plates direct you into a field of corruption. There is a clean path through the muck, but you must not only steer away from the poison, but also dodge a series of stone fixtures. Do not oversteer—-keep close to the middle and avoid making sudden moves. The path ends at a balcony overlooking the City of Light.

From the balcony, wall run to the left and use the ring at the edge of the building to whip around to the other side.

There are two green power plates out here. Activate the first one to stomp directly to the second. Use Elika's magic on the second green power plate to race straight to the top of the tower—and into the waiting Warrior.

RETURN OF THE PRINCE
MOVES IN MYSTERIOUS WAYS
DYNAMIC WORLD
DESERT
RUINED CITADEL
THE VALE
ROYAL PALACE
CITY OF LIGHT
TREE OF LIFE
SECRETS

The Warrior

The Corrupted has learned from his previous encounters with you. There are no immediately visible ledges in this chamber at the top of the Queen's Tower. Instead, four doors randomly open and shut—one on each wall. You must drive the Warrior up to one of the open doors and knock him off the top of the tower before the door closes. To complicate your efforts, the Warrior makes an extra effort to stay near the center of the room. You must repeatedly attack him to push the Warrior up to one of the doors and then time your final attack perfectly to nudge him right through the door as it opens.

TIP

As before, the only way to weaken the Warrior is a combo that begins with an acrobatic move.

Position yourself with your back to the open door and get the Warrior to look at you. When the Warrior starts to advance, immediately slide between his legs and start your weakening combo. The Warrior will not tread too far from the center of the room unprompted, so use an extended combo with lots of magic and sword strikes to inch him toward the door.

The Warrior will not drop without a fight. As you push him toward an open door, he swings those huge fists. You must deflect them. If you only guard—or get hit—the Warrior has a chance to recover.

The Warrior often uses one of Ahriman's Influences to make you retreat so it can recover.

If you back the Warrior up to an open door, but he's not weak enough to be pushed outside, go ahead and start your acrobatic combo—just make it is a short one. And as soon as you complete the combo, start another acrobatic combo with your sliding between the Warrior's legs so that you reverse positions again and turn the brute back around. As soon as he's vulnerable, go for the kill.

Slam the weakened Warrior with a sword attack when he's right in the doorway. Tap the attack button during the struggle to push the Warrior off balance and make him topple off the Queen's Tower.

As soon as the Warrior tumbles into the corruption below, purify the fertile ground in the middle of the chamber. Not only does this make the Light Seeds appear, but it also opens more of the sealed doors, giving you a way back down the tower.

Healed

There are just two paths leading into the Queen's Tower, so you must only search the tower and both the north and south routes to collect all the Light Seeds.

Tower

After you liberate the Queen's Tower from the Warrior and save the fertile ground, the Light Seeds spread across the area. Four of them are easily visible around the fertile ground—those are your first pick-ups. Once those have been collected, step through the gate that opened after you saved the tower. It's a long way down, but a series of wooden panels are useful for slowing your descent to a safe speed.

Jump toward the first wooden panel and grip fall down its face. There is a Light Seed on top of a slot in the plank. You automatically stop on the slot. From this hanging point, kick away from the panel to grab the slot in the wood panel to your right. Slide down that panel and use the ring at the bottom to cross under a narrow beam.

Link to the next ring and scramble up the panel above. When you have a firm grip on the panel, jump away from it to grab the slot in the opposite panel and pick up another Light Seed.

Slide down the panel and then jump over to the other wall just as you near the bottom. Use the three rings to cross under a ledge. There is another Light Seed down here.

Keep sliding down the series of wooden panels. When the gap widens between the panels, use Elika's help to bridge the distance.

When you reach the balcony at the bottom of the wooden panels, run to the open door that leads inside the tower. Don't go inside just yet, though. There are two Light Seeds on the rock wall opposite of the door. Jump up on top of the railing and then having Elika fling you to the Light Seeds. After picking them up, kick back from the wall and call on Elika to return you to the balcony.

Now enter the tower. There are several Light Seeds within easy reach. One is in the center of the room. Two more Light Seeds are on the door to the right of the green power plate. Jump across the gap to grab the door, scramble up it to pick

up the treasures, and then kick back to the main floor. Repeat this on the opposite door, which has only one Light Seed.

RETURN OF THE PRINCE
MOVES IN MYSTERIOUS WAYS
DYNAMIC WORLD
DESERT
RUINED CITADEL
THE VALE
ROYAL PALACE
CITY OF LIGHT
TREE OF LIFE
SECRETS

Two Light Seeds beneath this floor. Look over the edge of the landing. There is a ring directly below you. Slide down and use this ring to pass beneath the floor.

Roof along the three rings to grab the two Light Seeds and then scramble up the opposite side to return to the middle floor.

Use the green power plate to climb up the wall and onto the ceiling. There is a Light Seed on the ceiling, just behind the hanging lamp you must avoid.

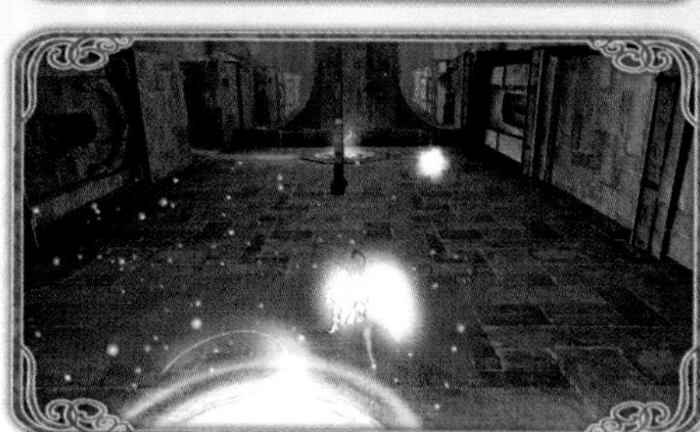

Keep following the trail of green power plates as it winds around the tower interior.

TIP

STEER INTO THE LIGHT SEEDS AS YOU CLIMB, BUT MAKE SURE TO IMMEDIATELY VEER BACK TO THE CENTER OF THE PATH SO YOU DON'T MISS THE NEXT POWER PLATE.

The green power plates direct you back to the small balcony that leads outside the tower. There is a Light Seed on the balcony, as well as one between the two carved wooden panels that flank it.

Wall run out to the ring to reach the next side of the tower. There is another Light Seed on the green power plate straight ahead.

The green power plates return you to the top of the Queen's Tower. Use the wooden panels to climb back down to the middle floor. Hang over the ledge that looks down on the bottom floor of the tower. If you have earned the Hand of Ormazd, the blue power plate below you is active. When you slide down the wall, use magic on the power plate to grab this area's hard-to-find Light Seeds.

BLUE POWER PLATE

The magic of the power plate launches you through the air. While arcing across the tower, you pick up an entire line of Light Seeds. The arc drops you down on the bottom floor of the Queen's Tower, ready to collect the rest of the Light Seeds. Now, if you do not have the Hand of Ormazd, you must come back after unlocking that special power.

Jump to the center of the room collect four Light Seeds.

SOUTH PATH

Several Light Seeds are found along the southern path leading away from the Queen's Tower. To reach them, do a double jump from the tower to a high wall. Scramble up to the scaffolding at the top of the wall and then carefully shimmy to the right. Pass around the side of the wall so your back is toward a slide. The slide takes you to the nexus platform between the Queen's Tower and Ahriman's Tower. If you have not purified the Tower of Ahriman just yet, there is a soldier waiting for you. Dispatch it so you can continue collecting Light Seeds.

RETURN OF THE PRINCE
MOVES IN MYSTERIOUS WAYS
DYNAMIC WORLD
DESERT
RUINED CITADEL
THE VALE
ROYAL PALACE
CITY OF LIGHT
TREE OF LIFE
SECRETS

Two Light Seeds await collection in an alcove just below the platform. To reach the Light Seeds, jump out to the wall to the left of the alcove and slide down to the narrow bits of exposed scaffolding below you. Next, crawl along the woodwork so you're inside the alcove. Wall run to the left and then jump to the wall with the Light Seeds. After grabbing them, kick away from the wall. Jump to the adjacent wall and then wall run back so you're pointed to the platform. Jump to it and crawl up to the ledge.

Jump back to the same wall, but instead of grip falling to the woodwork below, scramble to the planks above you.

Wall run to the left and jump out to the series of slides. Follow the slides as they curve back to the tower. Jump over the gaps between the tilted platforms. When the slide directs you into a wall, jump out and wall run along the wall so you can leap to the last platform and slide through a Light Seed on your way back to the base of the tower.

North Path

Exit the tower to the north to start along the path that leads to the City of Light. Jump out to the column straight ahead. After twirling around the column, kick to the wall and then wall run to the left. You run through a Light Seed just before reaching a brass ring. Grab the ring with your gauntlet to link around the building and close in on another column.

Wall run away from the ring and jump to the column. Slide to the bottom of the column to pick up a Light Seed. Climb back up the column and jump to the slide pointing away from it.

The slide leads to a ring in the wall directly ahead. Jump out and link from the ring to scramble up to the platform above. If you have not healed the City of Light, there's a soldier to be fought here.

TIP

If you run straight for the cloud of corruption as soon as you reach the platform, you can dispel it with a sword strike before the soldier has a chance to form.

From the platform, look south. There is a Light Seed right on top of a ring that's a quick wall run away. After linking another wall run from the ring, jump out to the column and then roof along the series of rings to pick up another Light Seed on your way back to the Queen's Tower.

The slide at the end of the rings drops you right next to a column. Jump out and grab the column. Two more Light Seeds are inside the corner, off to your right. Jump away from the column and wall run into the corner. Jump to the adjacent wall to pick up the Light Seeds and then hop back to the slide. Follow the slides back to the Queen's Tower.

City of Light

The City of Light was once a luminous corner of the Ahuras' world, a place to celebrate Ormazd and all of his blessings, despite his absence. But now the corruption has covered this sacred site, including the fertile ground inside the city. The Prince and Elika must weave through the winding corridors to locate the fertile ground and fight back against the Warrior in order to save the city.

Corrupt

Approach

There are two ways to approach the City of Light. If you come from the west—the Tower of Ormazd—you must cross a series of posts and poles. Vault through the air, which is thick with corruption, and spin around the flag poles as you close in on the City of Light's entrance. The city streets are sadly covered in corruption, leaving you with no choice but to stick to high ground as you hop across posts and slide to the blue power plate that marks the entrance of the city.

If you approach the City of Light from the Queen's Tower, you must cross a obstacle course of rings, slides, and columns. Use the column from the crossroads between the two areas to roof your way over to a slide. Ride the slide down to a river of corruption. Just before you slip into the gloom, jump out to the first in a line of columns.

Use Elika's help to jump to the semicircle of columns that lines the corruption-covered boulevard.

Bound from one column to another to close in on the entrance of the City of Light.

Slide down the ramp at the end of the columns and jump across the banner poles the reach the blue power plate.

City Sights

To enter the City of Light, slide down the edge of the landing in front of the huge black door that leads to the Warrior's lair. Use the blue power plate to arc over the pool of corruption that chokes the city streets and drop down on a long platform orphaned in the murkiness. From here, you can see the Warrior thrashing about the city square. Reaching the city square suddenly turns a lot more dangerous when swirling patches of corruption on the walls explode into masses of black tendrils. They retreat temporarily, giving you a quick chance to safely skirt by them.

CAUTION

ONCE THE TENDRIL TRAP APPEARS, THERE IS NO CALLING IT BACK—IT INFESTS THE REST OF THE CORRUPTED WORLD.

Wait for the tendrils to vanish and then wall run across the stone.

Jump out to the scaffolding around the corner and then look straight down. There are more tendrils below. Wait for those to pull back and then grip fall to the scaffolding closer to the bottom of the wall.

When the tendrils next to the blue power plate recede, wall run and use Elika's magic to escape.

The power plate arcs you across the street to another wall.

RETURN OF THE PRINCE
MOVES IN MYSTERIOUS WAYS
DYNAMIC WORLD
DESERT
RUINED CITADEL
THE VALE
ROYAL PALACE
CITY OF LIGHT
TREE OF LIFE
SECRETS

You automatically grab the fissure in the wall. Creep to the right and watch the rhythm of the tendrils popping out of the wall. When the tendrils retreat, wall run to the blue power plate. Use Elika's magic to bounce into the street to the right.

The walls narrow. There are six tendrils in this alley. The blue power plate slams you into the left wall, so link into a wall run as you land and rush across the receded tendrils. When the corruption on the right wall pulls back, jump across and wall run straight for the blue power plate at the end of the wall. Use it to jump over the corruption river and to a long slide.

Ride the slide as it banks to the right. More tendrils pop out of the walls. As you near the bottom, the tendrils to the left retreat. Jump out and wall run along the vacated tendrils before they reappear.

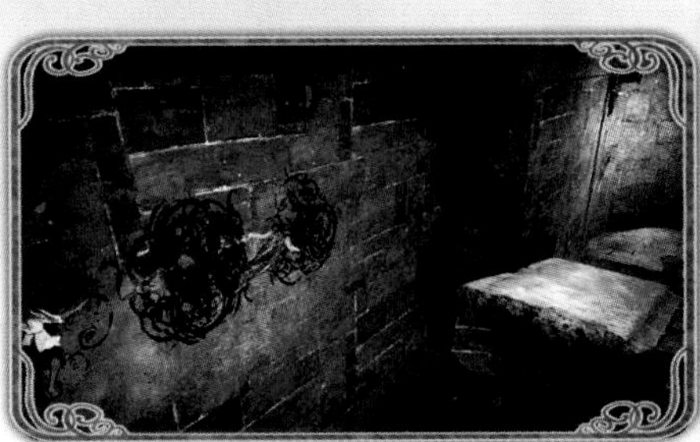

Jump to the adjacent wall when the next trio of tendrils pulls back. Wall run to the right and jump down to another slide just as the tips of the tendrils appear.

At the end of the slide, jump to flat ground and wait for the next set of tendrils to flail and then disappear before wall running to the right.

You must pass through the narrow alleys ahead, but there is nothing to hold onto and there are tendrils on every wall. Wait for the tendrils on the left to vanish and then start your wall run. At the end of the three tendrils, jump to the right wall and wall run. As you run, the tendrils on the adjacent wall pull back. Jump to that wall and wall run to the left. Just as you run out of steam, jump one last time away from the wall. You leap toward the side of a wall you cannot quite see—but at least there is some scaffolding to grab.

Follow the scaffolding along the wall until you reach another series of tendrils.

You are almost to the city square. The tendrils flip and flail on the walls ahead. But they retract and reappear in waves. So as soon as the tendrils closest to you pull back, start wall running. Just as you reach the end of the wall, the tendrils on the opposite side almost disappear—but the tendrils you're running over start to reemerge. Jump off the wall and wall run along the alley as it twists and turns, keeping ahead of the tendrils as they pull back for a few seconds. Whenever you see the curling tips of the tendrils reappear, you must jump away or they will grab you.

Use the blue power plate at the end of the alley to soar over the walls surrounding the city square.

The Warrior

When you finally land inside the city square, the Warrior wastes no time closing in on you. But as he stomps your way, look over his shoulder. Directly behind him is an illuminated alcove with a huge iron gate above it. Since there are no edges in the square to push the Warrior over, you must instead back the Warrior into that alcove and slam him against the wall so hard that the gate falls and traps him.

The Warrior tries to limit your combo options by using Ahriman's Influences. When the Warrior turns blue, you must pull back and keep Elika safe. If you try a combo while the Warrior is bright blue, Elika will be injured. The Warrior also shakes off any weakness after several seconds with a corruption storm. Back away when the black particles swirl around the Warrior and reposition yourself so you can goad the Warrior into following you toward the makeshift prison cell.

TIP

BACK TOWARD THE ALCOVE SO YOU ARE BETWEEN IT AND THE WARRIOR. WHEN THE WARRIOR CLOSES IN, YOU CAN SWITCH POSITIONS BY SLIDING BETWEEN HIS LEGS VIA AN ACROBATIC COMBO.

After slipping between the Warrior's legs, perform a lengthy combo to weaken the Corrupted. Work fast before he can react. Weave Elika's magic into your sword strikes so the Warrior is significantly weakened by the time the combo is complete. The Warrior needs to pop those blue sparks before you can shove him into the alcove and close the gate.

As soon as you see the blue sparks, rush in for another attack.

Tap the attack button repeatedly when you enter into the struggle with the Warrior.

The gate slams to the ground, trapping the Warrior in the cage like a zoo animal. Now, with the Warrior disposed of, quickly have Elika purify the fertile ground so the Corrupted's power over the area cannot find purchase again. Once the purification is complete, the Warrior disappears in a pool of corruption. Now it's time to collect the Light Seeds and escape the city.

Healed

There are two paths into the City of Light. Search both paths to the east and west, as well as the entirety of the city, to collect the 45 Light Seeds.

City of Light

RETURN OF THE PRINCE
MOVES IN MYSTERIOUS WAYS
DYNAMIC WORLD
DESERT
RUINED CITADEL
THE VALE
ROYAL PALACE
CITY OF LIGHT
TREE OF LIFE
SECRETS

After you defeat the Warrior, four Light Seeds appear inside the city square. Collect the Light Seeds and then approach the now-open gate opposite the Warrior's cage. A trail of Light Seeds leads out over the water and through the alleys.

Jump down to the Light Seed just over the water. Let Elika save you, drawing you back up to the city square.

From the exit of the city square, wall run along the right wall and then jump over to the left. Wall run to the blue power plate.

The power plate launches you up to a small platform in the middle of the water. From here, you can reach the entrance of the City of Light and blast open the door that leads to the Warrior's Fortress.

Follow the path to the door. Use the posts and poles in front of you to cross the water and then slide down the tilted platform to pick up a Light Seed. There is another Light Seed directly in front of the black door, right above the blue power plate. From the door, there are three directions you can travel to collect Light Seeds—east, west, and back into the city.

The blue power plate launches you across the water and to a platform. There is a small hole in the platform to your right. Drop into it to grab a Light Seed.

Retrace your steps toward the city square to collect a series of Light Seeds. Without the corruption tendrils, travel is easier—but there are still risks you must take to collect all the Light Seeds. Run to the wall in front of you and jump out. Wall run through the Light Seed.

Jump out to the scaffolding. Scramble straight up to pick up a Light Seed and then grip fall down to the lowest fissure on the wall. Another Light Seed is near the blue power plate. After picking it up, wall run to the blue power plate and bounce across the water. You automatically grab some scaffolding. Wall run to the next blue power plate.

The power plate blasts you up a narrow alley. Run wall through the Light Seed and bounce over to the opposite wall. Wall run to the blue power plate.

As you rush down the slide, steer to the left. Jump out to grab the Light Seed above the tilted platform.

Wall run around the corner, jumping to connect the two moves, to pick up a Light Seed. Jump to the next slide.

At the bottom of the slide, jump out and wall run down the alley for a Light Seed. Jump to the scaffolding and crawl along it to reach a Light Seed.

Keep wall running down the alley, bouncing from wall to wall.

Another blue power plate is at the end of the alley, right in front of the city square. Wall run through the Light Seed before using the power plate.

Back at the city entrance, look out to the west to spot more Light Seeds. Run out to the end of the post and jump out to start wall running to the left. Jump away from the wall run and slide down to a series of poles. Swing around the poles and drop to a post. Wall run up the wall from the post to fetch a Light Seed.

There is another pair of Light Seeds above the water on a balcony. Jump to the post between the two narrow walls south of the City of Light entrance. Scramble up the wall and jump back and forth to reach the Light Seeds on the balcony.

West Path

Jump out to the wall next to the platform. Scramble up it to reach the Light Seed.

RETURN OF THE PRINCE
MOVES IN MYSTERIOUS WAYS
DYNAMIC WORLD
DESERT
RUINED CITADEL
THE VALE
ROYAL PALACE
CITY OF LIGHT
TREE OF LIFE
SECRETS

There is a loop of slides and poles that stretches to the crossroads between the City of Light and the Queen's Tower. Steer to the left of the slide as you jump down and then loop around the poles to reach the platform where the two paths meet.

Turn around from the platform and jump out to the post. Turn to the wall and scramble up it to pick up the Light Seed. Jump out to the next post and then hang straight down. Drop down to the lower post to pick up two more Light Seeds.

East Path

Start at the post hanging over the water. Run to the end of the post and jump over to the wall in front of you. Wall run along that wall and then jump to the right to keep moving thought the alley. There are two posts lashed together just ahead, so keep bounding from one wall to the other to reach the posts. Once you reach them, face the wooden panel and scramble up it. A Light Seed is directly above you.

Jump between the two walls to reach the Light Seed on the ledge above the posts.

Wall run around the corner and then jump out to the slide. Stick to the center of the slide to pick up the Light Seed and then jump out to scramble up to the next platform.

From the platform, look west. There is a loop of columns and slides you must cross to collect the series of dangling Light Seeds. Jump down on the slide directly ahead of you and ride it to the bottom, collecting the Light Seed. Double jump out to the broken column hanging from the ceiling.

Climb up the column and turn so your back is against the Light Seed on the roof. Roof over to the ring to grab the Light Seed and then link to another roof scramble. You drop down on a slide with a Light Seed. At the bottom of the slide, jump to the crossroads platform between the City of Light and Tower of Ormazd.

Face the City of Light and jump on the left column. Roof over to the ring and then keep scrambling to shuffle through two Light Seeds. You drop down on a slide.

Double-jump at the bottom of the slide to reach a set of columns. Jump from one column to the next collecting the Light Seed between them.

Jump to the slide at the far end of the line of columns. There is a Light Seed on the slide. At the end of the slide, jump off to the wall and wall run to a series of poles.

Jump to the stable post between the poles. Wall run up to the yellow power plate to grab the Light Seed. If you have activated the yellow power plates, use Elika's magic to blast off.

Yellow Power Plate

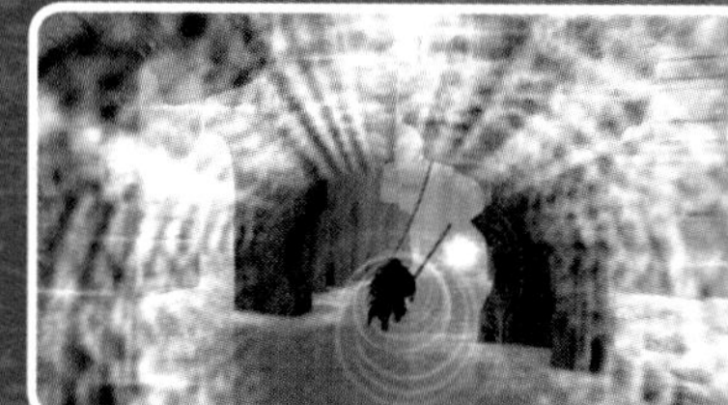

The yellow power plate blasts you through a quick tour of the city. The route swoops low over the water. As you fly, steer into the Light Seeds. But watch out for obstacles like posts and walls. If you slam into any of these, you are returned to the yellow power plate and must start the trip all over again to collect the rest of the Light Seeds. There are four Light Seeds on this flight.

Warrior's Fortress

RETURN OF THE PRINCE
MOVES IN MYSTERIOUS WAYS
DYNAMIC WORLD
DESERT
RUINED CITADEL
THE VALE
ROYAL PALACE
CITY OF LIGHT
TREE OF LIFE
SECRETS

After purifying all of the fertile ground in the City of Light, the Prince and Elika must take the fight directly to the Warrior. The Corrupted is defending his fortress to the north of the City of Light, waiting for the Prince to arrive. To the Warrior, it is a bittersweet challenge. The Prince is the mortal enemy of his master, Ahriman. But the Prince also represents a sliver of salvation. To die with honor would finally put the Warrior's corrupted soul to rest.

Approach

To reach the Warrior, you must navigate through a series of blue and green power plates. After passing through the black doors, walk out to the end of the post and jump to the green power plate. Steer to the right to line up with the next green power plate and then activate with Elika's magic. The ruins of the fortress force you to dodge rocks and debris as you stomp along the surface.

> **CAUTION**
>
> If you bump into any rocks or fixtures, you must start the whole approach over from the beginning.

Use the blue power plate at the top of the wall to launch to a green power plate. Hold the magic button so you wall run as soon as you land.

The green power plate propels you along the fortress walls. Dodge the rocks as the wall curves to the right.

A blue power plate at the end of the wall blasts you up to a wooden platform. If you fall after this, Elika brings you back to this platform.

Wall run out to the green power plate. The magic propels you along the wall, defiant of gravity. Follow the trail as it spins to the left.

The next green power plates push you along archways. Steer along the curves to keep from falling into the corruption below. There is a blue power plate at the end of the green power plate sequence that pushes you over the sea of corruption and toward the outer wall of the Warrior's Fortress.

Climb the wall below the green power plate. Follow the trail to the top as it curves to the left.

The blue power plate at the end of the trail sends you flying down into the Warrior's sanctum.

Final Showdown

The Warrior rises from the ground, covered in corruption. The corruption recedes from the Warrior and settles at the edges of the platform. There is little empty space to push the Warrior off the platform, save for a single naked patch of ground. To defeat the Warrior once and for all, the Prince must back the Warrior up to that exposed edge and attack with all his might, using the power of Elika's magic to shove the Corrupted to his doom.

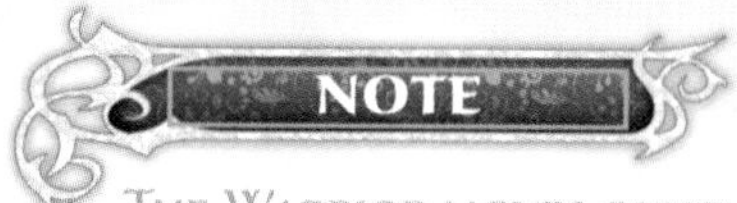

NOTE

The Warrior moves quite a bit in this battle—mostly away from the exposed ground you need to push him against.

Work to lure the Warrior to the exposed ground, but never back down from a fight. In fact, if the Warrior gets too far away from the edge, it's useful to push him into the corruption that lines the arena. Weaken the Warrior with an acrobatic combo and then shove him to the corruption. Repeatedly tap the attack button to tip the Warrior into the corruption. He regains his strength as a result, but he also moves back toward the middle of the arena.

Exchange blows with the Warrior, deflecting his attacks as you position yourself with your back to the exposed edge. When the Warrior closes in, start your acrobatic combo. Slide between the Warrior's legs to change places. Now that the Warrior has his back the edge, finish the combo to weaken him. When you see the blue sparks, rush in and attack to start the struggle.

CAUTION

You have only a second or two after weakening the Warrior to start the struggle. Otherwise, he surrounds himself with a cloud of corruption particles to keep you at arm's length while he heals.

The Warrior can grab you in his giant hands. As he tries to crush you, repeatedly tap the on-screen button to wrench free of his vice-like grip.

After freeing yourself, you climb around the Warrior's body, dishing out attacks. Tap the buttons displayed on-screen to hit the Warrior. If you complete the sequence successfully, you weaken the Warrior.

The struggle at the edge is not easy. Really hammer the attack button to knock the Warrior off balance and out of the arena.

The Warrior slips, but grabs the edge of the arena. Elika walks up to the Warrior as he hangs on. She reaches out to purify the Warrior and release his spirit. This was almost too easy. Why is this Corrupted giving up without a real fight? That's when the Warrior pushes away from the ledge and drops into the bubbling lava and corruption below. He means to deny you your victory.

After you watch the Warrior fall, the ground begins to shake. The arena cracks and tilts. With nothing to hold on to, the Prince and Elika slide off the edge of the platform. Fortunately, they land on a small slab of stone in the middle of the corruption.

Last Stand

They aren't alone for very long. The Warrior erupts from the corruption. He's consumed by both fire and his own rage. There is no way to attack the Warrior when he's covered with flames. The Prince and Elika must keep back and find a way to eliminate the Warrior without touching him.

The Warrior is very aggressive as he stalks you around the small arena. But check out his health meter. It's dropping. The fire is slowly killing him, so maintain your distance and let him die.

RETURN OF THE PRINCE
MOVES IN MYSTERIOUS WAYS
DYNAMIC WORLD
DESERT
RUINED CITADEL
THE VALE
ROYAL PALACE
CITY OF LIGHT
TREE OF LIFE
SECRETS

While dodging the Warrior around the arena, watch the edges. The platform is crumbling, reducing the size of the arena with every passing second. The less room you have to move, the easier it is for the Warrior to strike you. If the Warrior hits you, you will suffer great injury. But far worse is if the Warrior slams you again while you're hurt. If you fail to tap the button to make Elika save you at the last second, the Warrior hammers you. While you recover from your near-death experience, the Warrior actually gains back some health.

TIP

Use the dodge button to move quickly. Just walking the arena will not keep you out of the Warrior's reach.

Keep dodging to the side, rolling away from the Warrior as he stomps after you.

When the Warrior's health bar empties, he collapses to the ground. Elika can now safely approach the fallen Corrupted and set him free. With a light touch on his head, Elika releases his spirit. The corruption is completely blasted out of the City of Light. The sun is restored to the heavens. It is now time to leave the City of Light behind and seek out more fertile ground in the kingdom.

Tree of Life

Final Battle

All four of Ahriman's Corrupted have been purified. Their tortured spirits are free to slip into the afterlife without the burden of Ahriman's treachery. With each saved soul, Ahriman's hold over the world has weakened. And now that his four grotesque anchors have been cut, it is time for the Prince and Elika to strike at the heart of Ahriman inside the temple of the Tree of Life. This final battle against the root of evil will not only test the Prince's skills, but also teach him the ultimate lesson about love and sacrifice. What if the fate of the world relied on having the strength to live with a broken heart?

Temple

After defeating the fourth of the Corrupted, Elika announces to the Prince that they can now take the fight directly to Ahriman back at the temple of the Tree of Life. Whether you use the teleport skill to instantly warp to the temple or clamber through the paths, grabbing any remaining Light Seeds before you reach your destination, you must be ready for the full terror of Ahriman. The dark god will not go back into his prison without a fight, and in the history of wars between gods and men, the former have an imposing track record.

NOTE

If you want to finish your Light Seed collection, do so before going to fight Ahriman because if you manage to best the god, you can no longer visit the four regions of the world.

When you return to the temple, run up the stairs and approach the giant doors. The doors are sealed and give no indication of opening, but trust your instincts and the powers of Ormazd. Although the God of Light failed to rein in his evil brother's power when they shared this realm, his magic is still powerful enough to get you close enough to Ahriman to fight him. Walk into the sealed door. Ormazd's magic allows you to pass through the door and into a magical world. You must successfully activate the series of power plates in this magic world to push through the thick corruption that protects Ahriman. If you survive the sequence, you emerge inside the temple and at the foot of Ahriman.

CAUTION

You must complete this sequence without falling. Because there are no stable platforms to stand on except for the landing next to the first power plate, if you miss a plate, you are transported all the way back to the beginning of the course.

The course begins on a ledge in front of a blue power plate. Wall run to the power plate.

As soon as you touch the next wall, use the rings to link together four wall runs so that you reach the next blue power plate.

Hold the magic button and press the left control stick to the left so that you wall run to the red power plate as soon as you touch the wall.

TIP

Keep the magic button held after every flight so that you are ready with a wall run whenever you land. If you accidentally tap the jump button when you land, you'll kick off the wall and have to start the course over.

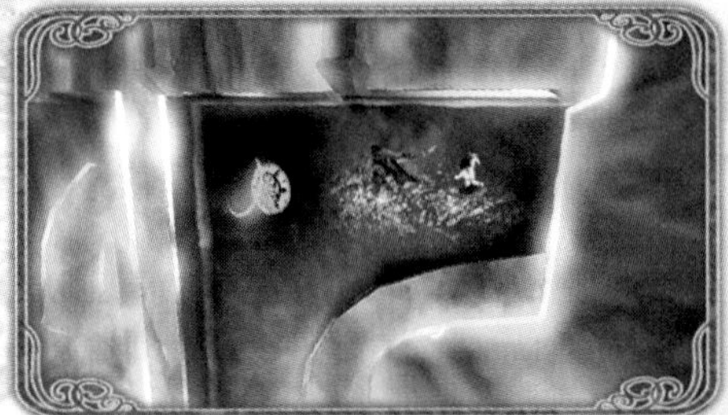

The power plate launches you through the air. When you land, wall run to the left to activate a green power plate.

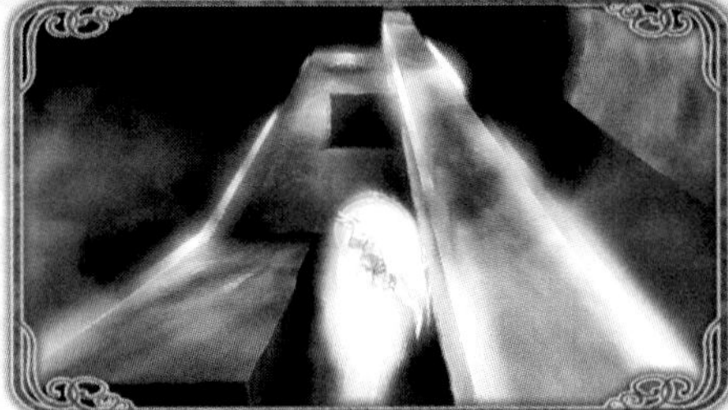

Dodge the blocks sticking out of the wall as you climb to the next power plate.

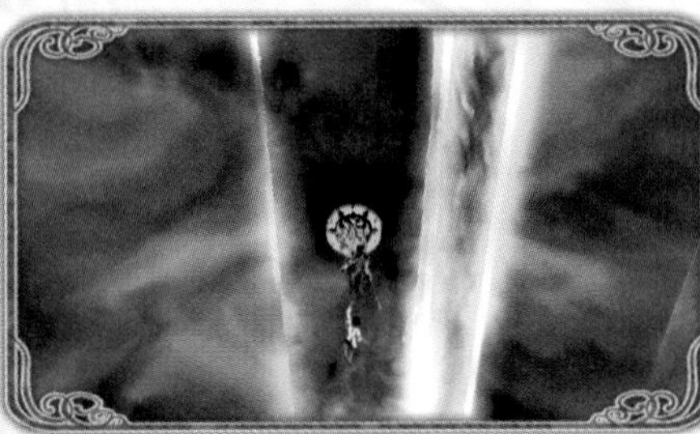

Two red power plates bounce you over to another green power plate. Wall run up to the green power plate so that you don't fall.

Avoid the blocks as you climb to the next green power plate.

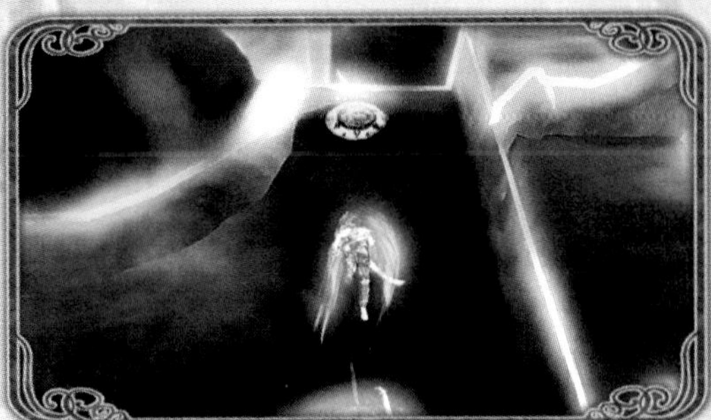

The green power plate at the end of the trail leads to a yellow plate.

RETURN OF THE PRINCE
MOVES IN MYSTERIOUS WAYS
DYNAMIC WORLD
DESERT
RUINED CITADEL
THE VALE
ROYAL PALACE
CITY OF LIGHT
TREE OF LIFE
SECRETS

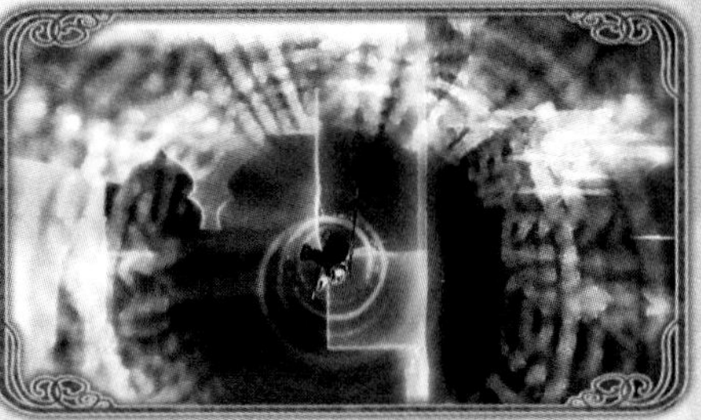

While flying through the air, get ready to dodge three walls in quick succession. In this order, dodge to the left, then up, and then duck down.

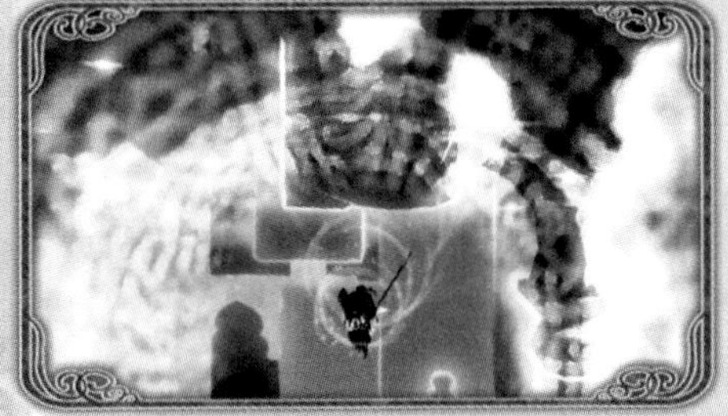

Another set of three obstacles appears later in the flight. Dodge down first, then right, and finally to the left.

Steer to the right as you approach the window in the tower to avoid crashing into the wall.

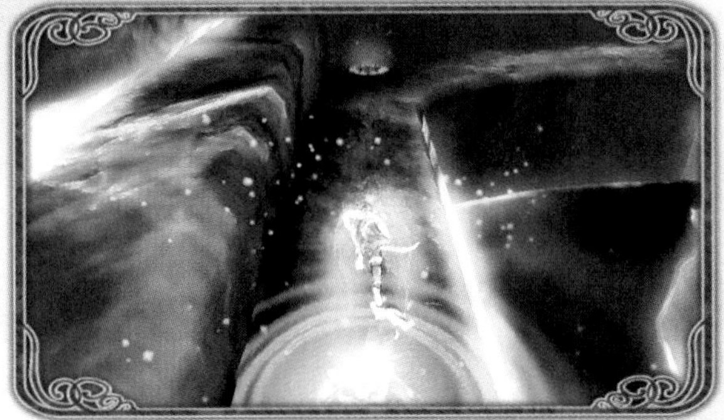

You land on a green power plate. This sends you climbing straight for another green power plate.

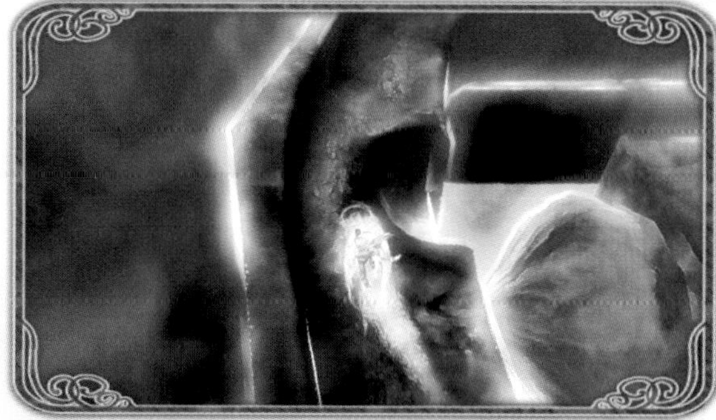

Keep to the left as you climb around an arch after activating the second green power plate. There is another green power plate on the far side of the arch.

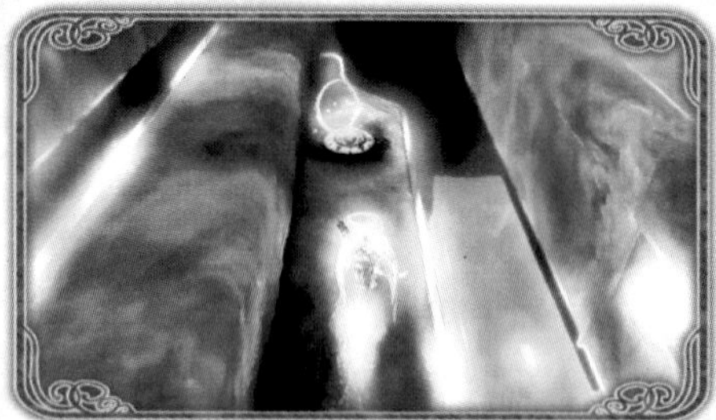

This power plate marches you directly to a yellow power plate.

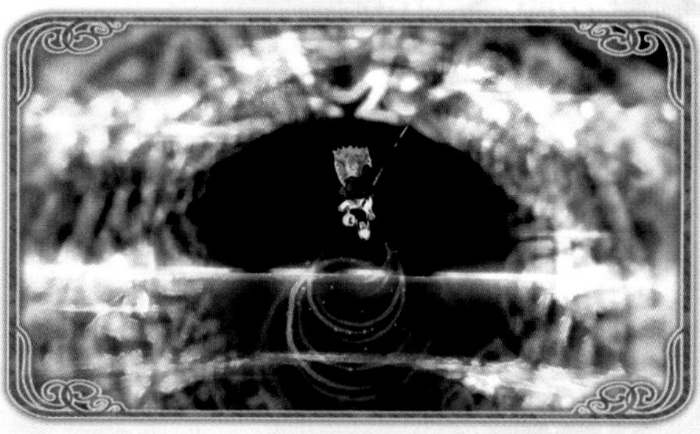

The yellow power plate blasts you into the air. You fly harmlessly between a series of columns before shooting skyward. Dodge up to avoid an archway as you ascend.

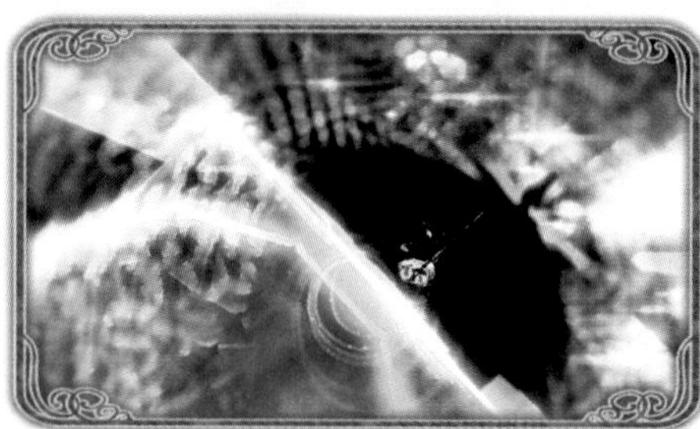

When you scream back down, dodge to the upper right to avoid a tower.

You land on a wall, so have the button held down and run to the right as soon as you touch down. Jump to the adjacent wall.

Use the ring to link another wall run so that you can reach the red power plate to the right.

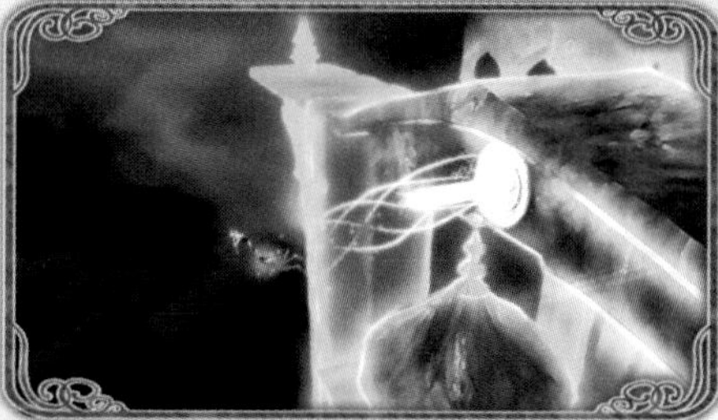

Bounce off another red power plate.

Then you must wall run to a ring, and link to another wall run. Then kick to the adjacent wall, run along it, and use the next ring. If you link it up correctly, you can then wall run to the last power plate in this course.

The blue power plate propels you to a platform in front of a glowing door. Walk into the light to enter the temple and confront the scourge of Ahriman.

The Mourning King

After stepping through the door, you can see the fertile ground at the heart of the temple. If Elika can reach that sacred soil and save it, she can resurrect the Tree of Life and bury Ahriman back under the temple. Unfortunately, that plan is interrupted by a vaguely familiar face. The Mourning King has been completely consumed by Ahriman's corruption—nothing of Elika's father remains.

RETURN OF THE PRINCE
MOVES IN MYSTERIOUS WAYS
DYNAMIC WORLD
DESERT
RUINED CITADEL
THE VALE
ROYAL PALACE
CITY OF LIGHT
TREE OF LIFE
SECRETS

Elika is devastated to see her father so transformed. But sympathy for the man will not defeat him. You must engage the Mourning King in one last battle. Maybe a shred of his soul can be salvaged from his poisoned body?

The Mourning King is aggressive. He starts the battle by attacking, so be ready to deflect his initial blows and try to slip in a counterattack.

If you can land an attack, immediately start a combo. Use Elika's magic to keep the Mourning King reeling. Keep the chain going as long as you can before bringing it to a close with a sword strike.

Watch for the Mourning King to undergo all of Ahriman's Influences. When the Mourning King is enveloped by blue light, keep Elika back. If she attacks while the Mourning King is blue, she will be injured. While she recovers, your combo options are limited. If the king is cloaked in black but yellow sparks jump from his torso, deflect and attack and then counter with a lift.

Well, maybe there's nothing good left under that corruption after all.

CAUTION

The Mourning King spits corruption that blocks your view. Guard while the screen is obscured. Unless, of course, you're feeling lucky and can time a sword attack blind. If you land a blow, the inky gloom disappears.

The Mourning King uses the same spell as the Concubine to confuse you. If the king explodes in pink, back away! If the spell reaches your eyes, you controls are temporarily reversed.

Back off when the Mourning King quakes and the air around him is full of corruption. There is no attack that can break through this, so keep your distance until it subsides.

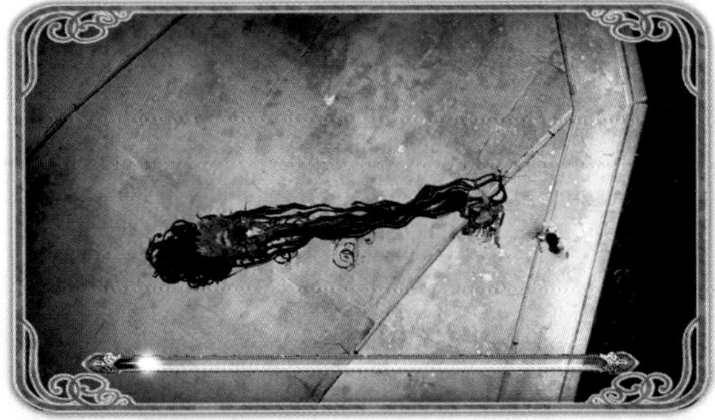

The Mourning King sometimes lashes out with corruption tendrils. Repel these attacks by pressing the buttons that appear on-screen.

Keep hammering the Mourning King with combos whenever possible. The longer the chain of successful moves, the more damage you inflict. While you should never pass up quick hits against the king because every slash helps, victory comes to those who really nail powerful chains.

After you zero out the king's health meter, he finally crumples in defeat. But a corrupted soul is hard to kill.

Racked with guilt and torn to shreds by Ahriman's corruption, the Mourning King—or what's left of him—turns away from his daughter and hurls himself into the poisonous filth that surrounds Ahriman's pit. The king's soul will never be at rest. But at least he can no longer hurt his little girl.

Ahriman

There is no time to rest after defeating the Mourning King. Ahriman has lost his last servant, leaving the god no choice but to finally rise from the corruption and fight the Prince and Elika himself. The macabre face of Ahriman bursts from the pool of darkness. His mouth opens, revealing a core made of the same energy that pulses from fertile ground. How could Ahriman possibly be powered by a similar force? And what will it take to extinguish that light forever?

To defeat Ahriman, you must reach three patches of fertile ground like the one you spotted when you first entered the temple. However, they are placed around the temple walls and there is no floor. You must scramble along the walls, using vines and rings to circle the room, and close in on the fertile ground. Ahriman fights back by raising the corruption in the hopes of swallowing you whole. However, if you can reach a power plate just as the poison rises, you cannot be hurt.

Frustrated by your ability to hide within the protection of Ormazd's magic, Ahriman will also lash out with giant fists. You must always be on the move to avoid those fists. If you pause, even for a second, Ahriman will strike and punch you off the wall.

NOTE

You see this sequence through Ahriman's eyes, which makes it difficult sometimes to spot the power plates. They are the bright spots on the wall. Aim for those and you will be safe when the corruption comes.

Fertile Ground 1

Wall run to the right and climb through the vines to reach the power plate. Stay there until the corruption rises and subsequently subsides. Once the poison drops back down, continue climbing along the vines to the right and then wall run to the fissure.

Scramble along the fissure to the right, never slowing down lest Ahriman pummel you with one of his colossal fists.

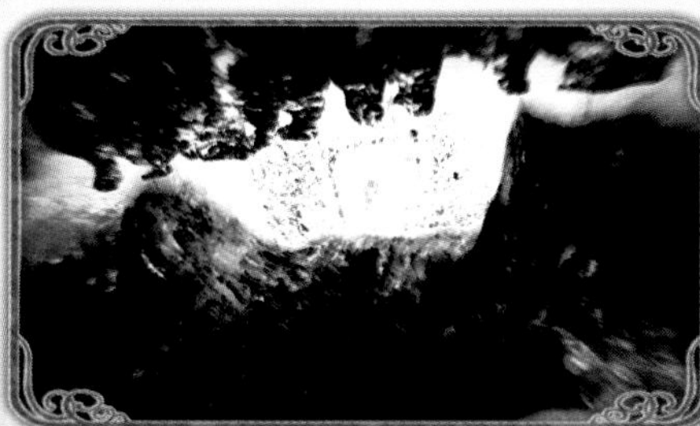

Wall run from the end of the fissure to another patch of vines. Keep crawling to the right, closing in on another power plate. As you get close, the corruption bubbles and pops. It's about to rise, so hurry into position.

When the corruption drops back down, wall run to the platform with the fertile ground. Run into the center of the fertile ground and repeatedly tap the magic button so Elika can purify the area.

Fertile Ground 2

Wall run away from the purified fertile ground and into a patch of vines. Ahriman lashes out with his fist as you leave the fertile ground, so make sure you do not pause. Crawl across the first vine patch, wall run to the next, and then climb up to the power plate.

RETURN OF THE PRINCE
MOVES IN MYSTERIOUS WAYS
DYNAMIC WORLD
DESERT
RUINED CITADEL
THE VALE
ROYAL PALACE
CITY OF LIGHT
TREE OF LIFE
SECRETS

As the corruption subsides, wall run to the right again. You must use the series of rings to negotiate around the outcropping. Press the gauntlet button as you touch each ring so you do not fall. After the third ring, wall run to a fissure and grab on to it.

Climb up the vines to reach the next power plate and avoid the corruption.

Now, use the next four vine fields to crawl between two patches of corruption on the wall. Wall run through the narrow bit of unaffected wall between the four vines. After the four-vine patch, run out and use the ring to propel yourself into another collection of vines.

Wait on the next power plate to avoid the rising corruption and then wall run to the next patch of fertile ground.

Fertile Ground 3

After Elika purifies the second patch of fertile ground, Ahriman recoils. He puts up his hands to guard against the power of the sacred soil and Elika's magic. His distorted vision even clears for a few seconds, giving you a clear view of the path to the next power plate. Climb along the lengthy collection of vines and then wall run to the power plate.

Wall run away from the vines next to the plate and use the ring to push toward the next series of vines.

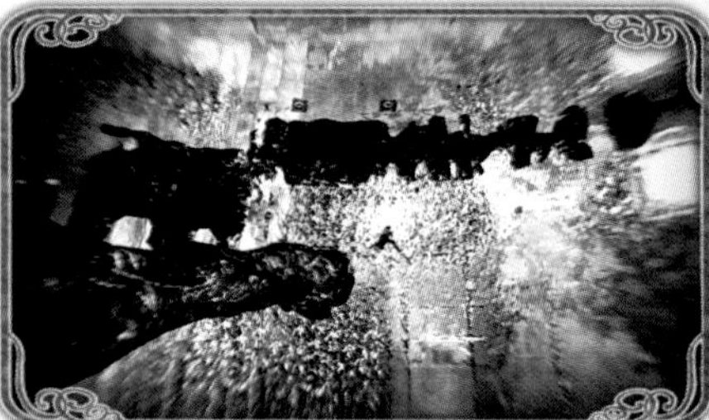

Climb up the vine. Scramble up the blank stretch of wall between the two sets of vines.

There is another power plate to the right. Wall run to it.

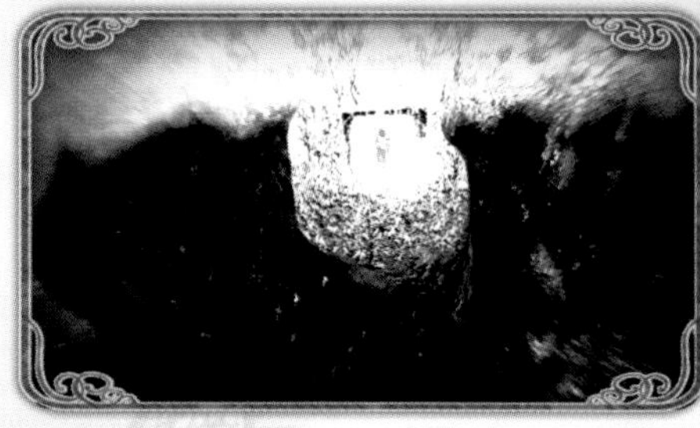

Wall run to the ring and then run to the solid ledge. The fertile ground is directly above you, but the lip of the platform keeps you from being able to scramble up to it. Instead, run along the ledge and then use the next ring to reach a patch of vines that surrounds a power plate.

After surviving the rising corruption again, use the vines to close in on what looks like another solid ledge. Wall run to it.

The ledge is anything but solid. As you run along it, pieces of it crumble under your feet. Jump over the gaps in the ledge as they appear. At the end of the ledge, jump to the wall and run along it to reach another patch of vines. Bound between the two rings on the wall to close in on another power plate.

After hanging on the power plate to survive the belching corruption, wall run out to the two rings and then dash to the third patch of fertile ground. Purify it.

After purifying the third patch of fertile ground, Ahriman is severely weakened. Elika must now strike at his core. Use the red power plates above the fertile ground to launch into the heart of Ahriman.

It's difficult for the Prince to see what Elika is doing through the frenzied air inside the temple. She appears to be using some sort of magic to seal the dark god. But where is this magic coming from? Only when it's too late does the Prince realize Elika's gambit, her sacrifice. Because the Mourning King used the power of Ahriman to bring his daughter back from the dead, part of the magic that bound Ahriman was inside her. Her life was being unnaturally extended. And to seal Ahriman back in the underworld and give birth to a new Tree of Life, Elika must give back what isn't really hers—life.

From Elika's death, the Tree of Life is renewed and Ahriman is sealed in. Order is restored. With a heavy heart, you pick up Elika's body. You must carry her out of the temple and to the altar just beyond the main gate. Once there, you set down her body.

Aftermath

After placing Elika's body on the altar, the Prince looks out across the desert. Four new Trees of Life are sprouting. These saplings represent a renewal of life for the Ahuras. The royal line is dead, but through the sacrifice of the princess, the world is given a second chance. The Prince fulfilled his promise to Elika to help her free her lands of Ahriman's dreadful corruption and lives to see the new day dawn.

But what good is a restored paradise without love?

What good is life without love?

And that's when the Prince makes the most selfish decision of his entire life....

CAUTION

If you're a fan of happy endings, you may want to stop playing right about now.

The Prince decides he does not want to live his life without Elika. There is one way to restore her life force—and that's to follow in the path of the Mourning King and cut down all four new Trees of Life.

Cross the desert and clamber up to each of the four saplings. Use the columns around the fertile ground to ascend to the platform with the new Tree of Life. Then cleave each trunk with your sword. With each destroyed sapling, the skies darken and the ground turns rotten. After all four trees have been chopped down, return to the altar.

The door to the temple is open again. Enter the temple and run to the Tree of Life atop Ahriman's prison.

Hack the Tree of Life with your sword.

Destroying the Tree of Life inside the temple gifts you with the essence of life. Carry it out of the temple interior and approach the altar.

When the Prince reaches the altar, he gives the essence to Elika. The princess wakes, sitting straight up, gasping for air. She looks at the Prince, sad. Her sacrifice was the price for the world, but now unnatural life has returned to her.

Love has returned to the Prince. Love has returned to Elika.

And hell has returned to earth.

Secrets

There are many badges of honor to win for playing *Prince of Persia*. Whether you play the Xbox 360 or PLAYSTATION 3 edition of the game, you have a host of special goals to aim for, such as finding special views in the game or defeating enemies under specific conditions. Here are all the Achievements and Trophies you can win in *Prince of Persia*, plus tips and tricks for banking some of the trickier ones.

Xbox 360 Achievements

Achievement	Description	Points
First Meet	Encounter Elika	10
Save Me Please	First time Elika saves you	10
All the Basics	Complete the opening scene in the canyon	10
Explorer	Use compass for the first time	10
Beginner Healer	Heal your first fertile ground	30
Master Healer	Heal all fertile ground	50
Hunter's End	Kill the Hunter in his lair	20
Warrior's End	Kill the Warrior in his lair	20
Concubine's End	Kill the Concubine in her lair	20
Alchemist's End	Kill the Alchemist in his lair	20
Ahriman's End	Kill Ahriman	30
Explorer	Explore every area of every region	20
Block Master	Block 50 attacks	20
Deflect Master	Deflect 20 attacks	20
Biggest Combo	Do 14 combo hits in a fight	20
Be Gentle with Her	Finish the game with less than 10 saves from Elika	100
Breaker	Use an enemy to break something	10
Against the Wall	Win a struggle	10
Race Ruined Citadel	Go from the fertile ground in Sun Temple to the fertile ground in Windmills in 8 minutes	10
Race Observatory	Go from the fertile ground in Construction to the fertile ground in Heaven's Stair in 7 minutes	20
Race Royal Palace	Go from the fertile ground in Royal Gardens to the fertile ground in Coronation Hall in 6 minutes	30
Race City of Light	Go from the fertile ground in Tower of Ahriman to the fertile ground in City of Light in 5 minutes	40

Achievement	Description	Points
Warrior Special	Dodge 20 Warrior attacks in one fight	20
Hunter Special	Deflect the Hunter 5 times in one fight	20
Alchemist Special	Defeat the Alchemist without using the acrobatic button	20
Concubine Special	Defeat the Concubine without using the gauntlet	20
Light Seeds Rookie	Collect 100 Light Seeds	10
Light Seeds Beginner	Collect 200 Light Seeds	10
Light Seeds Casual	Collect 300 Light Seeds	10
Light Seeds Novice	Collect 400 Light Seeds	10
Light Seeds Collector	Collect 500 Light Seeds	10
Light Seeds Chief	Collect 600 Light Seeds	10
Light Seeds Veteran	Collect 700 Light Seeds	10
Light Seeds Expert	Collect 800 Light Seeds	10
Light Seeds Hardcore	Collect 900 Light Seeds	10
Light Seeds Master	Collect 1001 Light Seeds	50
Speed and Peace	Kill 10 soldiers before they spawn	10
Thrower	Push 10 soldiers to their deaths	10
Assassin View	Find the Assassin View	10
Titanic View	Find the Titanic View	10
Jumper	1,000 co-op jumps	10
Precious Time	Take one minute to think (at the right time)	10
Beginner Listener	Trigger one dialogue with Elika	10
Good Listener	Trigger more dialogues with Elika	10

Achievement	Description	Points
Perfect Listener	Trigger a lot of dialogue with Elika	10
Climber	Find the highest point in the world	10
Diver	Find the lowest point in the world	10
Speed Demon	Finish the game in less than 10 hours	10
Gone Baby Gone	Complete the game	80
Combo Specialist	Unleash every combo in the game	50
	Total Gamerscore Points	1000

PLAYSTATION 3 Trophies

Trophy	Description	Value
First Meet	Encounter Elika	Bronze
Save Me Please	First time Elika saves you	Bronze
All the Basics	Complete the opening scene in the canyon	Bronze
Explorer	Use compass for the first time	Bronze
Beginner Healer	Heal your first fertile ground	Silver
Master Healer	Heal all fertile ground	Gold
Hunter's End	Kill the Hunter in his lair	Bronze
Warrior's End	Kill the Warrior in his lair	Bronze
Concubine's End	Kill the Concubine in her lair	Bronze
Alchemist's End	Kill the Alchemist in his lair	Bronze
Ahriman's End	Kill Ahriman	Silver
Explorer	Explore every area of every region	Bronze
Block Master	Block 50 attacks	Bronze
Deflect Master	Deflect 20 attacks	Bronze
Biggest Combo	Do 14 combo hits in a fight	Bronze
Be Gentle with Her	Finish the game with less than 10 saves from Elika	Gold
Breaker	Use an enemy to break something	Bronze
Against the Wall	Win a struggle	Bronze
Race Ruined Citadel	Go from the fertile ground in Sun Temple to the fertile ground in Windmills in 8 minutes	Bronze
Race Observatory	Go from the fertile ground in Construction to the fertile ground in Heaven's Stair in 7 minutes	Bronze
Race Royal Palace	Go from the fertile ground in Royal Gardens to the fertile ground in Coronation Hall in 6 minutes	Silver
Race City of Light	Go from the fertile ground in Tower of Ahriman to the fertile ground in City of Light in 5 minutes	Silver
Warrior Special	Dodge 20 Warrior attacks in one fight	Bronze
Hunter Special	Deflect the Hunter 5 times in one fight	Bronze
Alchemist Special	Defeat the Alchemist without using the acrobatic button	Bronze
Concubine Special	Defeat the Concubine without using the gauntlet	Bronze
Light Seeds Rookie	Collect 100 Light Seeds	Bronze
Light Seeds Beginner	Collect 200 Light Seeds	Bronze
Light Seeds Casual	Collect 300 Light Seeds	Bronze
Light Seeds Novice	Collect 400 Light Seeds	Bronze
Light Seeds Collector	Collect 500 Light Seeds	Bronze
Light Seeds Chief	Collect 600 Light Seeds	Bronze
Light Seeds Veteran	Collect 700 Light Seeds	Bronze
Light Seeds Expert	Collect 800 Light Seeds	Bronze
Light Seeds Hardcore	Collect 900 Light Seeds	Bronze
Light Seeds Master	Collect 1001 Light Seeds	Silver
Speed and Peace	Kill 10 soldiers before they spawn	Bronze
Thrower	Push 10 soldiers to their deaths	Bronze
Assassin View	Find the Assassin View	Bronze
Titanic View	Find the Titanic View	Bronze
Jumper	1,000 co-op jumps	Bronze
Precious Time	Take one minute to think (at the right time)	Bronze
Beginner Listener	Trigger one dialogue with Elika	Bronze
Good Listener	Trigger more dialogues with Elika	Bronze
Perfect Listener	Trigger a lot of dialogue with Elika	Bronze
Climber	Find the highest point in the world	Bronze
Diver	Find the lowest point in the world	Bronze
Speed Demon	Finish the game in less than 10 hours	Bronze
Gone Baby Gone	Complete the game	Gold
Combo Specialist	Unleash every combo in the game	Bronze

RETURN OF THE PRINCE
MOVES IN MYSTERIOUS WAYS
DYNAMIC WORLD
DESERT
RUINED CITADEL
THE VALE
ROYAL PALACE
CITY OF LIGHT
TREE OF LIFE
SECRETS

Breaker

Earn this accomplishment by smashing an enemy, such as one of the Corrupted, into a pillar in any of your showdowns. Many Corrupted fights have pillars in the arena, such as the Hunter and Alchemist, and the Warrior atop the Tower of Ahriman and the Tower of Ormazd. Back your enemy into the pillar while performing a combo and smash the Corrupted into it. Tossing the enemy with a gauntlet move is the easiest way to make this happen.

Biggest Combo

The biggest combo in the game is to string together 14 different attacks. Use the combo table to chart out your preferred combos, starting with a sword hit before segueing into another attack, such as throwing the enemy into the air and then bouncing him around with Elika's magic. Use acrobatics to keep the combo going and then rely on Elika to continue smashing the enemy before you end the combo with either a throw or aerial.

TIP

You need a large arena to pull this off, so try it out at the top of the King's Gate or the first arena in the Hunter's Lair.

Special Views

To earn Titanic View, head to the Machinery Ground of the Vale. Walk out to the tip of the broken ship's bow, right next to the fertile ground.

The Assassin's View is located at the Martyr's Tower in the Ruined Citadel region. To earn this accomplishment, you must first heal the area by defeating the Hunter inside the tower and then cure the fertile ground on the rooftop. Once Martyr's Tower is pure, you can dip back down into the tower to collect Light Seeds. The Assassin's View is on the second-to-top floor of the tower. Step out on to the balcony and then walk to the edge of the post overlooking the lake. When you set your toes against the end of the post, you earn the accomplishment.

Ascending to the very top of the Heaven's Stair will earn the Climber.

The Diver is earned by finding the lowest point in the world. This is actually back at the Tree of Life temple. Step into the small alcove to the left of the temple.

NOTE

To earn the Listener Achievements and Trophies, keep chatting with Elika as you explore each new area of the world. Whenever you see a new sight, initiate a conversation and learn more about the history of the Ahuras, Ahriman, and Elika herself.

The Making of a New Prince

After swinging from the heights of the Windmills to the towers of the City of Light and back, Prima made the most important trip of all in the world of *Prince of Persia* to Montreal, Canada, to visit the studio behind the game. While there, the good people of Ubisoft revealed the deepest secrets of the game to us, and not just secrets about how traps are unlocked. They shared secrets involving the emotional core of the game and how the studio wanted to make *Prince of Persia* bigger than an impressive acrobatic simulation.

Visit

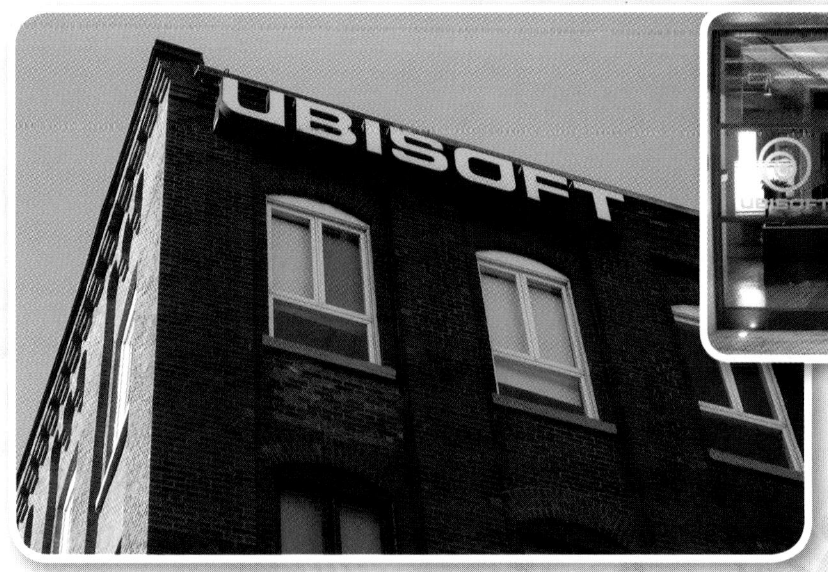

Ubisoft Montreal is housed inside a renovated textile factory, certainly a fitting locatio for a develope building a game from so many unique threads—acrobatics, combat, character development, and gorgeous environments.

Much of the old factory's charm remains inside the studio. Pillars are built out of brick and mortar, crafted by hand instead of machine. Old wooden floors have seen a billion steps over the last century. But no longer does this former mill produce cloth. Now, the output is purely digital. But even if the two products made here are worlds apart, the care and pride of the men and women inside the factory is the same, and that showed in each member of the *Prince of Persia* team we spoke with during our trip.

Producing the Prince

Ben Mattes, producer of *Prince of Persia*, doesn't want to make you cry. But he does want you to feel *something*. As producer of the newest adventure of the most famous Prince in video games, Mattes oversaw not just the creation of a game world, but also the installation of the game's heart: Elika. Mattes sat down with us to talk about the dynamic that exists between the Prince and Elika, how their relationship evolved over the development of the game, and exactly why you will never see a "game over" screen while playing.

Ben Mattes, Producer, Ubisoft

Prima: When you first envisioned this version of *Prince of Persia*, what was the starting point? What was the one idea that you wanted to build upon?

Ben Mattes: Cooperative gameplay between the Prince and an AI-controlled character. We knew from day one basically that was the hook that was going to replace *Sands of Time*. We were going to take a lot of the cool gameplay functionality that the *Sands of Time* brought to the player from the previous game. And we were going to inject those abilities into a human that would be integrated into the story so that you would have both story and character development, and a gameplay connection to this AI-controlled character.

We didn't always know that it was going to be Elika from day one. It took us maybe a couple of months to come to the idea of Elika. We sort of explored the idea of maybe a child or father figure or brother, or something like that. But in the end we decided, well, people like that sort of love interest angle so we'll make it a female.

Prima: And that's what made you decide on Elika, versus a child?

Mattes: Yeah. It came from the knowledge that Farrah as a character worked really well in *Sands of Time* from a storytelling and character-development point of view. So we sor of said, well, let's just build on that. We know that people like the sort of tension and the chemistry between the hero and this female who he's partnering with. So let's play off that but try and make that relationship even stronger and that partnership even stronger.

Prima: There are points in the game when I was surprised that I felt things. I mean, I wasn't sad or devastated. But there was actually palpable tensio with what happens with Elika.

Mattes: Well, I mean, between you and me, that was the intention from day one. It was, "How do we create something that people care about in a video game. In the world of video games, what do people care about?" People don't care about character so much because the one area where I think games are much weaker than film is in the devel-

opment of emotionally significant character art and story events. It's quite difficult to do in video games. You know to make people cry in video games or jump for joy in video games is difficult to do because of a character. It's maybe easy to do for other reasons, but it's difficult to do for character reasons because we still have not mastered the art of making digital avatars act the way that humans can act. I mean, that uncanny value thing is very, very much a significant challenge that the gaming industry has to overcome. So, what we did notice is that people do care about things in video games. Maybe they don't care about people as much, but they care about things.

If you ask a player in *Counterstrike* to describe, you know, how he feels about a particular weapon, he or she might use the word *love*. And they're probably not saying it in the, you know, that typical "I love my wife" sense.

Prima: But I "love" using my rifle.

Mattes: I LOVE using that gun! I LOVE the BFG in *Doom*. I love the chain saw gun. I love the Lancer in *Gears of War*, I love it! It's awesome!

So that when that gun in *Gears of War*, is pulled away from you and you no longer have the Lancer, there's that feeling of loss—there's that feeling of, "Oh … that really sucks!" That, "I am not as powerful now. I am not as happy now because I don't have that weapon."

So, what we wanted to do is to try and take that emotion, for lack of a better word, that feeling, and put it onto a person. So that people would have that feeling of loss, of separation from something that made them feel powerful. And because that thing that made them feel powerful was actually a character, to sort of get confused a little bit about what loss am I feeling here? "Am I feeling loss for the power that this character brings me? Or am I feeling loss for the person that I'm no longer with in the game?" And that was sort of the challenge that we set for ourselves. Because if we can bridge that gap for some people and have them confuse a little bit of the loss of power with the loss of a character, it'll be like we're faking in some way some of the emotions that Hollywood movies are good at eliciting from the audience, but that video games can't do. But replacing it with the video game version of it. Which is, it's not what you passively experience, it's what you actively experience that makes video games so powerful. So, if we can tie an active experience to an emotion, maybe it'll make something strong.

Prima: So, how then did you walk that line, though, because you describe Elika then almost as a thing?

Mattes: Yes, yes. Fair enough.

Prima: How do you cross, how do you walk that line of a thing verses a character?

Mattes: You know, that was one of the hardest challenges of the game. But I think how you walk that line, is you keep on coming back to what role does Elika serve.

I did an interview recently and we spoke for about 45 minutes about Elika, and only Elika, and I said something that they thought was very funny and it's been quoted and kind of bounced around the Internet a lot. Which is, it doesn't really matter to us if you love her. It doesn't really matter to us if you like her. You just can't hate her. You can't hate her. The second you hate Elika, the second you resent Elika, the second you're frustrated with Elika, the whole experience comes tumbling down. Because then suddenly you're going to resent having to use her power, right? You're not going to want her power. You're going to be like "Ugh, I've to do this stupid magic power with this dumb girl." And that's not at all the experience that we want. So, we had to be very careful to make sure that Elika was never a negative. And that was the kind of guiding light that helped us sort of pull together treating Elika as a thing rather than treating her as a person. It helped define her personality; it helped define her abilities; it helped define her game design; it helped define everything about her as this sort of guiding principle: Elika can never be a negative.

So, for example, we said, "If she can never be a negative, that means she can't die." Okay, well, that immediately set certain things about her. Like obviously she has to be magic. Okay, well *boom*. There's one thing that's already answered. She has to have magical powers. In terms of never being a negative, it helped us define her personality: She can't be too strong, but she also can't be too weak. If she's always kind of cowering in the corner, then immediately you're going to feel like you're babysitting her and it's going to be like, "You know, this isn't interesting to me." But if she takes too much initiative, if her personality is too strong, then it feels like she's in charge, she's the heroine and you're kind of following her. I mean, this is a game of a Prince, right, so he's the hero. He's got to be the star.

So, I think in order to come up with that balance between treating Elika as a thing and treating her as a person, we needed guiding lights. We needed sort of core fundamental principles to come back to every time we had a design or personality question to answer.

So, you know, for example, at one point in time we had a design for Elika to explore. If ever you stopped and you idled in a space, Elika would start walking off. And we would set all of these interest points in the world. And she would wander off to some interest point, and she would look at it and she would maybe start talking about it. And, it seemed great on paper. You know it was like, "Oh yeah, it's going to give her all this personality. She's going to feel so real and the world is going to feel so rich because Elika is going to be talking about it, or whatever." And w prototyped it and it was just horrible because she was always wandering off doing stuff. And then, you know, you'd stop, she'd wander off there, you'd start going this way and she wouldn't catch up. She wouldn't be there for you, she'd be off doing something else. So, you kind of had to go back and get her attention and then she would kind of start followin you again. And it was just not at all the kind of gameplay that we wanted which was really that it's the collaboration between the Prince and Elika that's so important.

There were certain features that we prototyped and even partially developed that we ended up cutting because it didn't line up with that sor

of core principle of Elika being only a positive and really helping reinforce for the player that feeling of power and ability in this world.

Prima: And so, you say that you wanted it that you never hated her, but you didn't care if you loved her. The emotional reaction I had, was that I needed her.

Mattes: Yes, well that's great. I mean I couldn't really ask for more. I mean, that is the best possible reaction that we could hope for from people. Because when you need her, when we play with that by having her thrown aside in combat, you feel weakened. And that need, like I said earlier, it kind of blurs the line between needing her for gameplay reasons and almost missing having her around. When we grab her and stick her in certain places, you know with the Concubine, and she gets locked in place, you suddenly have to play levels without her. You feel that separation, you feel that distance. And why we really like that is because we've said from the beginning this isn't a love story and it isn't. I mean this is not a game about the love between the Prince and Elika.

And that was also a very conscious decision on our part because we don't think games can tell love stories very well. I mean, again, it's not a movie, we are not going to get the quality of performance that makes you feel love between characters. But if we can have people feel some of the components of love, like, for example, missing or needing someone, then isn't that somehow more powerful than us telling you through narrative that these two characters are in love? If instead, the player experiences a component of love from that relationship through gameplay and narrative threads, we think that's even more powerful than having us say, "Okay, they're in love; look they kissed. Happy ending kind of

thing. So, the fact that you said you felt like you needed her is really great to hear. It's really something we were aiming for.

Prima: Well, because it's interesting, at some points in the game you take care of her ...

Mattes: Uh-huh.

Prima: But there are other points in the game where she takes care of you.

Mattes: Yeah, they there's certainly a kind of codependence thing there.

Prima: She's certainly a strong character and she makes you stronger for it, but it's not overbearing. The focus is still definitely on the Prince.

Mattes: And that was another sort of balancing act in terms of "How much power do we give her?" Obviously she's magic. So, we have to counterbalance that a lot. For example, in combat, it's all you. She jumps in and she does stuff, but she's basically just the combo extender, and it's really the Prince's fighting that allows them to defeat all of these enemies that are standing in their way. And that's sort of one of the ways that we counterbalance and really reinforce that sort of codependence rather than dependence. They both have strengths in terms of gameplay abilities, but also in terms of personality. I think that makes the pair of them stronger than the sum of their parts. It's the collaboration between them, making them more powerful than either of them could be as individuals, that I think is so interesting about the game.

Prima: Now, Elika feeds into what I think is one of the most interesting aspects of the game: that it is impossible to die.

Mattes: In the traditional video game sense of "Game over. You suck. Would you like to continue? Yes/No. Insert another quarter" kind of death. Yes, there is no game over screen.

Prima: I looked! I tried!

Mattes: Yeah, you cannot get a game over screen in the traditional sense. And, you know I think most people that complain about this right now on the forums, they just don't get it. They think it means there's no challenge in the game because as soon as you fall off something you immediately respawn on that same thing. But the fact of the matter is that game over screens are an archaic leftover of coin-op console arcade days. That's why game over screens were invented—to leech more quarters out of punters in the arcades. And now that gaming has evolved as an art form, as an entertainment medium, I personally find the game over screen to be a real waste. It pulls you out of the immersion; it completely eliminates any sense of flow. It breaks the story. It's an artificial penalty that I think most gamers don't need to have forced upon them anymore. I mean, I know when I've failed in a game. I don't need a game over screen to remind

me that I failed. It's pretty clear that I just fell down a hole. I don't need you to remind me that I fell down a hole. I've already internalized that sense of failure.

And so, we decided that we didn't want to break the immersion. We didn't want to penalize lapsed hard-core gamers or advanced casual gamers or the sort of more beginning action-adventure gamer who might play this game, who if we had a superhard-core death mechanic would give up after 10 minutes because it would just be too difficult for them. And, at the same time—the super hard-core gamers—they never die. That's what defines a superhard-core gamer, they're not going to fall down holes, they're not going to get killed in combat because they're going to be great at the game.

So, we developed all of these ideas, we prototyped all these ideas, we did tons of interviews and research with players and once they understood what our "save me" mechanic is, which is you're not going to actually see a game over screen, but if you fail at any point in time, whether it be in combat or acrobatics, Elika grabs you, she pulls you back to the previous safe ground, which might be 15 ingredients back—ball, run, jump, pole, column, slide, vines—none of those are stable ingredients, so you can't be pulled back safely to any of those. If you have a long acrobatic chain and you fail on the last ingredient right before landing on another platform, Elika's going to pull you all the way back to the previous stable platform. You're going to have redo that acrobatic sequence. It really is like a rewind, you rewind back to a previous stable platform. Except it's got a different coat of paint on it.

So, I personally think that because the media has sort of hooked onto this "there's no death in the game" just as something to talk about in *Prince of Persia*, we're getting a lot of attention. But I think a lot of games are moving in that direction of saying, "You know what? This rolling check point system is really the way to go to make a game that is challenging and yet forgiving, and therefore hopefully will be completed by a larger population of people." And, some people will try and wipe it over with fades to white and fades to black and some people like us will try and integrate it into the gameplay or integrate it into the story, such as Elika catching you and throwing you back onto the previous platform. But I do think that you'll see a lot of people moving in this direction.

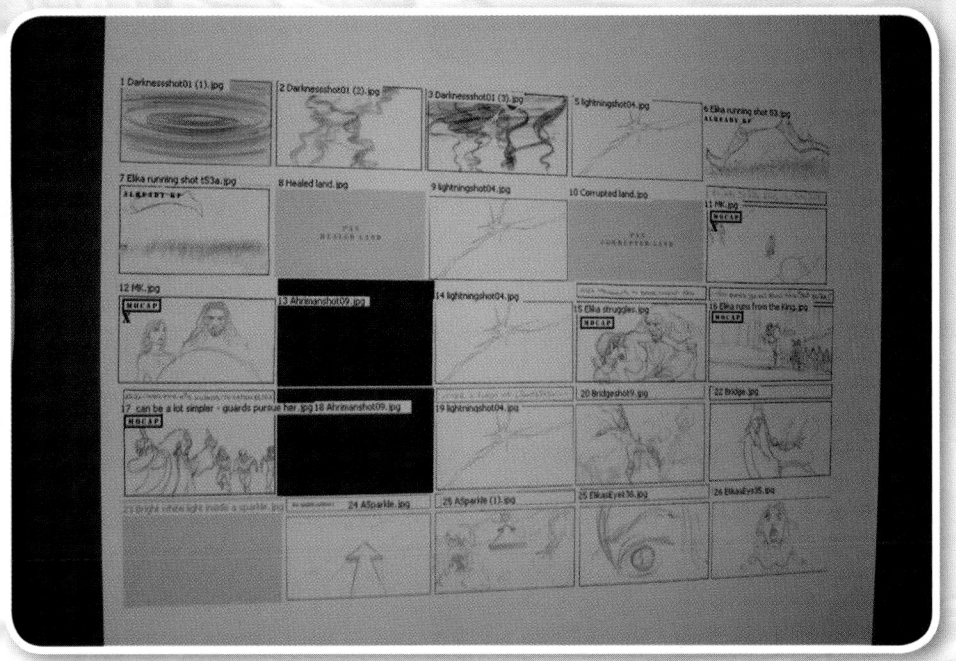

Prima: Elika's power is limitless, right?

Mattes: Yes. There's no meter; there's no mana gauge. Again, same reason as I was discussing before.... The mana gauge mechanic is often something that is very appropriate for the more hard-core gamers who are very good at managing resources, regardless of the type of game they are playing. But it can be very punishing for the non-hard-core gamer. *Sands of Time* is a perfect example. The hard-core gamer—they never ran out of sand, never. They always have sand; somehow they always manage to have sand. The beginning players were constantly running out of sand. They were rewinding too far, they weren't collecting sand powers, etc. So the fact that you had a limited resource of power in that game wasn't particularly rewarding for either group. Because the hard-core [players] were never penalized by the fact that you had a limited number and the casual players were never able to get over the fact that you had a limited number.

So, I'm not saying that a limited number, a limited amount of resources or a limited amount of mana, or whatever, is a bad thing. I think in certain games, in a certain context, it's great. But it's not what we wanted for this game. What we wanted for this game was not the feeling that you had to manage Elika's power. That wasn't what we were looking for.

It's going in line with what we're saying about Elika always being a positive. If ever you ran out of Elika's power right in the middle of a fight and she didn't do what you needed her to do, and you died because of it, you would immediately resent her for it. You wouldn't resent yourself.

I don't think players would say, "I suck for not better managing Elika's power!" I think, players would say, "Ugh, Elika ran out of power! I hate her; I hate the fact that Elika's here. I could have just done this fight on my own!" And then that would have invalidated what we are trying to do with this character.

Prima: Well, there's one thing that you do have to manage in the game, and that's collecting the Light Seeds.

Mattes: There is a collectible component, but not in the typical mana gauge sense. So, yes, the Light Seeds are a crucial component of the game. They are the currency that allows you to purchase the magical powers that unlock further parts of the world. They serve several purposes for us. They gave a value to the healed world, so once you've driven the corruption out, the Light Seeds appear to give value to that area. They create a collection mechanic which is fun. People like collecting stuff. We have beautiful game, with beautiful environments and beautiful little secret areas. So having the Light Seeds is a good way to encourage people to explore the world to its fullest and really see all of the attention to detail that has been invested in this world.

And they allowed us to create an open-world game in that there's true player choice of how the story progresses, etc. But we do it in a structured way, so it's not just, "Okay, here's your sandbox. Here's an overwhelming amount of possibility. Good luck! Let us know when you finish, kind of thing." In our opinion that's one of the weaknesses of some traditional sandbox

games. Unless you are used to sandbox games, they can be very overwhelming. That amount of choice presented to the player can be overwhelming. I have so much opportunity, I just don't know what to do about it. This is too much for me. I am going to go play a linear game because then I know that I am always doing the right thing.

Prima: Do you have a favorite part of the game?

Mattes: Yes, I have favorite things about the game but I also have favorite chunks of gameplay. My favorite thing about the game is our world structure. To me, it is a real masterpiece accomplishment. I'm not claiming that it's a true innovation. I mean people have done network structures before. *Metroid Prime* did it. *Burnout Paradise City* did it. *Burnout Paradise City* is effectively a network of interconnected nodes and sticks. The nodes, intersections, are your choice points where you decide, "Am I going down Mullholland Drive or am I going up Fifth Avenue?" And, once you get on Fifth Avenue, you're on a linear street, very much like our world structure. The circles and the map are the intersections, and once you make a decision, you drive on the highway to your next destination. So, the idea of an open-world game being represented through a network of interconnected nodes and sticks is not necessarily new, but what is good is how we kept the pace of acrobatics flowing so smoothly throughout the entire world, where you can literally navigate from one end of the world to the other in a single uninterrupted acrobatic chain....

Prima: "I'm going to go from the Marshalling Ground all the way over to the Royal Gardens. I want to see if I can do this without falling."

Mattes: And that's just, you know, that's cool. There's no popping, there's no loading, there's just flowing through the world. The environments are changing as you pass from the Ruined Citadel to the Observatory. It goes from kind of red to sort of green and then you move into Royal Palace and it sort of becomes blue and then you move into the City of Light. That's so cool, when you just sort of see the world changing around you as you flow from one end to the other. But also cool is how the game play evolves in different ways depending on the choices you make when you navigate in the world.

Prima: Where does this game exist on the Prince's time line? Or does it not?

Mattes: There isn't a Prince time line. Jordan Mechner uses a phrase to explain it. "It's *A* Prince of Persia, not *THE* Prince of Persia." The original Prince that he created 20 years ago wasn't actually a prince. He was some pauper off of the street who was dropped in a dungeon. That was a *Prince of Persia*. *Shadow in the Flame* had a chronological connection. Those two were related. *Prince of Persia 3D*, new chapter in the book—no connection whatsoever. *Sands of Time*, new chapter in the book—no connection whatsoever. *Sands of Time* was a thick chapter because there were two sequels which were connected. And now there's going to be a Disney movie, that may or may not, you know, tie into that *Sands of Time* trilogy. And then there's a new chapter, which is the one that we're telling now. So, the parallel is really direct with the original influence, which is a *1001 Arabian Nights*, a book of stories where each chapter tells a story of some hero or villain within a universe. None of which are necessarily chronologically connected. You can kind of imagine them all taking place in parallel universes. But it's through reading the entire book that you get the full appreciation for this world of *1001 Arabian Nights*. That's the analogy we use when describing *Prince of Persia*. Each chapter tells of a different young, agile warrior who saves the world by running, jumping, flipping, and fighting. But there's not necessarily a chronological connection of, "I'm your father. You're my son. We're brothers, or whatever." They all sort of take place in alternate time lines.

Fights of Fancy

Despite spending so much time in the air, the Prince also knows just how to get down in the dirt and take down a monster. Thomas Delbuguet, the combat designer for *Prince of Persia*, sat down with us to explain how the Prince can be so elegant when ripping an enemy limb from limb. He even told us how to score the elusive 14-hit combo—the longest combo in the game. And now we're passing his secrets along to you.

Thomas Delbuguet, Combat Designer

Prima: How did the combat system evolve over the last few years?

Thomas Delbuguet: It evolved quite a bit actually. Because when we initially started development on the fight system, we were given a mandate to rethink how fighting was approached in action-adventure games, and more importantly, in *Prince of Persia*. So, we thought long and hard about what we can do to bring a *Prince of Persia* acrobatic feeling to the fight, and keeping it rewarding, and so on. We focused more on these challenges and mini-events where you had to react to situations, just like you might have in the acrobatic sequences where you have to react to the traps that are being released. And more so than just purely mashing: You find the combo that you like doing the most, and destroy the enemy with it. So that was really our approach. Put in a little bit more thought process and puzzling aspects within a fight. So, therefore, when we started developing it, we knew that it was going to be something different. We knew that it was not going to be a traditional fighting system versus/one-on-one type of mechanics. We knew that we needed to keep it open and keep it iterative, so we really allowed the system to grow. We had our main guidelines, our general sets of rules, but our finer rules were determined as we got feedback from players and so on. So it was a very iterative process.

Prima: One of the things that is most interesting not just about the fighting, but the whole game, is the combo tree. How did that come about?

Delbuguet: The combo tree is actually very interesting. And we all shared a lot of frustration with the previous trilogy, where you had all these wonderful combos, they did some really cool stuff, but the players would stick to the same one combo because it worked. It just worked.

I did it all the time. As soon as there was a wall close by, I'd jump on the wall, run it, and *bang*! Blow everything up and then, that was perfect. But it wasn't very strategic. You really had a divide between

the acrobatic fans and the fighting fans, and we want to bring that back together. So, the first thing we looked at was the combo tree. What could we do so that the player doesn't have to go into a list and see all these input sequences and say, "Okay, I got to memorize that one, and memorize that one, and it's got this weird funky name and I've got no idea what it's really going to do." So, we decided to get rid of all of that and just create a branching system, which is very natural.

You don't need to think so much of, "Okay, I'm going to do a heavy attack, and then a light attack." And so on, it's just more of "What do you want to do at this point?" "Okay, I want to attack him." So, you're going to start using your sword and say, "Okay, I want to make my combo longer." So you start using Elika to make your combos longer. "Okay, I want to juggle him in the air." So, you lift him up in the air with your gauntlet and now you can juggle him. And the process continues, using Elika to make your combo longer. And then, you have the acrobatic button, which is used to swap positions.

So, basically what we did is gave a function to each of your inputs, so that they didn't really matter how you would chain them because you would chain them according to what you need to do in that combat sequence or what you want to do in that combat sequence.

Prima: What is the longest combo possible?

Delbuguet: The longest combo possible is a 14-hit combo. We have a new Achievement for it. It can be tricky to pull off and it can be very easy to pull off. It depends on your situation, depends on how you position yourself in the area. It depends on what kind of arena you're in as well, what enemy you're fighting.

Prima: So, how do you do the 14-hit combo?

Delbuguet: My recommendation would most definitely be find the largest arena and try it there. We interrupt your combos when we get to the end, to the perimeter of an arena. And, depending on the nature of the perimeter, you have extra bonuses. If it's a ledge, you have an opportunity to potentially kill your opponent instantly. If it's corruption, well, your opponent is going to take the advantage because it's corruption. If it's a wall, well, it's fair game for both of you. And, basically if you want to pull off the long combos, you've got to be aware of where

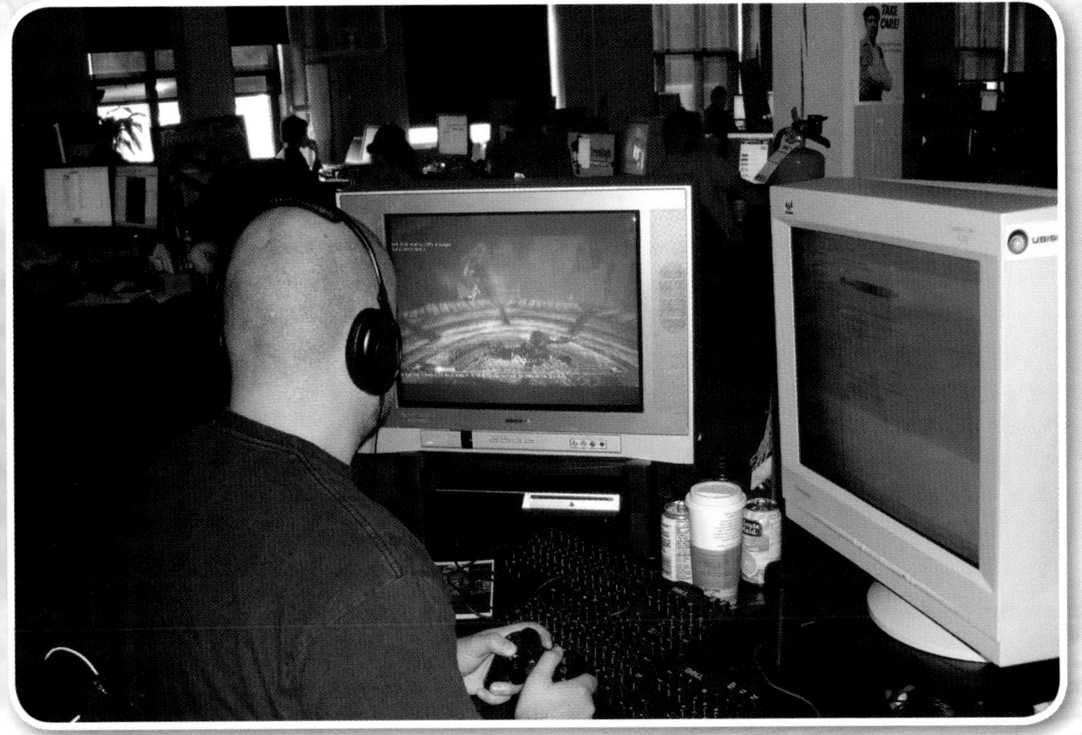

the perimeter is and start your combo far enough from that perimeter to also move him closer toward the parameter. So this strategy isn't necessarily just get close to a wall, do a couple of hits, throw him in a wall, do damage. We really reward the player who decides, "Okay, let's bring him back toward the middle." Start your big combo chain, do about ten hits of damage, then at that point you could start deciding which inputs you need to do if you want to branch off to an aerial combo or not. Or, if you want to grab and just kind of throw the enemy directly into the perimeter and then take advantage of the bonus damage that you'll do, hitting him against the wall or falling off a ledge.

Prima: Can you do the 14-hit combos against the soldiers at the crossroads?

Delbuguet: There are some fights that you could do it at the crossroads against the soldiers. But, it'll require some skills. It'll really require you knowing the positioning and the knowing the nature of the combo. Is the combo going to change directions? I don't know if I want to spoil that too much for players, but since you're using all your inputs, using your lift, your gauntlet, you're using your acrobatic, the nature and the orientation of the combo can change and you might loose track of where you are in your environment. So it's a little tricky, but doable I think. I've been able to do it in one area specifically.

Prima: Which area?

Delbuguet: If you want a great spot to do it, the Hunter's Lair—the first part of the Hunter's Lair—because it's divided into three portions. The first part—you could definitely do it there. The challenge will be to do it before he tries to trap you or run away. And there's a couple of them with the Concubine also that should be pretty straightforward, pretty easy to do.

Prima: When you go for the full 14, how do you start it out? How do you do it?

Delbuguet: I always go on the defense. I actually rarely try to gain the offensive right from the start. Because it pays to be a little bit more patient. We built the system to be defensive, but it's also because I like the feeling of what happens. When you are just blocking, you're letting the enemy go on, do his combo string, and you never know exactly what he's going to do. It's very rewarding to interrupt that sequence when you decide to, when you just remain very patient, and have him push you toward a perimeter and hit that deflect button. You break his combo. You immediately counterattack with your sword because it's the one counterattack that would do the most damage. And then you start chaining up with your sword attacks and you start chaining it up with Elika and you start pushing him away from the perimeter. And, at that point, you're going to have to do the acrobatics and reverse it back toward the same area. So, that's generally how I approach my trying to do the 14-hit combo. The other tricky element is the enemies' abilities to deflect. And that could pose an interesting challenge for doing the combos, so for that I recommend maybe trying to do the 14-hit combo a little earlier on in the game before the enemies get more powerful.

Building a Kingdom

Michael McIntyre, Level Designer

Vhat good is creating an incredible sense of reedom without an amazing world within which to xercise that freedom? Michael McIntyre, one of he level designers for *Prince of Persia*, talked about he sweat and joy that went into constructing the vorld of the Ahuras.

rima: Of all the different stages, which one is your favorite?

Iichael McIntyre: In terms of specific levels that I've worked on, or just in the game as a whole?

rima: How about both?

AcIntyre: As far as regions that are favorites, of course, I do like them all but I was asked this question before and I think the Vale beats out the other ones. There's just something about it that looks really different, really new. Just in looking around the place, you really want to explore it. With balloons floating around and the huge Observatory tower and all these pipes going around ... it's just a really cool, very different sort of vibe for *Prince of Persia*. And I think that's my favorite region.

As far as specific stages that are in the game, I think I'm really happy with the final challenge that the players have to do, which I did work on. I'm just quite excited about how well that whole thing turned out. When the player gets to the very end of the game and you have to face Ahriman, that turned out quite well. It was one of those things where we weren't sure how it was going to be pulled off because we couldn't build a full Ahriman. We had to get out the tape and make this kind of cool experience based on smoke and mirrors kind of, but it turned out really well.

Prima: So, what kind of preparation did you do when you were designing these levels?

McIntyre: There was a lot. For most of the team, the way it started was that we'd have concept art. The concept artists were the ones that were basically pulling ideas out of thin air, and saying, "Oh, maybe this looks cool; this feels cool. This is a neat sort of space to play around in." Because your environment is an important part of *Prince of Persia*. With all the acrobatics, essentially what you're doing is interacting with the environment.

Working on puzzles is also a big challenge for *Prince of Persia*. It's challenging to build a 2-D puzzle, something that's just on paper and for people to work out. Then you move that into 3D, and that becomes mind-blowingly more complex. So you have to find a puzzle that is both challenging and yet can be understood in 3D without having to print rules. It's really tricky to build intuitive, challenging 3-D puzzles. But I was very pleased that I got to work on a couple of puzzles in the game, the Windmill being one. And that was one that involved probably the most gameplay research for me, to the point where I actually was building flash prototypes of the puzzle to gauge its difficulty. I could pass that around

to people to evaluate ways to increase the challenge of it and whatnot, and that was really valuable.

And I suppose there was even further research into puzzle making, I actually did a lot of research into mazes and labyrinths in terms of a maze as a puzzle. There's an interesting sort of modern maze—I guess you could say—that is interactive. You do things that change the maze and it's a question of actually finding out the order that you have to do things in to pass through them. And I thought this was interesting—and it ended up becoming, not so much building a maze for a player, but it's almost like a theoretical maze where you are trying to find the correct path through the puzzle, or trying to find the correct sequence in order to pass through it. And I think that informed a lot of the stuff that I did for the puzzle.

And then, as far as gameplay went, the entire level design team together did a lot of research and development in terms of, How do we do the acrobatics in this game? It's an open world; it's not linear any more. We want to be fast and fluid and yet still challenging, fun. It's not *Assassin's Creed*. You don't just hold down buttons and steer around like a car. It requires timing. It took a lot of work and a lot of misses—a lot of us coming up with stuff that did not work in order to come up with that sort of magic mix that we have now. It's like really fast circulation, and then challenging, more hard-core objective paths.

Prima: Did you work on the Royal Gardens puzzle?

McIntyre: No, that was another one of our level designers. Mustafa worked on that.That one's a pretty good, it such a *Prince of Persia* puzzle. It's a really tricky one.

Prima: It's interesting that you should say labyrinth, because that's how I began to look at the game—almost as one of those hedge mazes.

McIntyre: Yeah, and that's, I think, an easy correlation to make because it has a very similar appeal. And it's something that really had informed me because as a designer you're not trying to come up with these abstract challenges. You are trying to create an experience. And I think that is what has informed me through a lot of it—that sort of charm and almost romance of traveling through a maze and basically being in a space that is intriguing and challenging. And you are trying to figure out how to get through it. And the difference with this *Prince of Persia* is that it's like a maze that has multiple exits, so you're kind of finding which one you want to get to.

Prima: So, how do you design a level when you have such an emphasis on the acrobatics? On being able to be so vertical as well as horizontal?

McIntyre: It really starts with these rough cubes, these volumes that essentially say, "Okay, this will be the gameplay space." I need to make certain that there's nothing that they can interact with outside of that. I have to create these boundaries that even with his amazing abilities, he cannot get past. And then once you define that, then you come in and try to think of what cool moves you could do in that space.

And then there's the other layer of that, of course—the acrobatic sequences. How you travel and how you get past the corrupted obstacles. But then, once the corruption's gone, you're exploring and looking for the collectibles. And then all surfaces are game and suddenly you can grip fall down and do rebounds and all this stuff. And so, you get to use those moves to explore every little nook and cranny, which is a fun part.

To Elika, with Love

Matthew Clarke, Elika AI Designer

After playing through *Prince of Persia* several times, we no longer saw Elika as just a tagalong companion. She's a real, breathing part of the Prince's world. It's now impossible to imagine how the Prince got by without her. Matthew Clarke, the AI programmer for Elika, chatted with us about the creation of Elika as a living force and the steps he took to make sure you felt like you were standing on a three-legged stool without her.

Prima: What was the biggest challenge with creating Elika?

Clarke: Well, in the beginning, what design wanted was to have a character that the player falls in love with and yet, at the same time, would not be a burden. I worked on Farrah on *Sands of Time* before, so I had a bit of experience with sidekicks and companion characters. It's difficult to get the player to fall in love with a character that he's not controlling because there's not this established recipe to have the player fall in love with him or her. Sometimes it's difficult to get people to fall in love and it's like forced weddings.

If you try to shove love down people's throats, well, the first thing they are going to say is, "No, I don't want that." It has to happen out of itself. So, we started with a couple of ideas, and saw what had been done in the past. *Ico* was a big inspiration in terms of what we wanted to reach, but Elika's character was less frail and less weak than Yorda. Yorda, the way she moved, the way her texture was transparent, showed that the character needs help. Whereas Elika—she's a princess. She's grown woman. She's able to do magic. So, it was about getting away from that "save the princess" type of cliché.

Prima: It was interesting to watch the way she would interact. For instance, when you are climbing vines, she has to climb on your back. Why does she require your help then but not in other situations like wall running?

Clarke: Two reasons—and a lot of things in our design process or our production processes are based on two decisions. At first we didn't have the safe entry system. We did the vines behavior before we had any sort of interaction and we thought, "Hey, why not have a bit of physical intimacy or interaction." And, at the same time, it solved a lot of technical problems as well because, you know how it happens on a vine, where is the player going, are there traps coming along? So, it was hard to say what is the best position on the vines.

Prima: It's easier to just bring them together?

Clarke: Yes, exactly. Let the player basically carry Elika around.

Prima: Were there things with Elika that got removed, say, for example, you have the cooperative jump in there, but were there Elika actions that got pulled?

Clarke: In terms of moves, most of the time we adapted to what we needed. We had magic powers that were in development, but sometimes, it's about choosing between quality and quantity, so some magic powers were left aside. We have a certain amount of animations where the Prince and Elika interact. We have fancy, complex versions and then we have simple versions. At the beginning of the story, they're going to interact in a certain way, you know—kind of cold, kind of like strangers. And, as that evolves, we have more of the intimate, shall I say, interactions.

Prima: In regards to Elika's compass move, I found after about three maps, I stopped using it. Thinking to myself, "No, I think I want to do this." Have you noticed other people that might stop using the compass?

Clarke: No, but that's a very good point, and that brings us back to our previous question about features with Elika that were left aside. At some point we had the compass, and we had pointing by Elika at the same time, saying, "Well, should we use this ledge, or we should climb these for vines?" Elika was the compass herself, or she was more directing or giving you advice. But it was a lot of blabber and stuff that, when you are trying to create a relationship between two characters, didn't work. If the character itself is seen as a tool, it's more difficult than if it's just a human being. So we decided to focus on emotional stuff more than on her pointing the direction because the compass does that job. And, the compass is optional. It's part of the *Prince of Persia* franchise to know where my objective is but not know how to get there. And it's part of the fun to resolve it, resolving that enigma of, "How can I interact with the environment to get to that objective?"

Prima: About halfway through the game, the first time I played it, I began to see the Prince and Elika almost as newlyweds. It's interesting to watch the way that they kind of figure each other out. And I was curious, how do you take the narrative elements, like the story line, and convey that through their physical interactions in the game?

Clarke: Well, there are two things. Obviously in the narrative, there's a part that's purely linear. When you go back to the Temple to buy a new power, we know where you are in the game. So, for this part, we can show some evolution. I don't know if you've noticed, but at the beginning of the game, if you wait at a point in front of a vista or in a corridor, she's going to position herself in front of you, and not face you. At the beginning, it's *her* quest. But as the story evolves, she's going to run side-by-side with you and look at you a bit more. And at the end of the game, if you stop and you just let the controller sit there, she's going to stay behind you and she's looking at you all the time. So it does evolve over time. It doesn't influence the gameplay, but it's something you can notice—or not.

So, yes, it kind of feels like they're newlyweds. But as I said, forced love stories are often failed ones, so we just tried to put the tension in between them and let the players create the love stories in their heads instead of our saying, "Well, hold hands and be in love with Elika." It doesn't work that way.

Prince of Persia

Art Gallery

PRINCE OF PERSIA

PRINCE OF PERSIA

RUINED CITY : RICH FACADE 02
RUINED CITY : RICH FACADE 01

Prince of Persia

Prince of Persia
Observatoire

Observatoire

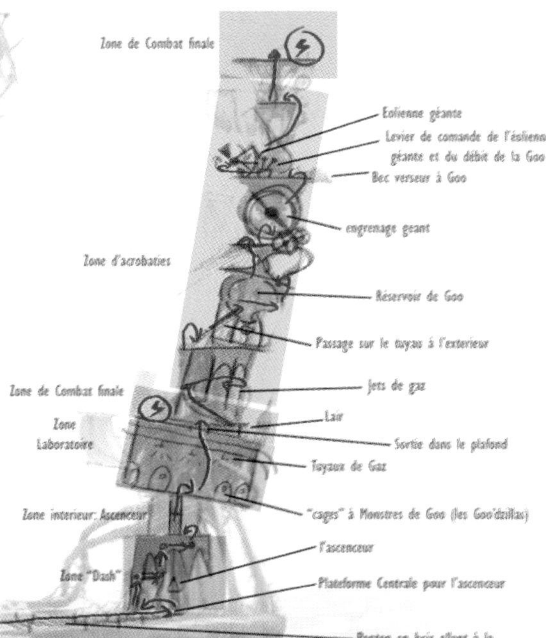
Zone de Combat finale
Eolienne géante
Levier de comande de l'éolienne géante et du débit de la Goo
Bec verseur à Goo
engrenage geant
Zone d'acrobaties
Réservoir de Goo
Passage sur le tuyau à l'exterieur
Zone de Combat finale
Jets de gaz
Lair
Zone Laboratoire
Sortie dans le plafond
Tuyaux de Gaz
Zone interieur: Ascenceur
"cages" à Monstres de Goo (les Goo'dzillas)
l'ascenceur
Zone "Dash"
Plateforme Centrale pour l'ascenceur
Ponton en bois allant à la plateforme Centrale de l'ascenceur

BASSINS DE GOD
A CIEL OUVERT
BASSINS DE GOD
A CIEL OUVERT

Prince of Persia

Prince of Persia